Managing Supply Chain Risk

Integrating with Risk Management

Managing Supply Chain Risk

Integrating with Risk Management

Sime Curkovic
Thomas Scannell
Bret Wagner

CRC Press
Taylor & Francis Group
Boca Raton   London   New York

CRC Press is an imprint of the
Taylor & Francis Group, an **informa** business

CRC Press
Taylor & Francis Group
6000 Broken Sound Parkway NW, Suite 300
Boca Raton, FL 33487-2742

© 2016 by Taylor & Francis Group, LLC
CRC Press is an imprint of Taylor & Francis Group, an Informa business

No claim to original U.S. Government works

Printed on acid-free paper
Version Date: 20150520

International Standard Book Number-13: 978-1-4987-0710-7 (Hardback)

Visit the Taylor & Francis Web site at
http://www.taylorandfrancis.com

and the CRC Press Web site at
http://www.crcpress.com

Contents

Preface

Managing supply chain risks is emerging as a viable, proactive, and strategic supply chain management (SCM) application. This book's focus is on the structure, implementation, and maintenance of a formal system for managing risks in the supply chain. A common theme is that the decision to manage supply chain risks constitutes a major undertaking for most firms. Such an undertaking, it is argued, does not take place in a vacuum. Rather, it is a response to a number of factors or influences. However, no book to date has empirically identified these factors and explained how they can be leveraged into a competitive advantage. In this book, we use data from firms and SCM managers to identify which factors affect the decision to develop a system for managing supply chain risks and then explain how these factors can influence the level of success.

Certain factors have been identified as having a critical impact on predisposition and progress toward managing risks in SCM. These factors described a situation where the respondents saw managing risks as an extension of their SCM movement. There seems to be recognition that succeeding requires more than simply creating a new program or department. It is argued that these various factors act to pre-condition the firm and its systems to the introduction, acceptance, and progress on managing SCM risks. The book identifies the factors underlying the decision to develop a system for managing supply chain risks and how these factors can be leveraged into a competitive advantage.

About the Authors

Sime Curkovic, Ph.D., is a professor of supply chain management at Western Michigan University (WMU) and is a former director of the WMU Integrated Supply Management program. He received his undergraduate degree in management systems from Kettering University and his Ph.D. degree from Michigan State University. Dr. Curkovic has taught several courses in sourcing, operations, logistics, process, environmental, and multinational management. His research interests include environmentally responsible manufacturing, green purchasing, total quality management, supply chain management, and integrated global strategic sourcing. Dr. Curkovic's publications have appeared in the *Journal of Supply Chain Management*, the *IEEE Transactions on Engineering Management*, the *Decision Sciences Journal*, the *International Journal of Operations and Production Management*, the *International Journal of Production Research*, the *Journal of Quality Management*, the *Journal of Operations Management*, and the *International Journal of Production Economics*. His professional memberships include ASQ, APICS, DSI, INFORMS, ISM, and POMS. Dr. Curkovic's previous work experience was with General Motors in the midwestern United States, Mexico, and Germany. His dissertation on the relationship between total quality management and environmentally responsible manufacturing has received the following awards: (1) the *APICS Educational Foundation Edward & Marion Plossl Fellowship*; (2) the *Richard J. Lewis Quality of Excellence Award*; and (3) the *National Decision Sciences Institute Elwood S. Buffa Doctoral Dissertation*. Dr. Curkovic is an American-born citizen of Croatian descent.

Thomas (Tom) Scannell, Ph.D., a professor of management at Western Michigan University, teaches process and operations management, purchasing, ethics, sustainable operations, business strategy, quantitative analysis, and quality management at the graduate and undergraduate levels. He received his Ph.D. in operations and sourcing management from Michigan State University, and his MBA and B.S. in electrical engineering from WMU. He has served on and chaired many committees and was the director of the MBA program. Dr. Scannell's publications have appeared in numerous journals, including the *Decision Sciences Journal,* the *Journal of Operations Management,* the *Journal of Business Logistics,* the *Sloan Management Review,* the *Journal of Supply Chain Management,* the *Journal of Product Innovation Management, Modern Management Science and Engineering,* and *The World Financial Review.* He is the co-author of a book regarding supplier integration into new product development and has published industry reports with CAPS Research regarding innovation. Dr. Scannell helped establish the Supply Chain Management Council of West Michigan. His 11 years of industry experience include work as an electronics design engineer, systems engineer, program and project manager, and new product development manager.

Bret Wagner, Ph.D., is an associate professor in the management department at Western Michigan University. He was the director of the integrated supply management (ISM) program from 2004 to 2012, during which time enrollment in the program increased by 79% and the Gartner Group ranked the program #5 in the nation. With a Ph.D. in operations management from Michigan State and a master of engineering administration from George Washington University, he brings his strength in production planning to the ISM program. His research interests

include production planning and scheduling and optimization modeling. Dr. Wagner has spearheaded the SAP initiative at the College of Business. He has received numerous grants to support the initiative and has helped integrate SAP's software into the ISM curriculum. He is widely sought to provide workshops on using SAP software in business curriculums. Dr. Wagner was the first recipient of the *Majdi Najm Service Award* from the SAP University Alliance. He is the co-author of the book *Concepts in Enterprise Resource Planning* and has published research articles in *Decision Sciences,* the *International Journal of Operational Research*, and the *Journal of Operations Management.*

1

Introduction

On behalf of Western Michigan University (WMU) and the Center for Integrated Supply Management, our group conducted a research project about the potential for managing risks in supply chain management (SCM). Managing supply chain risks is emerging as a viable, proactive, and strategic SCM application. This project's focus is on the structure, implementation, and maintenance of a formal system for managing risks in the supply chain. A common theme is that the decision to manage supply chain risks constitutes a major undertaking for most firms. Such an undertaking, it is argued, does not take place in a vacuum. Rather, it is a response to a number of factors or influences. However, no research to date has empirically identified these factors and explained how they can be leveraged into a competitive advantage. In this study, we use data from 46 firms and SCM managers to identify which factors affect the decision to develop a system for managing supply chain risks, and we explain how these factors can influence the level of success.

Certain factors were identified as having a critical impact on predisposition and progress toward managing risks in SCM. These factors included corporate strategy, supply chain organization, process management, performance metrics, and information and technology. These factors characterize a situation where the respondents saw managing risks as an extension of their SCM movement. There seems to be recognition that succeeding requires more than simply creating a new program or department. It is argued that these various factors act to pre-condition the firm and its systems to the introduction, acceptance, and progress on managing SCM risks. The report begins with a profile of the respondents and how they manage supply chain risks. The report then concludes with an evaluation of the factors underlying the decision to develop a system for managing supply chain risks and how these factors can be leveraged into a competitive advantage.

RESPONDENT PROFILE

Sample job titles: supply chain leader, strategic buyer, senior buyer, director of supply chain, vice president of purchasing, purchasing manager, senior supply chain manager, global sourcing business unit manager, director of global procurement, strategic procurement manager, commodity manager, and plant manager.

Main activities of companies: Manufacturing (39/46): *11* automotive first tier suppliers, *4* automotive original equipment manufacturers (OEMs), *3* electronics manufacturers, and *21* other (e.g., office furniture, home appliance, pumps, seals, gauges, valves, hydraulics, aerospace, medical equipment, plumbing fixtures, seats, recreational vehicles, safety equipment, industrial doors, automation equipment, pharmaceuticals, cosmetics, home building material, child care goods, food). 28/46 of the manufacturers can be classified as capital-intensive, high-volume producers that make use of assembly lines in operations, and 11/46 of the above can be classified as low-volume producers of highly customized products.

Non-manufacturing (7/46): *3* distributors, *1* logistics, *1* telecommunications, *1* clinical testing, and *1* retailer.

Annual sales revenue:

$1B–$9B:	32%
$10B–$49B:	34%
$50M–$99M:	4%
$50B–$99B:	7%
$100M–$499M:	14%
$500M–$999M:	7%
Over $100B:	2%

Number of employees:

Under 50:	2%
50–99:	2%
100–499:	9%
500–999:	5%
1,000–4,999:	24%

| 5,000–9,999: | 9% |
| Over 10,000: | 49% |

Ownership structure:

Privately owned:	33%
Publicly owned:	60%
Publicly/privately owned:	7%

Geographical regions accounting for sales revenue:

Africa:	16/46 firms
Europe:	31/46 firms
North America:	46/46 firms
South America:	30/46 firms
Asia:	34/46 firms

HOW RESPONDENTS MANAGE SUPPLY CHAIN RISK

Q1. Usage of supply chain risk evaluation tools, techniques, and methodologies:

Plan to implement an application within 1–2 years: 6%
Currently using an application: 61%[*]
Plan to evaluate an application within 1–2 years: 13%
No plans to use anything: 20%

Q2. Spending plans next year for managing risks in the supply chain (e.g., IT, support services, process changes, etc.):

Less than $500,000: 52%	$500,000–$1,000,000: 2%
$1,000,000–$5,000,000: 9%	More than $5,000,000: 7%
Unanswered: 30%	

---

[*] All firms agreed there is no obvious single application for managing supply chain risks on the market today. These 61% are actually only using existing SCM applications for managing risk.

Q3. Budget for managing supply chain risks increase, decrease, or stay the same next year:

Increase: 45%
Decrease: 14%
No change: 41%

Q4. Area within company that usually takes ownership of investments for managing supply chain risks:

Risk Management: 3%   Supply Chain/Purchasing: 60%
Legal: 6%   Logistics: 3%
Accounting/Finance: 7%   Manufacturing/Operations: 12%
IT: 3%   Quality: 6%

Q5. Funding for managing supply chain risks comes from:

General operations budget: 26%   Specific departmental budget: 42%
General finance budget: 11%   General IT budget: 4%
Specific budget to address supply chain issues: 17%

Q6. Techniques used to identify and analyze risk in supply chain:

Sample of responses: Initial supplier evaluations, financial risk assessment, supplier quality audits, capacity planning for operations and suppliers, lead time analysis for project management, supplier scorecard, management review, supplier risk analysis based on accounts payable performance, contingency plans, on-site capability review, forecasting techniques, safety stock, capacity and network planning, multi-sourcing, price hedging for commodities, back-up carriers, historical data, cross-functional teams, risk management group, project service levels, information sharing with suppliers, total spend management, open communication, supplier competency reviews, benchmarking, lifecycle management, failure mode and effects analysis, develop local supply base, contract management and leverage, demand planning, inventory management, and vendor management inventory.

FACTOR 1: CORPORATE STRATEGY

Factor 1—Data and Observations

Firms overwhelmingly agreed there is no obvious single application for managing supply chain risks on the market. Most firms (61%) are only using existing SCM applications for managing risk (see Q1). In the absence of risk management applications, these firms are building risk considerations into traditional SCM applications (e.g., spending, contract, inventory management, demand planning, benchmarking, building long-term partnerships, etc.). An additional 6% said they would like to implement a SCM risk application in 1–2 years, and another 13% said they are considering it. This indicates that while specific supply chain risk applications do not exist, interest levels are very high (80%). The 80/20 rule resurfaces as 80% of the firms have placed a priority on managing supply chain risks. The following questions were also asked on a 1 to 7 scale (strongly disagree to strongly agree): (1) Managing supply chain risk is an increasingly important initiative for our operations; and (2) without a systematic analysis technique to assess risk, much can go wrong in a supply chain. The means for both questions were well above 5.00 and had very small amounts of variance. Again, interest and need levels for supply chain risk applications remains high.

Eighteen percent of the firms said they would spend over $1M in services, technology, and personnel to support managing supply chain risks, while 7% actually plan to spend over $5M. Another 52% said they plan to spend more modest amounts of less than $500,000. Thirty percent would not answer the question because of its proprietary nature, but indicated a moderately large amount of spending was planned. Not surprisingly, larger companies will invest more than smaller ones. The manufacturing firms look very similar in their higher spending efforts with a focus on supplier failure, whereas the non-manufacturing firms indicate lower spending levels with a focus on logistics failures.

These questions were also asked on a 1 to 7 scale (strongly disagree to strongly agree): (1) Our spending intentions for managing supply chain risks are very high (mean = 3.37, var. = 2.47); and (2) we do plan on investing nontrivial amounts in managing supply chain risks (mean = 4.30, var. = 3.77). In this study, there was dedicated funding for managing supply chain risks and 86% indicated that such budgets would increase or stay the same (see Q3). However, only 42% will come from specific SCM departmental budgets and 60% indicated that SCM takes ownership of such investments (see Q4 and Q5). While spending intentions for managing supply chain risks are moderate, funding is poorly targeted and ownership is not centered within the SCM discipline. Managing risks is just now reaching the core of traditional and mature SCM applications.

Factor 1—Conclusions and Recommendations

A common theme identified from the cases was that while there were few examples of best practice, there were valuable lessons to be learned from the way individual companies managed risks. It was agreed that the management of risk should be a core issue in the planning of any organization. Firms have increased their exposure to risk through their SCM initiatives, which focus on cost reduction. Few firms in this study made a formal assessment of supply chain risks or had a strategy in place. These findings indicate the importance of dedicated resources and aligning risk management with corporate strategy.

Formulating an appropriately aligned organizational strategy can, to a certain extent, mitigate risks in the supply chain. While the actions of competitors, customers, and suppliers external to the company cannot be strictly controlled, formulation of an appropriate strategy can help a company prepare for many events. The companies in this study have a strategy committed to investing heavily in the development of their supply chains to increase cost efficiency in alignment with corporate strategy. However, they also need to limit their exposure to risk by investing in the implementation of systems to increase monitoring and control of their suppliers, while also aligning their strategies with corporate risk management groups. With significant opportunities for improvement, there was no indication that such systems and alignment were in place.

Most professional bodies that deal with risk take the view that risk management should be a continuous process, which runs throughout the organization's strategy. It should address methodically all risks surrounding the organization's activities past, present, and in particular, future. It must be integrated into the culture of the organization with an effective policy and process led by senior management. It must also translate the strategy into tactical and operational objectives, assigning ownership throughout the organization with each manager and employee responsible for the management of risk as part of their job description. It must support accountability, performance metrics, and rewards, thus promoting operational efficiency at all levels, including SCM.

Most of the risk management strategies in this study appear to be fragmented—one group buys insurance, another administers claims, another handles everything related to safety or security, and so forth. The perspective of a holistic and enterprise-wide approach is a new approach concerned with managing risks to provide reasonable assurance to all stakeholders (including SCM) regarding the achievement of company objectives. In reality, SCM covers the supply chain from suppliers to your company and not from your company to customers. Only the corporate risk management group can address risks for the entire supply chain and lifecycle of a program. An effective strategy for managing risks in the supply chain requires a closely aligned strategy and relationship between risk managers and others in the organization. Risk management can provide its traditional expertise and information. Other functions such as purchasing, sales, marketing, finance, operations, and logistics can bring additional expertise. As a cross-functional collaborative team, these holistic and enterprise-wide functions can create and implement a supply chain risk strategy that is strategically aligned with corporate objectives. This will require obtaining senior management understanding and approval, and setting up organizational responsibilities.

Gaining management support is often the most challenging part of implementing a proactive system for managing risks in the supply chain. It is necessary to emphasize the importance of supply chain risk management to senior management in order to get the properly targeted resources necessary to implement such a system (rather than the poorly targeted budgets seen in this study). Depending on the management culture, this should be the first step but could be the last. The firms in this study strongly disagreed that supply chain risk initiatives are driven from the bottom up. This indicates the strong potential for a proactive approach since supply chain risk initiatives appear to be driven from the top down.

This study recommends having an organizational strategy fully committed to undertaking risk assessments in the supply chain and at the very least the need for business continuity planning when the company is exposed to the supply chain. As a part of organizational strategy, it would behoove these firms to build a valued and respected risk management function. Progressive organizations will implement a risk management strategy to enable them to react to potential issues in a streamlined fashion. By having a plan, organizations are able to minimize a large ripple effect in other operations within their organization and across their supply chain.

FACTOR 2: SUPPLY CHAIN ORGANIZATION

Factor 2—Data and Observations

Risk management in this study was mostly handled by a corporate function, usually dealing with insurance companies and some security issues. However, risk management in the supply chain has emerged rather recently, and it appears many managers and functional areas are not involved. The following questions were asked on a 1 to 7 scale (strongly disagree to strongly agree): (1) My workplace uses supply chain risk managers who work closely with corporate risk management (mean = 2.53, var. = 3.03); and (2) I fully understand the activities being performed by our risk management group (mean = 4.00, var. = 2.66). On a higher level, the corporate function is involved with risk management and has contact with insurance companies, but does not necessarily coordinate risk management activities in the whole group, nor does it appear to develop directives.

Most of the firms in this study have outsourced one or more of their non-core business functions. For financial reasons, resource constraints, and/or the need to tap into expertise they do not have, outsourcing has become a key aspect of many strategic initiatives. The following question was asked on a 1 to 7 scale (strongly disagree to strongly agree): (1) We are planning to outsource all or some of our risk management functions. The mean was only 2.25 with little variance. The organizations in this study have no intention to outsource risk management and are strongly inclined to develop these skills internally by purchasing a risk management application for internal use, and specifically in the SCM area. However, the following questions were asked on a 1 to 7 scale (strongly disagree to strongly agree): (1) There is no single set of tools or technologies on the market for managing supply chain risks; and (2) managing supply chain risk is an increasingly important initiative for our operations. The means were well above 5.00 and had small amounts of variance. Again, interest and need levels for supply chain risk applications remains high.

Respondents in our study saw a broad set of risk factors that pose a disruption to their supply chains. These risks did not vary much by industry, and most were shared (see Appendix A, Table A.1). Supplier failure/reliability was the top risk factor and common across all respondents. Bankruptcies of suppliers, logistics failure, commodity cost volatility, natural disasters, and strikes/labor disputes were distant seconds. The non-manufacturing respondents were more inclined to place a higher priority on logistics failure, which is not surprising since they were mostly made up of distributors and a retailer.

Respondents were asked to rank order five of the following risks which would have the greatest severity or impact on the supply chain if it occurred (e.g., 1 = most severe, 2 = second most severe, etc.). The numbers in Table 1.1 indicate the frequency of responses.

While the majority of the manufacturing respondents identified supplier failure as their top risk factor, they also attributed the majority of their downtime in operations to supplier failure. In general, these firms have reacted to manage this risk factor, along with others such as natural disasters, strikes, and so on, by building risk considerations into current SCM applications. Commodity cost volatility was also a growing concern,

TABLE 1.1

Frequency of Responses

Risk factor	Frequency
Supplier failure/reliability	41
Bankruptcy, ruin, or default of suppliers, shippers, etc.	22
Logistic failure	20
Commodity cost volatility	18
Natural disasters or accidents	15
Strikes — labor, buyers, and shippers	15
Diminishing capacity	10
Government regulations	9
Attracting and retaining skilled labor	8
Customer-related (demand change, system failure)	8
Lack of trust with partners	7
Currency exchange, interest, and/or inflation rate fluctuations	7
Intellectual property infringement	7
Energy/raw material shortages and power outages	6
Geopolitical event	6
Ethical issues	5
Legal liabilities and litigation	5
Information delays, scarcity, sharing, and infrastructure breakdown	5
Customs acts/trade restrictions and protectionism	4
Contract failure	4
Degree of control over operations	3
Contamination exposure — food, germs, infections	3
Measuring tools — metrics translate differently	2
Weakness in the local infrastructure	2
Internal and external theft	2
Return policy and product recall requirements	2
Banking regulations and tighter financing conditions	2
Port/cargo security	1
Tax issues	1

but with limited amounts of systems to manage its risk. For example, the majority of the firms strongly disagreed that they were using hedging strategies (to protect against commodity price swings) and speculation (forward placement of inventory, forward buying of raw materials, etc.) for managing supply chain risks (and yet it was identified as one of the top risk factors). Not surprisingly, firms were very disappointed with their supply chain's performance on lower commodity prices and reduced material price volatility. Only one firm in the entire sample had a system in place to proactively manage commodity prices. This firm had a dedicated staff that used a price sliding system on key commodities, which were tied to market indices (e.g., plastics, metals, rubbers, etc.).

Notice that some of the top risk factors are largely beyond the control of buying organizations (e.g., natural disasters, default or ruin of supplier, geopolitical events, or perhaps even supplier failure). Managers insisted that while preventing these factors is not possible, reacting to them quickly is an option through contingency planning. The firms in this study are recognized as leaders in SCM and several have received formal recognition by industry associations for their ability to use SCM applications in a customer-driven manner. For example, these firms were very satisfied with their supply chain group's performance on the following issues: after sales service performance, supplier reliability, inventory management, delivery reliability, order completeness, damage-free delivery, and meeting customer service levels. However, they did not show a proactive commitment to risk management. However, these questions were asked on a 1 to 7 scale (strongly disagree to strongly agree): (1) We are prepared to minimize the effects of disruptions (terrorism, weather, theft, etc.); (2) proactive risk mitigation efforts applied to the supply chain is common practice for us; and (3) we can actually exploit risk to an advantage by taking calculated risks in the supply chain. The means were very low and had small amounts of variance.

Most of the firms strongly agreed that managing supply chain risks is driven by reactions to failures rather than being proactively driven. Most managers agreed that they have had supply disruptions that have caused financial hardships in the past 24 months. There was no indication that managing risk was being driven by anything other than failure and remediation. However, the largest gaps in performance for reducing disruptions were in tighter financing conditions, exchange rate fluctuations, and commodity cost volatility (Table 1.2). While supplier failure is a high risk factor for all the firms and will increase in risk for several of the

TABLE 1.2

Increase, Decrease, or No Change in Supply Chain Risk

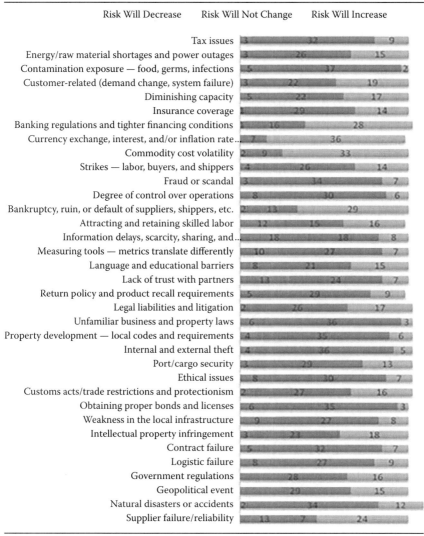

	Risk Will Decrease	Risk Will Not Change	Risk Will Increase
Tax issues	3	32	9
Energy/raw material shortages and power outages	3	26	15
Contamination exposure — food, germs, infections	5	37	2
Customer-related (demand change, system failure)	3	22	19
Diminishing capacity	5	22	17
Insurance coverage		29	14
Banking regulations and tighter financing conditions	16	28	
Currency exchange, interest, and/or inflation rate...	7	36	
Commodity cost volatility	2	9	33
Strikes — labor, buyers, and shippers	4	26	14
Fraud or scandal	3	34	7
Degree of control over operations	8	30	6
Bankruptcy, ruin, or default of suppliers, shippers, etc.	2	13	29
Attracting and retaining skilled labor	12	15	16
Information delays, scarcity, sharing, and...	18	18	8
Measuring tools — metrics translate differently	10	27	7
Language and educational barriers	8	21	15
Lack of trust with partners	13	24	7
Return policy and product recall requirements	5	29	9
Legal liabilities and litigation	2	26	17
Unfamiliar business and property laws	6	36	3
Property development — local codes and requirements	4	35	6
Internal and external theft	4	36	5
Port/cargo security	3	29	13
Ethical issues	8	30	7
Customs acts/trade restrictions and protectionism	2	27	16
Obtaining proper bonds and licenses	6	35	3
Weakness in the local infrastructure	9	27	8
Intellectual property infringement	3	21	18
Contract failure	5	32	7
Logistic failure	8	27	9
Government regulations		28	16
Geopolitical event		29	15
Natural disasters or accidents	2	34	12
Supplier failure/reliability	13	7	24

firms, 13 firms did say that they expect supplier failure to be less of a risk in the future. A close assessment of these 13 firms reveals that they have done the most to build risk considerations into as many SCM applications as possible.

The respondents were each asked if supply chain risks would increase, stay the same, or decrease in the next 1 to 2 years. See Table 1.2 for the results.

Factor 2—Conclusions and Recommendations

There was no indication that risk management has become a main part of the firms' SCM activities or that it even helped SCM meet the organization's objectives. It is recommended that corporate risk management groups focus on positioning the entire organization to try to avoid supply chain disruptions, and to develop strategies to manage the impact of them should avoidance not be possible. More tools are needed to assist in risk management at the supply chain level and not just at the level of the individual firm. This study concluded that the use of managing risks in the supply chain was complacent. It appears that in developing supply chain strategies that focus on cost reduction, these firms have played down the risks from supply chain disruptions. Risk considerations are still reactive in nature but have the potential of adding value in a proactive, strategic, and long-term manner.

The recommendations of this study describes ideal conditions as being where there is a supply chain risk manager who is responsible for development and implementation of managing risks in the supply chain. This supply chain risk manager should also work closely together with corporate risk management, as well as with the supply chain managers. In this study, a gap was suggested as firms failed to use supply chain managers who work closely with corporate risk management and managers did not fully understand the activities being performed by their risk management groups.

Supply chain managers should also use the tools and processes that supply chain risk managers have developed to analyze, assess, and manage risk in their supply chains. In the absence of risk management applications, the supply chain managers in this study are building risk considerations into existing traditional SCM applications (e.g., spending, contract, and inventory management, demand planning, benchmarking, etc.). This study shows that mostly supply chain managers run and coordinate the work to maintain an optimal balance between risk exposures and costs for damages versus protection activities. Supply chain managers are the interface to other functional areas and they are responsible for risk management in the supply chain. Core production should of course support SCM with risk management issues. This means that many different players could be involved in sharing responsibility for implementing and maintaining a system for risk management. This could make roles unclear, so responsibilities need to be defined. However, the key responsibility lies with supply chain managers that should run risk management work in their respective parts of the supply chain.

FACTOR 3: PROCESS MANAGEMENT

Factor 3—Data and Observations

This study showed that documenting the likelihood and impact of risks was not a key part of SCM and that supply chain risk information was not readily available to key decision makers. Furthermore, very few of the firms were actually able to exploit risk to an advantage by taking calculated risks in the supply chain and even fewer were prepared to minimize the effects of disruptions. These questions were asked on a 1 to 7 scale (strongly disagree to strongly agree): (1) A key part of our supply chain management is documenting the likelihood and impact of risks (mean = 4.20, var. = 2.86); and (2) supply chain risk information is accurate and readily available to key decision makers (mean = 3.87, var. = 2.78). There was some debate as to the validity and usefulness of tools to operationalize the process. The managers did tend to prefer approaches that combine subjective and objective measures because this allows them some freedom rather than being pushed into taking decisions solely on complicated numerical analysis. Failure mode and effects analysis (FMEA) is a mainstream tool used to collect information related to risk management decisions for most companies in an engineering capacity, but not in a supply chain capacity. There were several documented procedures to complete an FMEA across industries in this study, especially in automotive. Most managers supported a modified version of the tool that could be used to help evaluate the risk of SCM decisions.

Several of the firms used financial reports and questionnaires during supplier approval to compare supply candidates to the business requirements of the buyers or project teams. When justified by a perceived level of risk, a few of the firms went one step further and had candidate comparison matrices (e.g., supplier profiling form and supply chain PFMEA). Additionally, most had formal processes for supplier visits (e.g., rapid plant assessment, site verification of the supplier questionnaire, etc.). Some firms actually used lifecycle management with supplier report cards and their buyers would conduct periodic supply chain reviews. In one firm, sourcing was assigned risk ownership and they used FMEA principles to evaluate risk impact. For each risk, they would assess what the financial impact would be in the event of a disruption. They then assigned a probability to each risk area and then they prioritized by multiplying the financial impact by the risk probability. Again, most firms are only using existing SCM applications for managing risk with no formal risk management system in place. In the absence of risk management applications, these firms are building risk considerations into traditional SCM applications.

Factor 3—Conclusions and Recommendations

Managing supply chain risks should occur at all levels of the supply chain, and the process should support integration with supplier and customer risk management activities. The process should be active in all stages of the acquisition lifecycle, starting with technology development and continuing through acquisition, production, maintenance, repair, and disposal. The scope of the process should include all types of risks appropriate for the supply chain. In addition to the common causes of disruption, risk identification should consider economic, political, environmental, regulatory, manufacturing readiness, and technological obsolescence issues. All levels of management should be actively engaged in risk management, including strategic, business, program, technical, and tactical levels. The process should both leverage common tools for assessing risk, but also develop specific SCM mitigation tools and solutions.

A method for analyzing supply chain risk must be a cross-functional process that involves senior management as well as key stakeholders from finance, operations, internal audit, and risk management. However, the companies in this study have not adopted this boundary spanning process. Instead, they have managed risks within functional areas. However, it was acknowledged that the most effective forms of risk management demands involvement across multiple areas of the organization.

The process begins with an assessment of the supply chain. This can usually be done with internal resources, but might require the assistance of outside consultants. In either case, it was agreed that this assessment would take the most effort. While generally lacking among firms, this study indicates the importance of having a process that will allow an organization to analyze, prioritize, and measure the economic impact of risks in the supply chain. Such a process should provide decision makers with financially justified value propositions for initiatives that are aligned with the company's strategic goals. Though a number of different risk management processes have been put forward, most tend to follow the generic process offered in this study with the following key elements.

- SCM Risk *Planning*: Develops an overall plan for assessing, handling, and communicating supply chain risks. It identifies how risk priorities are established, how risks are communicated, the training resources required, and the stakeholders responsible for each of the risk management activities.
- SCM Risk *Identification*: Uses tools that enable a thorough investigation of all possible sources of risk within a supply chain. To be effective, this part of the process must be conducted throughout the supply chain and lifecycle of the program.
- SCM Risk *Analysis*: Assesses each risk in terms of its likelihood of occurrence, and the estimated impact should the risk occur. This study recommends a modified version of the FMEA tool that could be used to help evaluate the risk of SCM decisions.
- SCM Risk *Handling*: Stakeholders rank order the risks and determine what options exist to mitigate the most likely and/or serious risks. Mitigation strategies can either lower the likelihood that the risk will occur or reduce or eliminate the impact should it occur. These plans must be assessed both in terms of their cost as well as in terms of their impact on the likelihood and severity of the risk. Based on this analysis, mitigation strategies are selected that provide the greatest return to the company. Our study shows that many risks are actually common across a large number of suppliers and industries. What is implied is that the same mitigation strategy may be successful in addressing a broad range of supply chain risks.
- SCM Risk *Monitoring*: Systematically tracks the risks and the risk handling plans against cost, schedule, and performance metrics, to ensure that risks are being managed as planned. In other words, measures and monitors performance to maintain a balanced risk profile.

Understanding the risks within a supply chain requires an in-depth knowledge of business operations. To develop this understanding, the company must begin with interviews and workshops typically involving a cross-functional team of subject matter experts representing sourcing, manufacturing, and logistics. The company must collect its financial and risk performance data (e.g., average lead times, safety stock levels, other inventory levels, etc.) and benchmark it against industry and functional comparisons. This process enables the organization to develop a detailed picture of its supply chain, which in turn helps it identify potential risks more easily.

A few managers took the view that effective supply chain risk management does not need to be a highly formalized and structured process. However, this study favors a more formal, structured process for managing risk.

FACTOR 4: PERFORMANCE METRICS

Factor 4—Data and Observations

All of the firms in this study have developed and monitor a set of performance metrics to maintain a risk profile for their supply chains. They do so by using an assortment of tools and techniques such as: initial supplier evaluations, QS audits, industry benchmarking, supplier questionnaires, report cards, capacity planning, lead-time analysis, financial risk assessment, business continuity plans, risk analysis based on accounts payable performance, historical data, technical capability assessment, on-site capability reviews, forecasting techniques and analysis, data tracking with customers to identify demand trends, supplier performance measurement, and so on. The majority of the firms also used supplier risk rankings, similar to credit scores used in the financial industry, to measure suppliers on stability, contingency planning, and on-target delivery performance. These tools allow the firms to ask some basic questions such as: do suppliers maintain consistent quality and delivery performance and is lead-time volatility increasing? While most of the firms track this type of performance through supplier scorecards to monitor leading indicators that impact risk, none had an ongoing risk-review process to ensure that they keep their risk profile within an optimal range of economic impact.

This study also demonstrates that the measurement of risk factors does not necessarily require a new or unique set of performance measures. For example, one firm used average on-time delivery as a measure of supplier performance and chose to look more closely at the peaks and valleys of this indicator to determine the supplier's risk impact on its own delivery performance. In another example, key metrics were established to measure the risk associated with key suppliers and their performance against service level agreements. Supplier agreements were then aligned with the established levels negotiated with the company's key customer agreements.

In general, the development of proactive risk management performance metrics in the supply chain was lacking in this study. The supplier scorecards were not balanced or optimal, and supported reactive decision making. The firms in this study do equip themselves with management scorecards that can identify some trends in advance. They often referred to them as dashboards, reviews, audits, and so on, and they allowed managers to view the progress of their supply chains according to a collection of performance indicators. In this manner, they do get some early warning signs if suppliers or carriers are underperforming. However, they fall short on having systems with event-based alerts that notify them when their supply chains are at risk. Until that happens, managers will not take appropriate and well-managed risks (e.g., they will outsource to low cost regions to meet their cost savings goals and not stay within an optimal range on the risk management side).

In general, no one was compensated or incented in their day-to-day job to look at and evaluate the risks within an optimal range of economic impact. For example, a typical offshore target for several supply chain managers was to achieve x million dollars of components offshore in y years. Such situations forced managers to inevitably compromise on risk issues as they focused on achieving cost efficiency. None of the firms have developed some sort of on-demand platform that helps them predict supplier failures before they occur. Managers were mostly concerned with risks on the supply and demand sides of the supply chain. It is not that they ignored operations risk, but typically, operations risk management resides in other departments such as corporate risk or finance, and is covered by buying insurance or hedging foreign exchange exposure.

Factor 4—Conclusions and Recommendations

A key component of the supply chain risk management framework is to develop and monitor a set of performance metrics to maintain an optimal risk profile of an organization's supply chain. In response to this, it is recommended that a risk-adjusted view of current and traditional SCM performance metrics be used. In addition, key risk measures may be added to monitor potential upstream and downstream disruptions in the supply chain. New measures might also be added to monitor supplier contingency planning processes and procedures that already exist as traditional SCM applications. Establishing a set of supply chain risk measures across an organization's supply chain can culturally institutionalize the importance of managing risks in the supply chain. As decisions are weighed in terms of both the financial benefits and the impact to supply chain risks, the results should lead to a more proactive approach with long-term benefits to the entire supply chain.

This study suggests that performance metrics are an important determinant of the temporal perspective of supply chain managers. If the reward system only rewards those who achieve their objectives irrespective of due attention to risks, then managers will strive to achieve objectives at the cost of disproportionate risks. In most of the firms in this study, the major objectives were to reduce inventory, improve in-stock availability, and cut costs. Most of these firms had specific targets for offshore sourcing that forced managers to inevitably compromise on risk issues. Managing risks in the supply chain was perceived as something that contradicts the process of achieving these company objectives.

The most appropriate strategy might not be adopted because of factors such as performance metrics. Developing metrics that accurately and fully tap the impact of effectively managing risks in supply chains will drive managers to take appropriate and well-managed risks. Although the development of specific performance metrics is beyond the scope of this study, it is certainly an area ripe for future research.

FACTOR 5: INFORMATION AND TECHNOLOGY

Factor 5—Data and Observations

In this study, firms had information regarding what occurs in other parts of the supply chain. An issue on information was not suggested as it was asked on a 1 to 7 scale (not satisfied to very satisfied): How satisfied are you with your supply chain group's performance on "Visibility" (detailed knowledge of what goes on in other parts of the supply chain, for example, finished goods inventory, material inventory, work in progress (WIP), pipeline inventory, actual demands and forecasts, production plans, capacity, yields, and order status). The mean was modestly high (4.26) with a very small amount of variance, as was their agreement that their company uses real-time inventory information and analytics in managing the supply chain. Furthermore, the questions were also asked on a 1 to 7 scale (not used to extensively used): To what extent are the following used in managing your supply chain and risks within it: (1) information gathering; and (2) establishing good communications with suppliers. The means for both questions were very high (well above 5.00) and had small amounts of variance. Also in this study, information delays, scarcity, sharing, and infrastructure breakdown were seen overwhelmingly as the lowest-rated risk factors both currently and for the future.

These findings are not surprising given that firms in this study showed that a wide variety of information-based technology and applications are being spent for their SCM efforts (e.g., ERP configuration systems, electronics reverse auctioning, radio frequency identification, collaborative planning forecasting and replenishment—CPFR, etc.), but very few firms showed that their technologies are being used to support risk considerations. Respondents agreed that the key to improved supply chain visibility was sharing information among supply chain members. However, there was only one company that demonstrated an increased focus on inventory optimization to deal with the risk of out-of-stocks or to buffer against the increased risk of supply disruptions. The role of supply network design and optimizations tools is still evolving on the SCM side. Some of the firms in this study do indeed make use of network design tools for infrequent, long-range decision making, such as manufacturing location or distribution capacity given long-term demand expectations. However, there was no indication that there are new cases of usage, such as helping companies understand, model, and cope with increasing levels of uncertainty in the supply chain or network.

Few of the firms used technology applications to do the following (with the exception of the three electronics firms and one food manufacturer): joint technology development initiatives, data warehousing, network design analysis programs, demand signal repositories, inventory optimization tools, and forecasting techniques (e.g., to pre-build and carry additional inventory of critical items). These techniques would be useful in managing risk and continuity with regard to new product launches as might be required moreso for electronics manufacturers than say automotive manufacturers. These firms were more inclined to embrace techniques such as scenario planning and capacity modeling. The electronics industry is known for risk stemming from short product lifecycles and high demand uncertainty. The food manufacturer made use of exploring a range of alternative supply sources and transportation routes between its distribution centers and customers. This was the only indication of a firm turning network analysis into a continuous process of refinement that allows them to reduce risk while identifying opportunities.

The firms in this study did not use their technology to evaluate their supply chain networks and lacked disciplined network-analysis programs. The more advanced firms in this study did leverage their technology to periodically assess strategic decisions about where to locate distribution centers and manufacturing capacity. They did look at what network design would allow them to service customer demand at the lowest cost and risk. None of them, however, were using network-design tools in innovative ways such as modeling the networks of their key competitors to test various scenarios and to perform frequent what-if analysis. None were also employing network-design tools to assess risks in the design of the network or even using simulation techniques to test network-configuration options.

Most of the technology supported the following SCM applications for the purposes of managing risk: information gathering, partnership formation and long-term agreements, supplier development initiatives, supplier performance measurement systems, consistent monitoring and auditing of a supplier's processes, using an approved list of suppliers, visiting supplier operations, establishing good communications with suppliers, inventory management (buffers, safety stock levels, optimal order and production quantity), spending management and analysis, credit and financial data analysis, business process management, contract management (e.g., leverage tools to monitor performance against commitments), and contingency planning (jointly with suppliers).

Inventory management in particular was a critical SCM application used to buffer risk and serve as a de-coupler between echelons of the supply chain. Some companies have adopted software tools to address multi-echelon inventory optimization. Firms are using these tools to apply probabilistic forecasting techniques to make inventory policy and configuration decisions and to evaluate different inventory strategies, though none of them used it to evaluate postponement strategies. Used effectively, they can help companies improve customer-service levels and fill rates, dampen the impact of supply disruptions, reduce risk, and yield better trade-off decisions between customer-service levels and required inventory investment.

Overall, the firms in this study did not engage in proactive modeling exercises as part of a concerted sales and operations planning process. As an example, they lacked a strong what-if capability and could not do cost versus delivery trade-offs. It was agreed though that Internet-based systems will become the common platform for supply chain integration and that the use of supply chain planning software will increase dramatically.

Factor 5—Conclusions and Recommendations

Technology has emerged as a key enabler to realize data and information integration in the supply chain. Making use of technology, in general, results in reducing disruption risks in the supply chain. Current information technologies allow for improved integration of information flows and supply chain visibility among all participants. Shared information reduces uncertainty and reduces the need for non-value added cost drivers such as safety stocks. As a result, the system becomes more responsive and eventually could become demand driven rather than forecast driven. A few select samples from this study demonstrate that information-driven supply chains hold the potential to perform significantly better than those that do not have access to information beyond their corporate boundaries.

Confidence in a supply chain is weakened when the length of time it takes to complete all the needed steps in the end-to-end pipeline process is longer and inconsistent. Associated with this length and inconsistency is the lack of visible, accurate, and real-time data. A key element in dealing with supply chain risk goes beyond documenting the likelihood and impact of risks, but also getting visibility to risks when they occur and translating that risk information to key decision makers so that they can evaluate and act on information. Throughout the supply chain, key operational data and information such as inventory, demand, forecasts, production and shipment plans, work in progress, yields, capacities, and backlogs should be easily accessible by key members of the supply chains. Such information should be accurate and timely, rendering it useful for all parties for planning and re-planning purposes. Thus, it is important that data and information are tightly managed and that any updates are made as timely as possible. The accuracy of the data should be a source of confidence to the parties using the data.

CONCLUDING COMMENTS

Managers agreed that without a systematic analysis technique to assess risk, much can go wrong in a supply chain (i.e., unexpected costs, extended lead times, poor quality, or numerous other negative performance variables). Analyzing the risk associated with SCM is a relatively new subject, and little has been done to assist managers with this process. However, one thing is certain, documenting and analyzing risk must be an essential part of continuous improvement. It becomes critical to have an easily understood method to identify and manage risk.

FMEA is a mainstream tool used to collect information related to risk management decisions for most companies in an engineering capacity, but not in a supply chain capacity. There were several documented procedures to complete a FMEA across industries in this study, especially in automotive. Most managers supported a modified version of the tool that could be used to help evaluate the risk of SCM decisions. For several of the firms in this study, FMEA is a well-documented and proven technique commonly used to evaluate the risk for failures in product and process designs. SCM decisions can be evaluated in much the same manner as product and process defects.

Most managers felt that proactive risk mitigation efforts applied to the supply chain is not common practice, but is required for minimizing disturbances. There was a general impression that with an FMEA-based SCM risk assessment tool, unforeseen problems that might have impacted the success of SCM efforts can be avoided. Most managers want to develop an implementation tool for FMEA in a supply chain environment, as well as know the issues occurring during the implementation process. They also want a procedure to integrate FMEA across the supply chain; and know how to implement the procedure in the supply chain, as well as to know the common problems occurring in its implementation under a supply chain environment. Managers were concerned with the inconsistencies in the ranking of severity, occurrence, and detection, and the inaccuracies that may delay effective FMEA implementation in a supply chain. Managers want guidelines for customers to correct these problems in FMEA applications, so they can adopt and integrate their FMEA process into a supply chain environment.

While many factors have been cited as influencing the predisposition toward having a system for managing risks in the supply chain, certain factors were identified as having a critical impact on predisposition and progress toward this. These factors included: corporate strategy, supply chain organization, process management, performance metrics, and information and technology. These factors describe a situation where the respondents saw managing supply chain risks as an extension of SCM. They also described a situation in which respondents recognized that success with managing risks requires cross-functional teams and cooperation. There seems to be recognition that succeeding requires more than simply introducing a new program or department. Rather, it is an undertaking that requires the participation of multiple parties working together. It is argued that these various factors act to pre-condition the firm and its systems to the introduction, acceptance, and progress on managing risks in the supply chain.

2

Using FMEA for Supply Chain Risk Management

INTRODUCTION

A key component of reducing overall corporate risk is supply chain risk management (SCRM) (Hauser 2003; VanderBok, Sauter, Bryan, & Horan 2007). Proactive SCRM can lead to greater customer satisfaction, lower total costs, improved delivery performance, and higher quality outcomes (Sodhi, Son, & Tang 2012). There is currently no obvious single application for managing supply chain risks. Most firms are using existing supply chain applications for managing risk (Zsidisin 2003a,b). In the absence of risk management applications, these firms are building risk considerations into traditional supply chain applications such as: initial supplier evaluations, financial risk assessment, supplier quality audits, capacity planning for operations and suppliers, lead time analysis for project management, supplier scorecard, management review, supplier risk analysis based on accounts payable performance, contingency plans, forecasting techniques, and safety stock to name just a few.

While there has been some research on supply chain risk management, there are still more questions than answers (Zsidisin and Ellram 2003; Zsidisin, Ellram, Carter, & Cavinato 2004). Sodhi et al. (2012) note that there is an "absence of any consensus on a definition or scope for supply chain risk." A number of processes of SCRM have also been proposed. Kleindorfer and Saad (2005) presented a three-step process: (1) specifying sources of risks and vulnerabilities, (2) assessment, and (3) mitigation; while both Jüttner, Peck, and Christopher (2003) and Hallikas, Karvonen, Pulkkinen, Virolainen, and Tuominem (2004) suggested a four-step process. Manuj and Mentzer (2008) provided a five-step process, and Tummala and Schoenherr (2011) extended risk management process to supply chains. Clearly, there is not yet agreement on what components and definitions constitute a "standard" supply chain risk management process. Sodhi et al. (2012) also note that "there is a shortage of empirical research in the area of SCRM" and this shortage is especially critical in addressing the question of current practice.

Jüttner (2005) has assessed the practice of SCRM, noting that "all traditional risk assessment processes/tools are being adopted more widely than the supply chain-specific processes" and that there is a "trend towards the less formalized and 'softer' tools." Failure mode and effects analysis (FMEA) has been suggested as such a tool (Teng, Ho, Shumar, & Liu 2006; Welborn 2007). Documenting the likelihood and impact of risks must be a key part of managing the supply chain and managers must have access to readily available risk information to make decisions. FMEA is a tool used to collect such information related to risk management decisions (Roshan et al. 2003; Walewski, Gibson, & Ellworth 2002; Welborn 2007).

FMEA is a long-standing technique used to assess the risk failures in product and process designs. All potential failures are evaluated in terms of likelihood, severity, and detectability. A higher FMEA score implies higher risks. Common variables used to quantify risk are frequency of an activity associated with the defect, quantity of parts associated with the defect, ability to detect the defect, probability of the defect, and severity of the defect. A risk priority number (RPN) is calculated for each potential failure. A common RPN is the product of: probability of failure * detectability of failure * severity of failure (Carbone & Tippett 2004; Stamatis 1995; Welborn 2007). The steps to complete a FMEA are as follows: (1) identify risk categories, (2) identify potential risks, (3) rate the opportunity, probability, and severity of each risk, (4) calculate the RPN for each risk, (5) analyze risks by RPN by using techniques such as a Pareto distribution, (6) develop actions to mitigate risks with a high RPN, and (7) reassess risks with another cycle of FMEA (Welborn 2007). The supply chain can actually be managed in much the same way as product and process defects. This will be demonstrated in the remaining sections of this chapter by actually showing how FMEA can play a major role in the process of managing risks through supplier assessment and selection.

RESEARCH METHOD

The purpose of this study was to identify how companies manage risks through supplier assessment and selection, and if FMEA plays a role in that process. The research was largely exploratory, so a purposeful sample was used (Eisenhardt 1989; Miles & Huberman 1994). The research questions were explored in two steps.

First, a survey was sent to 67 perceived supporters of the effort. The companies and people contacted were those that had supported supply management higher education and research programs, and were generally active in supply management professional organizations. Several industries were chosen for this study to achieve some level of generalizability. A 69% response rate was realized (46 responses). Most non-respondents indicated that either they did not have sufficient time to complete the survey or that company policy prevented them from discussing the particular research topics.

Second, after reviewing the survey data, respondents who indicated they had used FMEA as part of a supplier qualification process were contacted. One firm was asked to participate in follow-up research to further explore supplier qualification and FMEA processes as they relate to risk management. The three authors conducted a semi-structured interview with the supply chain manager and the director of supplier development at an office furniture manufacturer.

SURVEY RESULTS

The companies responding to the survey were based in North America and had global sales. Table 2.1 indicates that most of the responses (84.8%)

TABLE 2.1

Respondent Industry Profile

Description	Number
Manufacturing	
Automotive first tier suppliers	11
Automotive OEMs	4
Electronics manufacturers	3
Other (e.g., office furniture, home appliance, aerospace, medical equipment, plumbing fixtures, seats, recreational vehicles, etc.)	21
Non-Manufacturing	
Distributors	3
Other (logistics, telecommunications, clinical testing, retailer)	4

TABLE 2.2

Respondent Sales Profile

Sales ($)	Percent
50M–99M	4%
100M–499M	14%
500M–999M	7%
1B–9B	32%
10B–49B	34%
50B–99B	7%
Over 100B	2%

TABLE 2.3

Respondent Employment Profile

Employees	Percent
Under 50	2%
50–99	2%
100–499	9%
500–999	5%
1,000–4,999	24%
5,000–9,999	9%
Over 10,000	49%

TABLE 2.4

Respondent Titles

	Percent
Procurement or Supply Chain Leader/Manager/Coordinator	37%
Supply Chain Director/Vice President	16%
Materials/Inventory Manager	16%
Strategic/Senior Buyer	13%
Plant Manager	6%
Supply Chain Analyst	6%
Account/Sales Director	6%

were from manufacturing companies. Tables 2.2 and 2.3 list the sales and number of employees for each firm, respectively. Table 2.4 provides the job titles of the respondents.

The survey consisted of multiple sections, including Likert-scaled and open-ended questions. Some sections addressed issues such as what were the greatest risks the companies faced and what were the common techniques for identifying and mitigating risks, for example. This chapter focuses on the results specific to FMEA.

Respondents were asked to indicate whether they used FMEA for SCRM. Depending on that response, respondents were directed to respond to an appropriate set of questions. The majority of respondents (30 out of 46) indicated that they did not use FMEA for SCRM. Responses to open-ended questions suggested that FMEA is reserved for high-risk situations and is not used on a routine basis, as one firm indicated: "…we only use it in the very highest risk situations." Another manager commented, "I personally feel that most companies will not incorporate FMEA to all functional areas of the company. Unfortunately, it is and will continue to be considered a tool for engineering and quality until it is taught and pushed through supply chain issues."

Table 2.5 lists other reasons why FMEA was not used for SCRM, ranked from the highest to lowest average. The general lack of knowledge regarding how to apply FMEA in a supply chain context seems to be the biggest challenge to more widespread adoption. Perhaps it is this lack of knowledge that keeps the explicit value of FMEA from being recognized—or perhaps it is the perceived lack of value that keeps firms from learning more about FMEA. Either way, the other reasons for not adopting FMEA do not seem substantial and could likely be overcome through more knowledge about the process and proving its value.

The 16 firms that did use FMEA indicated that it could provide substantial benefits (see Table 2.6). However, measuring the effectiveness of

TABLE 2.5

Reasons Why Non-Users Do Not Adopt FMEA

Item	Mean	SD
There is not enough knowledge of the FMEA procedure.	5.27	1.48
There is no noticeable "explicit" value yet.	4.43	1.79
It is not recognized or required by our industry.	4.21	1.64
FMEA is too time-consuming.	4.10	1.52
It is difficult for us to estimate failure modes using tools such as the FMEA model.	3.96	1.32
Not enough failures are experienced to justify using it.	3.62	1.82
It would not be compatible with our software or processes.	3.57	1.81
It is too confusing or complicated.	3.50	1.48
My organization is only considering future FMEA usage.	3.19	1.47
Never heard of FMEA.	2.69	2.38

Note: 1 = not an important reason, 7 = very important reason.

TABLE 2.6

The Impact of Using FMEA

The Use of FMEA Has Led to:	Mean	SD
Higher product quality.	5.74	1.24
Higher product reliability.	5.42	1.64
Better quality planning.	5.37	1.57
Continuous improvement in product and process design.	5.37	1.34
Lower manufacturing costs.	4.74	1.79

Note: 1 = strongly disagree, 7 = strongly agree.

any risk reduction process by using standard supply chain performance measures (e.g., cost, quality) does not directly assess the relative success of the risk mitigation effort. It can only be inferred that the FMEA mitigated risks and thus supported better supply performance.

Table 2.7 indicates that FMEA processes can be improved, that FMEAs are intended to be applied globally, and that the effort is cross functional though it needs to be championed by a few personnel. There are some concerns that FMEA is executed consistently, however. One manager suggested that FMEA has significant benefits "…if treated as the living document it is and if it used properly and consistently. [It is an] excellent tool for conveying lessons learned to current and new processes."

Respondents were also asked what issue or source of difficulty a variety of factors have been with regard to FMEA usage. Table 2.8 groups these

TABLE 2.7

FMEA Processes and Approaches

Item	Mean	SD
The current FMEA could be improved in terms of organization and efficiency.	5.16	1.21
Customer requirements were used when developing FMEA.	4.95	1.84
Global suppliers of your organization are encouraged to implement FMEA.	4.74	1.73
FMEA is a group-oriented assignment.	4.74	1.48
Management has provided the resources and provisions for enabling employees to use FMEA.	4.68	1.49
The FMEA process is the job of a few personnel and implementation is not widespread.	4.37	1.50
The FMEA process covers the entire global supply chain.	4.21	1.87
I would be more likely to use FMEA if our IT/ERP system included it.	4.16	1.64
FMEA is often too vague and causes confusion for those in the supply chain.	4.11	0.88
FMEA is applied in all functional areas of the company, including supply chain management.	4.05	1.58
The process ensures the inclusion of input from both suppliers and customers in SCM.	3.95	1.39
Design requirements are defined in quantifiable terms to all parts of the supply chain.	3.58	1.26
The format of FMEA software and documentation is consistent within all participants.	3.32	1.42

Note: 1 = strongly disagree, 7 = strongly agree.

TABLE 2.8

FMEA Issues and Sources of Difficulty

Item	Mean	SD
Culture and Commitment		
Lack of time, inability to work around members' schedules to set up time.	4.68	1.42
Team commitment, members know and understand the importance.	4.37	1.42
Getting the team involved, motivated, trained, and focused.	4.32	1.38
Lack of management support.	3.32	1.60
Knowledge and Skills		
Most personnel from various functions do not have adequate knowledge on failures.	4.74	1.63
Determining how much detail is necessary to complete the analysis.	4.53	1.35
Consistency in the assessment of each failure.	4.21	1.47
The ability to explain a defect clearly and understandably.	3.95	1.35
Identifying preventative actions for each failure.	3.84	1.38
Difficulty in identifying and ranking severity of the failures.	3.74	1.41
The team's ability to agree on potential failures and why they occur.	3.68	1.11
Confusion in FMEA terminology.	3.68	1.57
Finding risk priority numbers (RPN).	3.58	1.07
Lack of creativity.	3.37	1.30
Information		
Obtaining accurate quality information.	4.11	1.24
Finding reliable data.	4.11	1.29
Documenting all the data and requirements needed to complete the FMEA.	4.00	1.56
The ability to overlook sets of data that are needed to assess the severity of a failure.	3.79	1.47

Note: 1 = not an issue, 7 = major issue.

into three categories: culture and commitment, knowledge and skills, and information. It does not appear that access to information is the key challenge. Rather, culture/commitment and knowledge seem to be the major barrier to more widespread implementation (coupled with perceived need for FMEA). One manager suggested that FMEA "…is a tool utilized during green belt certification; however it appears for the most part it is put back in the 'tool box' to collect dust once individuals are certified." Another manager suggested that FMEA could be more effectively used at her firm: "Training and time. We need to train everyone on how to do them the *same* way, as consistency is necessary, and we need time and resources available to dedicate to this cause as everyone recognizes the importance."

This study also showed that documenting the likelihood and impact of risks was not a key part of supply chain management and that supply chain risk information was not readily available to key decision makers. Furthermore, very few of the firms were actually able to exploit risk to an advantage by taking calculated risks in the supply chain and even fewer were prepared to minimize the effects of disruptions. These questions were asked on a 1 to 7 scale (strongly disagree to strongly agree): (1) A key part of our supply chain management is documenting the likelihood and impact of risks (mean = 4.20, var. = 2.86). (2) Supply chain risk information is accurate and readily available to key decision makers (mean = 3.87, var. = 2.78). There was some debate as to the validity and usefulness of tools to operationalize the process. The managers did tend to prefer approaches that combine subjective and objective measures because this allows them some freedom rather than being pushed into taking decisions solely on complicated numerical analysis.

Several of the firms used financial reports and questionnaires during supplier approval to compare supply candidates to the business requirements of the buyers or project teams. When justified by a perceived level of risk, a few of the firms went one step further and had candidate comparison matrices (e.g., supplier profiling form and supply chain FMEA). Additionally, most had formal processes for supplier visits (e.g., rapid plant assessment, site verification of the supplier questionnaire, etc.). Some firms actually used lifecycle management with supplier report cards and their buyers would conduct periodic supply chain reviews. In one firm, sourcing was assigned risk ownership and they used FMEA principles to evaluate risk impact. For each risk, they would assess what the financial impact would be in the event of a disruption. They then assigned a probability to each risk area and then they prioritized by multiplying the financial impact by the risk probability. Again, most firms are only using existing supply chain applications for managing risk with no formal risk management system in place. In the absence of risk management applications, these firms are building risk considerations into traditional supply applications (e.g., spend, contract, and inventory management, demand planning, benchmarking, building long-term partnerships, etc.). The case below highlights how FMEA is used to mitigate supply chain risks at an office furniture manufacturer that has requested to remain anonymous and will henceforth be referred to as Company1.

COMPANY1 BACKGROUND

Company1 is a global, publicly traded company with a 2012 revenue of $2.75 billion and around 10,000 employees. They compete in the global office furniture industry with a portfolio that addresses three core elements of an office environment: interior architecture, furniture, and technology. Suppliers provide design, production, and service support and are a key to Company1's success. Suppliers are evaluated and selected using a range of criteria including sustainable business practices, financial stability, legal and ethical compliance, quality, cost, delivery, and technical competence.

Failure Mode and Effects Analysis

In rare cases of extremely high risk, Company1 may conduct a complete FMEA. Only one FMEA in the supply chain has been conducted in the last seven years. It involved a new supplier and material that could have resulted in very high risk. The existing tools were not sufficient to assess risk, so a member of the Supplier Quality Group (SQG) who had been involved with the design of the FMEA, utilized a cross-functional team to apply FMEA. It proved to be an effective tool, as the supplier was not pursued in large part due to this assessment.

The initial FMEA template and guidelines were developed using information gathered from published articles. Rather than gathering information by directly using the FMEA templates, the interview guide shown in Table 2.9 was used to simplify the interview process. This interview guide put FMEA topics into non-FMEA language and ensured that the data gathered would be in terms that were familiar to the buyers. For example, the buyers would be asked, "What do you see as potential problems or causes of problems? How severe are the problems? How often do you think this might occur? How could we detect the problem or know about it?"

TABLE 2.9

FMEA Worksheet

Cause/ Problem Statement	Result of Problem	Severity	Occurrence	Detection	Action Item	Assigned to	Target Date

The SQG then populated the FMEA form shown in Table 2.10. It is an Excel-based form that guides the user. The "Item and Function" column in the FMEA form would be populated using the terms recorded during the interviews so that the process and issues would be familiar to all stakeholders. Each project would have a new set of topics that were derived from the interviews.

Each major heading in the FMEA form has a comment box that provides instructions. Scales were developed for the severity, likelihood of occurrence, and likelihood of detection columns as shown in Table 2.11 through Table 2.13. People generally agreed to and understood the meaning of the scales, but there was often disagreement regarding actual assignment of a number to a risk issue. The probability ranking was the most challenging because the ranges are more difficult to interpret and agree upon.

Agreement on a number was only part of the process. The greatest benefit of the process was the discussions that enabled the team to identify the critical issues from a cross-functional point of view. It was expected that people from different functions would perceive risk differently, so the discussions gave the team an opportunity to explore what the issues really were from a variety of perspectives. This process facilitates a fact-based, decision-making agreement by following a process of engaging all the stakeholders in a formal risk review.

Though FMEA proved to be effective, it has not jumped out to Company1 as something that needs to become part of the standard tool set, so for the short term there will likely be limited use of supply chain FMEA. However, there is some consideration that FMEA will be updated as supply becomes more involved in new product development processes and to support the company's strategic objectives of moving into new markets. FMEA might be more efficiently adopted because as the supply manager for Company1 indicated, "I believe the process will become more acceptable since we are seeing an influx of people with engineering and quality backgrounds in our sourcing organization."

Finished Goods FMEA

One of Company1's highest risk supply issues is the purchase of finished goods (FG). FG items are delivered directly to a Company1 customer from the supplier, so Company1 does not see the FG prior to customer installation. FG items are generally low volume and specialized products that may require specific capital equipment. Items might include a special lighting

TABLE 2.10

Supply Process FMEA

Supply Process Failure Mode Effects Analysis

Review team:		Process stakeholders:		Date	
Supplier:		Key project dates:		Tollgate 1 completed:	
Product:				Tollgate 2 completed:	
				Tollgate 3 completed:	

													Anticipated Results to Proposed Action(s)			
Item and Function	Potential Failure Mode	Effects of Failure	Projected Severity at 1st ship Rank 1-10	Cause(s) or Mechanism(s) of Failure	Projected Probability of Occurrence at 1st ship Rank 1-10	Key Process or Product Characteristic Yes/No	Current Design Controls	Projected Probability of Detection at 1st ship Rank 1-10	Ranking or Priority Number (Calculated 4×6×9)	Proposed Action(s)	Responsibility and Planned Completion Date	Severity Rank 1-10	Probability of Occurrence Rank 1-10	Probability of Detection Rank 1-10	Ranking or Priority Number (Calculated 13×14×15)
1	2	3	4	5	6	7	8	9	10	11	12	13	14	15	16
Part and/or Product															
Liability									0						0
New Technology									0						0
Process Complexity (Delivery, Performance)									0						0
Process Complexity (Cost)									0						0
Specifications (Incoming quality)									0						0
Business															
Core Competency									0						0
Ownership									0						0

Continued

TABLE 2.10 (Continued)

Supply Process FMEA

Item and Function	Potential Failure Mode	Effects of Failure	Projected Severity at 1st ship Rank 1–10	Cause(s) or Mechanism(s) of Failure	Projected Probability of Occurrence at 1st ship Rank 1–10	Key Process or Product Characteristic Yes/No	Current Design Controls	Projected Probability of Detection at 1st ship Rank 1–10	Ranking or Priority Number (Calculated 4×6×9)	Proposed Action(s)	Responsibility and Planned Completion Date	Anticipated Results to Proposed Action(s)			
												Severity Rank 1–10	Probability of Occurrence Rank 1–10	Probability of Detection Rank 1–10	Ranking or Priority Number (Calculated) 13×14×15
1	2	3	4	5	6	7	8	9	10	11	12	13	14	15	16
Capacity									0						0
Quality System									0						0
Financial									0						0
Environmental									0						0
Facilities									0						0
EDI/TradeWeb									0						0
Relationship															
Segmentation									0						0
Finished Goods									0						0
Sole/Single/Multi Source									0						0
Lead Time									0						0
Logistics									0						0

TABLE 2.11

FMEA Degree of Risk Severity Ranking

Degree of Severity Ranking

Degree	Description	Median Ranking
Very high	When a potential failure mode affects safe operation of the product and/or involves non-conformance with government regulations. May endanger people or product. Assign "9" if there will be a warning before failure, assign "10" if there will *not* be a warning before failure.	10 9
High	When a high degree of customer dissatisfaction is caused by the failure. Does not involve safety of people or product or compliance with government regulations. May cause disruption to subsequent processes/operations and/or require rework.	8 7
Moderate	When a moderate degree of customer dissatisfaction is caused by the failure. Customer is made uncomfortable or is annoyed by the failure. May cause rework or result in damage to equipment.	6 5 4
Low	When a failure will cause only slight annoyance to the customer.	3 2
Minor	When a failure is not likely to cause any real effect on subsequent processes/operations or require rework. Most customers are not likely to notice any failure. Any rework that might be required is minor.	1

fixture or a unique chair. Company1 still owns the FG design as the supplier builds to specifications.

There are two keys to mitigating FG risks. First, the initial supplier qualification process conducted by the SQG provides confidence in the supplier process. Second, the FG services group, with support from the SQG, conducts a "Probability/Likelihood of Discontinuance in Service" with an associated "Severity/Impact" analysis on a periodic basis or when market conditions change (reference Table 2.14). This process is similar to, but it is not a textbook FMEA. This "scorecard" provides a closed loop analysis in the qualification and lifecycle management process.

CONCLUSION

Managers agreed that without a systematic technique to assess risk, much could go wrong in a supply chain (i.e., unexpected costs, extended lead times, poor quality, etc.). Analyzing the risk associated with SCM is a

TABLE 2.12

FMEA Degree of Risk Occurrence Ranking

Degree of Occurrence Ranking

Chance	Description	Probability	Median Ranking
Very high	Failure is almost inevitable.	1 in 2	10
		1 in 3	9
High	Process is "similar" to previous processes with a high rate of failure.	1 in 8	8
		1 in 20	7
Moderate	Process is "similar" to previous processes, which have occasional failures.	1 in 80	6
		1 in 400	5
		1 in 2,000	4
Low	Process is "similar" to previous processes with isolated failures.	1 in 15,000	3
Very low	Process is "similar" to previous processes with very isolated failures.	1 in 150,000	2
Remote	Process is "similar" to previous processes with no known failures.	1 in 1,500,000	1

TABLE 2.13

FMEA Degree of Risk Detection Ranking

Degree of Detection Ranking

Degree	Degree in %	Description	Median Ranking
Detection is not possible	0	Control method(s) cannot or will not detect the existence of a problem.	10
Very low	0 to 50	Control method(s) probably will not detect the existence of a problem.	9
Low	50 to 60	Control method(s) has a poor chance of detecting the existence of a problem.	8
	60 to 70		7
Moderate	70 to 80	Control method(s) may detect the existence of a problem.	6
	80 to 85		5
High	85 to 90	Control method(s) has a good chance of detecting the existence of a problem.	4
	90 to 95		3
Very high	95 to 100	Control method(s) will almost certainly detect the existence of a problem.	2
			1

TABLE 2.14

FG "Scorecard"

Supplier List			Probability/Likelihood (Discontinuance in Service)				
			Weight per probability				
			Viable financial stability 40%				
			Change in ownership 20%				
			Tier two reliance 20%				
			Strategy change 20%				
Supplier	Product	SCL	Viable—Financial Stability	Change in Ownership	Tier Two Reliance	Strategy Change	Overall probability
			40% Weight	20% Weight	20% Weight	20% Weight	
			1 Low	1 Low	1 Low	1 Low	
			2 Medium	2 Medium	2 Medium	2 Medium	
			3 High	3 High	3 High	3 High	

Continued

TABLE 2.14 (Continued)
FG "Scorecard"

Supplier List			Severity/Impact					
Supplier	Product	SCL	Product Spending	Tooling Cost	Product Criticality	Recovery Time	Contingency Sources	Overall impact
			15% weight	10% weight	30% Weight	30% Weight	15% Weight	
			1 Very low 0–100k	1 Very low No tooling	1 Very low	1 Very Low 1 to 4 wks recovery	1 Very low—off the shelf	
			2 Low 100k– 250k	2 Low Transferable/ Under 10k	2 Low	2 Low 4 to 8 wks	2 Low—multiple sources	
			3 Medium 250k–500k	3 Medium 10k–25k	3 Medium	3 Medium 9 to 12 wks	3 Medium—2–5 available suppliers	
			4 High 500k–1 MM	4 High 25k–50k	4 High	4 High 3 to 6 months	4 High—1–2 suppliers	
			5 Very high 1 MM— above	5 Very high 50k and above	5 Very high	5 Very high 6 months or more	5 Very high— proprietary products/process	
								0

relatively new subject, and little has been done to assist managers with this process. But one thing is certain, documenting and analyzing risk must be an essential part of continuous improvement. It becomes critical to have an easily understood method to identify and manage risk.

FMEA is a mainstream tool used to collect information related to risk management decisions for most companies in an engineering capacity, but not in a supply chain capacity. There were several documented procedures to complete an FMEA across industries in this study, especially in automotive. Most managers supported a modified version of the tool that could be used to help evaluate the risk of SCM decisions. For several of the firms in this study, FMEA is a well-documented and proven technique commonly used to evaluate the risk for failures in product and process designs. SCM decisions can be evaluated in much the same manner as product and process defects.

Most managers felt that proactive risk mitigation efforts applied to the supply chain is not common practice, but is required for minimizing disturbances. There was a general impression that with an FMEA-based SCM risk assessment tool, unforeseen problems that might have impacted the success of SCM efforts can be avoided. Most managers want tools and procedures for implementing FMEA in a supply chain environment. They also want to know the critical success factors to the implementation process. Managers were concerned with the inconsistencies in the ranking of severity, occurrence, and detection and the inaccuracies that may delay effective FMEA implementation in a supply chain. Managers want guidelines for customers in correcting these problems in FMEA applications, so they can adopt and integrate their FMEA process into a supply chain environment. The case example provides direction for managers by emphasizing that supply chain FMEA cannot be viewed as purely an engineering exercise, and by ensuring that the terms and measures used in FMEA are driven by the key stakeholders.

REFERENCES

Carbone, T.A & Tippett, D.D. 2004. Project Risk Management Using the Project Risk FMEA. *Engineering Management Journal*, 16(4): 28–35.

Eisenhardt, K. 1989. Building Theories from Case Study Research. *The Academy of Management Review*, 14(4): 532–550.

Hallikas, J., Karvonen, I., Pulkkinen, U., Virolainen, V.M., & Tuominem, M. 2004. Risk Management Processes in Supplier Networks. *International Journal of Production Economics*, 90(1): 47–58.

Hauser, L. 2003. Risk Adjusted Supply Chain Management. *Supply Chain Management Review*, 7(6): 64–71.

Jüttner, U. 2005. Supply Chain Risk Management: Understanding the Business Requirements from a Practitioner Perspective. *The International Journal of Logistics Management*, 16(1): 120–141.

Jüttner, U., Peck, H., & Christopher, M. 2003. Supply Chain Risk Management: Outlining an Agenda for Future Research. *International Journal of Logistics*, 6(4): 197–210.

Kleindorfer, P.R. & Saad, G.H. 2005. Managing Disruptions in Supply Chains. *Production and Operations Management*, 14(1): 53–68.

Manuj, I. & Mentzer, J.T. 2008. Global Supply Chain Risk Management. *Journal of Business Logistics*, 29(1): 133–156.

Miles, M. & Huberman, A. 1994. *Qualitative Data Analysis: A Sourcebook of New Methods*, Newbury Park, CA: Sage Publications.

Roshan, R.P., Venkata, R.K., Reggie, J.C., & Meng, C.Z. 2003. Methods Towards Supply Chain Risk Analaysis. *Proceedings of the IEEE International Conference on Systems, Man, & Cybernetics*, 5(1): 4560–4565.

Sodhi, M.S., Son, B.G., & Tang, C.S. 2012. Researcher's Perspective on Supply Risk Management. *Productions and Operations Management*, 21(1): 1–15.

Stamatis, D.H. 1995. *Failure Mode Effect Analysis—FMEA from Theory to Execution.* Milwaukee, WI: ASQ Quality Press.

Teng, S.G., Ho, S.M., Shumar, D., & Liu, P.C. 2006. Implementing FMEA in a Collaborative Supply Chain Environment. *The International Journal of Quality and Reliability Management*, 23(2/3): 179–196.

Tummala, R. & Schoenherr, T. 2011. Assessing and Managing Risks Using the Supply Chain Risk Management Process SCRMP. *Supply Chain Management*, 16(6): 474–483.

VanderBok, R., Sauter, J., Bryan, C., & Horan, J. 2007. Manage Your Supply Chain Risk. *Manufacturing Engineering*, 138(3): 153–161.

Walewski, J.A., Gibson, E.G., & Ellworth, V.F. 2002. Improving International Capital Project Risk Analysis and Management. *Proceedings of Project Management Institute Research Conference*, July.

Welborn, C. 2007. Using FMEA to Assess Outsourcing Risk. *Quality Progress*, 40(8): 17–21.

Zsidisin, G.A. 2003a. Managerial Perceptions of Supply Risk. *Journal of Supply Chain Management: A Global Review of Purchasing & Supply*, 39(1): 14–23.

Zsidisin, G.A. 2003b. A Grounded Definition of Supply Risk. *Journal of Purchasing and Supply Management*, 9(5): 217–224.

Zsidisin, G.A. & Ellram, L.M. 2003. An Agency Theory Investigation of Supply Risk Management. *Journal of Supply Chain Management: A Global Review of Purchasing & Supply*, 39(3): 15–27.

Zsidisin, G.A., Ellram, L.M., Carter, J.R., & Cavinato, J.L. 2004. An Analysis of Supply Risk Assessment Techniques. *International Journal of Physical Distribution & Logistics Management*, 34(5): 397–413.

3

Supply Chain Risk Management within the Context of COSO's Enterprise Risk Management Framework

INTRODUCTION

Every firm is engaged in some type of risk management. However, few firms conduct risk management using a systematic approach (Beasley, Clune, & Hermanson 2005; Bowling & Rieger 2005). Enterprise risk management (ERM), though not widely adopted, provides a framework and set of tools for managing risks holistically. ERM has been defined a variety of ways, but most definitions focus on holistically identifying, assessing, and managing risks throughout an organization and its value chain (COSO 2004).

Supply chain risk management (SCRM), one element of ERM, is emerging as a viable, proactive, and strategic supply chain management (SCM) application. However, existing SCRM models do not explicitly make the linkage to ERM. This research focuses on the structure, implementation, and maintenance of a formal SCRM system and how such a system may be integrated with ERM. The ERM framework proposed by the Committee of Sponsoring Organizations (COSO) of the Treadway Commission is used to examine such integration (COSO 2004). It is suggested that explicitly linking SCRM with ERM will more readily advance research regarding these important issues and support supply managers in their efforts to develop SCRM strategies, garner the necessary resources, and execute SCRM at their firms.

Data from 46 firms were analyzed to identify which factors affect the decision to develop an SCRM system and how these factors can influence the level of ERM and SCRM success. The decision to manage supply chain risks constitutes a major undertaking for most firms. Such an undertaking is a response to a number of factors or influences. There seems to be recognition that succeeding requires more than simply creating a new program or department. It is suggested that various factors act to pre-condition the firm and its systems to the introduction, acceptance, and progress on managing supply risks.

The remainder of this chapter begins with a review of the literature, followed by the methods section. The survey data are then analyzed to profile the respondents and identify how they manage supply chain risks. The chapter then concludes with an evaluation of the factors underlying the decision to develop a system for managing supply chain risks and how these factors can be leveraged into a competitive advantage through ERM.

LITERATURE REVIEW

The literature review consists of four related sections. First, the rationale for pursuing a standard risk framework is presented. Next, an established ERM framework is explored. Proposed SCRM frameworks are then discussed relative to the ERM framework. Finally, an overview of supply risks and approaches that were included in the survey is presented.

Rationale for a Standard Framework

The advancement of research in a discipline (e.g., just-in-time manufacturing, supply chain management) may be accelerated through the development and validation of frameworks and concepts generated through exploratory empirical research. For example, the total quality management (TQM) discipline leverages standardized frameworks to advance theory building and testing (see for example, Black & Porter 1996; Capon, Kaye, & Wood 1994; Curkovic, Melnyk, Calantone, & Handfield 2000; Dean & Bowen 1994; Flynn, Schroeder, & Sakakibara 1994; Saraph, Benson, & Schroeder 1989). By leveraging such frameworks, TQM research has moved from a focus on case studies (the current state of SCRM research) to testable models and specific research hypotheses, linking the theoretical concept of TQM to empirical indicants. Operational definitions and standardized frameworks have contributed to TQM theory building by identifying the constructs associated with TQM, developing scales for measuring these constructs, and empirically validating the scales. SCRM research is still in its infancy stages and would benefit from development of standardized frameworks and concepts.

Sodhi, Son, and Tang (2012) identified the lack of consensus regarding the scope of SCRM as a critical gap in SCRM research. They suggested that there is a great need to reach a consensus on such issues in order to better communicate with company executives and practitioners, and to more quickly advance SCRM research. They also suggested that SCRM is a subset or extension of ERM (Sodhi, Son, & Tang 2012). Given their suggestions, the COSO ERM framework was identified as a potential consensus framework for SCRM that could fill the research gap while also contributing to the efforts of managers to link SCRM to corporate-wide risk management efforts.

Enterprise Risk Management and the COSO Framework

Global competitive landscapes and increasingly complex supply chain processes and partnerships, coupled with increased requirements to comply with regulations, laws, and industry guidelines has heightened awareness that firms may benefit from a systematic approach to risk management. Enterprise risk management (ERM) has garnered significant academic, consultant, and practitioner interest over the last decade as a way to not only mitigate risk but to take advantage of risk opportunities (Hoyt & Liebenberg 2011; Nocco & Stulz 2006). ERM is a process for identifying, analyzing, and proactively planning responses to a portfolio of risks (Bowling & Rieger 2005; Chapman 2003).

Though effective ERM can provide significant benefits for a firm (Hoyt & Liebenberg 2011; Smithson & Simkins 2005), a relatively small percentage of firms have a detailed understanding of this integrated process and adoption of ERM is rather limited (Chapman 2003; COSO 2010). Ad hoc approaches to risk management by various "silos" in an organization leads to duplication of resources, uncoordinated planning, and less efficient and effective risk management processes (Hoyt & Liebenberg 2011).

Varying frameworks have been proposed to support and standardize implementation of systematic ERM. Sample frameworks include the Joint Australia/New Zealand AS/NZ 4360-2004, the Turnbull Guidance, and the ISO standards for risk management. This research adopts the framework developed by the Committee of Sponsoring Organizations (COSO) of the Treadway Commission (COSO 2004), shown in Figure 3.1.

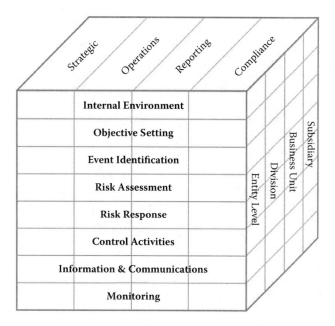

FIGURE 3.1
The COSO ERM framework.

This framework is perhaps the most widely discussed and familiar ERM framework (COSO 2010). COSO is a voluntary private sector organization, led by the Institute of Management Accountants, The Institute of Internal Auditors, Financial Executives International, the American Accounting Association, and the American Institute of Public Accountants. COSO provides executive management with guidance regarding effective, efficient, and ethical business practices.

COSO's ERM framework consists of eight components of ERM that are needed to help a firm achieve its objectives, as described in Table 3.1 (COSO 2004; Sobel 2006). All eight components need to be implemented and integrated to provide effective ERM. The framework also emphasizes entity-wide risk management across the four objectives (strategic, operations, reporting, compliance) as described in Table 3.2 (Ballou & Heitger 2005; COSO 2004). The COSO framework also emphasizes that risks be examined at each level of the organization (i.e., subsidiary, business unit, division, entity) beginning with the entity level and aggregated across all levels so that a portfolio of risks can be managed holistically (Chapman 2003; COSO 2004). This research focuses on the "entity" level and "operational" objectives across the eight components of ERM.

TABLE 3.1

Interrelated Components of the COSO ERM Framework

Component	Description
Internal environment	Reflects alignment of the firm's risk philosophy, its appetite for risk, the risk management and ethical culture, human resource policies and practices, assignment of responsibility, and the organizational structure to manage risks.
Objective setting	Identifies the firm's competitive strategy or positioning (e.g., low cost, high quality, etc.) and related objectives in four areas: strategy, operations, reporting, and compliance, which in turn drives objectives throughout the value chain.
Event identification	Identifies possible internal and external events, and the potential interrelatedness of those events, that impact a firm's ability to realize its strategy and objectives. Positive impact events are "opportunities" that are channeled back to strategic planning, while negative impact events are risks that should be managed through an integrated risk management process to help determine how such risks might be managed.
Risk assessment	Examines the likelihood, frequency, and the impact (e.g., financial, reputation, etc.) of events across a range (e.g., best to worst case) of possible outcomes associated with the events.
Risk response	Identifies, assesses, and selects risk response options that align with the organization's risk tolerances and risk appetite. Options include avoidance (e.g., not engaging in the activity), reduction (e.g., rebalancing the risk, reallocating resources, robust business process, etc.), sharing (e.g., insurance, partnering, contractual agreements, hedging, etc.) and acceptance.
Control activities	Establishes that risk policies and procedures are in place and properly executed, and that the risk management initiatives are effective. Such controls may include required authorizations, supervision, and segregation of duties, reconciliations, and verifications, for example.
Information and communications	Requires that internal and external sources be used to provide appropriate and timely risk related information that enables people to execute their responsibilities. Such communications need to be integrated throughout the value chain and impacted organizations.
Monitoring	Ensures that an ERM is present and determines how well it is working so that it can be revised and/or expanded.

COSO defines risk as the probability that an event may occur which adversely impacts the achievement of the entity's objectives (Chapman 2003). However, given that some risks if managed proactively may lead to a positive outcome for a firm, the framework supports the management of positive risk opportunities and negative risk impacts.

TABLE 3.2

Objectives of the COSO ERM Framework

Objective	Description
Strategic	Mission driven high-level goals and objectives (governance, strategic objectives, business model, external forces, etc.)
Operations	Resource development, management, and allocation (business processes, upstream value chain, downstream value chain, etc.)
Reporting	Information gathering, analysis, and communication (information technology, financial, internal, intellectual property, etc.)
Compliance	Conformance with laws and regulations (Securities & Exchange Commission, environmental, legal, contractual, etc.)

COSO formally defines ERM as:

> ...a process, effected by an entity's board of directors, management and other personnel, applied in a strategy setting and across the enterprise, designed to identify potential events that may affect the entity, and manage risks to be within its risk appetite, to provide reasonable assurance regarding the achievement of entity objectives. (COSO 2004)

ERM and related frameworks are not without detractors. Even COSO states that its ERM framework is not a panacea and is a challenge to implement, and it invites research based on better understanding the framework (Landsittel & Rittenberg 2010). There is a lack of empirical research into the effectiveness of ERM in general (Hoyt & Liebenberg 2011) and the specific frameworks in particular. Other detractors note that implementing ERM requires a substantial commitment of resources (time, personnel, money) that are not likely to be available during lean times, and a cultural shift of the entire organization (Ballou & Heitger 2005) without an appropriate return on such efforts (Samad-Khan 2005). However, with appropriate planning and execution COSO's ERM framework may be implemented by any organization, from large to small firms (Ballou & Heitger 2005; Chapman 2003; COSO 2004).

Linking ERM and SCRM Frameworks

SCRM frameworks have also been proposed (Hallikas, Karvonen, Pulkkinen, Virolainen, & Tuominem 2004; Kleindorfer & Saad 2005; Manuj & Mentzer 2008; Tummala & Schoenherr 2011). There are many similarities in these frameworks, though there is no consensus on the scope of SCRM.

In some cases, the concepts are the same, but the terms used are slightly different (e.g., risk assessment versus risk evaluation) and some frameworks do not explicitly identify key processes (e.g., monitoring and review). Table 3.3 compares four SCRM frameworks with the COSO framework.

Though SCRM frameworks and COSO share many similarities, there are significant differences. Most noticeably, the COSO framework explicitly identifies internal environment, objective setting, control activities, and information and communications as key components of risk management. Some of those components are implied and/or integrated into some of the SCRM frameworks, but the COSO framework provides a more explicit and comprehensive framework. This might be expected as COSO is an enterprise framework while the SCRM frameworks are "operational." But that is the point. Until SCRM is positioned as a key component of ERM, supply managers will continue to struggle to secure the resources and to make risk decisions that support corporate-wide strategy and objectives, and researchers will struggle to identify and measure risk management factors.

Supply Chain Risks and Practices

Firms face multiple supply risks, whether in combination or isolation. Sample risks include supplier reliability/failure, information errors, natural disasters, shrinkage, capacity shortages, financial instability, currency exchange rate fluctuations, port security, and increased government regulations, for example (Blackhurst, Wu, & O'Grady 2005; Kumar & Verruso 2008; Liu & Cruz 2012; Manuj & Mentzer 2008; Tummala & Schoenherr 2011; Zsidisin & Hartley 2012). Each risk might require a specific SCRM technique (Zsidisin & Wagner 2010).

For example, SCRM treatment options include evaluation and trust building (Laeequddin, Sardana, Sahay, Abdul Waheed, & Sahay 2009), use of dual sources (Khan & Burnes 2007), environmental scanning (Zsidisin, Ellram, Carter, & Cavinato 2004), combined capacity reservation contracts and spot markets (Inderfurth & Kelle 2011), supply chain modeling and information systems integration (Giannakis & Louis 2001), qualification and use of capable suppliers (Manuj & Mentzer 2008), supplier quality management initiatives (Holschbach & Hofmann 2011), buffer inventory (Tang 2006), contingency plans (Kleindorfer & Saad 2005), credit analysis (Kern, Moser, Hartman, & Moder 2012), strategic sourcing and flexibility (Chiang, Kocabasoglu-Hillmer, & Suresh 2012), forward buying or hedging (Zsidisin & Hartley 2012), and supplier development (Matook, Lasch,

TABLE 3.3

Comparison of SCRM Frameworks to COSO

COSO 2004	Hallikas, Karvonen, Pulkkinen et al. 2004	Kleindorfer & Saad 2005	Manuj & Mentzer 2008	Tummala & Schoenherr 2011
Internal environment				
Objective setting				
Event identification	Risk identification	Specifying sources of risks and vulnerabilities	Risk identification	Risk identification
				Risk measurement
Risk assessment	Risk assessment	Assessment	Risk assessment and evaluation	Risk assessment
				Risk evaluation
Risk response	Decision and implementation of risk management actions	Mitigation	Selection of appropriate risk management strategies	Risk mitigation and contingency plans
			Implementation of supply chain risk management strategies	
			Mitigation of supply chain risks	
Control activities				
Information and communications				
Monitoring	Risk monitoring			Risk control and monitoring

& Tamaschke 2009). Despite the plethora of risks and risk management approaches, few firms have a structured SCRM approach (Martin, Mena, Khan, & Yurt 2011).

RESEARCH METHOD

The purpose of this study was to identify how companies identify and manage supply chain risks and how those actions relate to systemic ERM. The research was exploratory in nature. A purposeful sample was selected to support the research objectives and methodology (Eisenhardt 1989; Miles & Huberman 1994). Key criterion included the following: the company would agree to identify an informed respondent, reply in a timely manner to a scaled and open-ended survey, and be willing to participate in follow-up questions as needed. All targeted companies were known to support supply management educational programs and professional associations.

A total of 67 surveys were sent to perceived supporters of the effort. Several industries were chosen for this study to achieve some level of generalizability. A total of 46 completed responses were received. Early to late respondent survey comparisons were made to analyze potential non-response bias (Armstrong & Overton 1977). The mean values for seven randomly selected questions were compared between the first 25% of responses and the last 25% of responses. No statistically significant differences were found between responses. The majority of non-respondents indicated that either company policy prevented them from participation in this particular survey or that resources were constrained when the survey was distributed.

DATA ANALYSIS

Respondent Profiles

The majority of responses (84.8%) were from manufacturing firms (see Table 3.4). All of the companies were based in North America and had global sales. The sales and number of employees for respondents are shown in Tables 3.5 and 3.6. Approximately 60% of the companies were publicly owned, 33% were privately owned, and 7% were publicly/privately owned.

TABLE 3.4

Respondent Industry Profile

Description	Number
Manufacturing	
Automotive first tier suppliers	11
Automotive OEMs	4
Electronics manufacturers	3
Other (e.g., office furniture, home appliances, aerospace, medical equipment, plumbing fixtures, seats, recreational vehicles, etc.)	21
Non-Manufacturing	
Distributors	3
Other (logistics, telecommunications, clinical testing, retailers)	4

TABLE 3.5

Respondent Sales Profile

Sales ($)	Percent
50M–99M	4%
100M–499M	14%
500M–999M	7%
1B–9B	32%
10B–49B	34%
50B–99B	7%
Over 100B	2%

TABLE 3.6

Respondent Employment Profile

Employees	Percent
Under 50	2%
50–99	2%
100–499	9%
500–999	5%
1,000–4,999	24%
5,000–9,999	9%
Over 10,000	49%

Companies were asked to have the survey completed by the person most familiar with supply risk management in their organizations. Different companies often use significantly different titles for similar responsibilities, while some companies may use the same title for significantly different responsibilities. Nonetheless, Table 3.7 suggests that informed respondents replied to the survey.

RESULTS AND DISCUSSION

Enterprise and supply chain risk management is a highly integrated process that requires coordination of strategy, process, policy, and tools throughout the value chain. Though discussed in separate sections below, each of the categories of the COSO ERM framework should be present and integrated in order to most effectively manage risks.

TABLE 3.7

Respondent Titles

	Percent
Procurement or Supply Chain Leader/Manager/Coordinator	37%
Supply Chain Director/Vice President	16%
Materials/Inventory Manager	16%
Strategic/Senior Buyer	13%
Plant Manager	6%
Supply Chain Analyst	6%
Account/Sales Director	6%

Internal Environment and Objective Setting

Table 3.8 provides descriptive statistics related to the internal environment and objective setting. All "agree/disagree" questions are scaled from 1 = strongly disagree to 7 = strongly agree. All "extent of use" questions are scaled from 1 = not used to 7 = extensively used.

Need: Respondents clearly believe that risk management is a critically important strategic initiative for their firms and that the management of risk should be a core issue in the planning of any organization. However, the concomitant development of resources, tools, and budgets appears lacking as suggested below.

Approach: Managing risks requires an integrated and systemic approach as the COSO framework suggests. Firms recognize that no single set of tools or technologies exists to manage all risks, so despite the clear need there is a significant challenge in implementation. Approximately half the firms agreed that supply chain risks are managed reactively rather than proactively, and that risk initiatives are driven top–down. It appears that in the absence of risk management applications, these firms are building risk considerations into traditional SCM applications (e.g., spend, contract, and inventory management, demand planning, benchmarking, building long-term partnerships, etc.) on an ad hoc basis.

Budget: Respondents suggested that firms are spending funds on supply risk management, but few suggested that spending was "very high" (only 26% of firms agreed that spending was very high). Budget allocations varied depending on firm size (larger firms having larger budgets) and industry type (service firms spending more on logistics issues, manufacturing firms spending more on supplier failure issues). With regard to potential change in budget for the next year, 45% indicated an increase, 41% no

TABLE 3.8

Internal Environment and Objective Setting

Need	Mean	SD
Managing supply chain risk is an increasingly important initiative for our operations.	5.65	1.30
Without a systematic analysis technique to assess risk, much can go wrong in a supply chain.	5.54	1.03
It is critical for us to have an easily understood method to identify and manage supply chain risk.	5.30	1.23
My workplace plans on evaluating or implementing supply chain risk tools and technologies.	4.98	1.58
We are very concerned about our supply chain resiliency, and the failure implications.	4.78	1.59
Approach		
There is no single set of tools or technologies on the market for managing supply chain risks.	5.24	1.49
We are currently using some form of supply chain risk management tools and services.	4.46	1.93
Managing supply chain risks is driven by reactions to failures rather than being proactively driven.	4.39	1.36
Proactive risk mitigation efforts applied to the supply chain is common practice for us.	4.33	1.49
Supply chain risk initiatives are driven from the bottom up rather than top down.	3.67	1.56
Budget		
We do plan on investing nontrivial amounts in managing supply chain risks.	4.30	1.86
Funding for managing supply chain risks will come from a general operations budget.	3.91	1.94
We have a dedicated budget for activities associated with managing supply chain risks.	3.65	1.96
Our spending intentions for managing supply chain risks are very high.	3.37	1.58
Organization		
I fully understand the activities being performed by our risk management group.	4.00	1.86
Supply chain employees understand government legislation and geopolitical issues.	3.70	1.26
My workplace uses supply chain risk managers who work closely with corporate risk management.	2.53	1.74
We are planning to outsource all or some of our risk management functions.	2.25	1.28

change, and only 14% indicated a decrease. Companies also indicated that ownership of investments for managing supply chain risks generally resides with Supply Chain/Purchasing (60%), though in some firms other areas had ownership (Manufacturing/Operations = 12%, Accounting/Finance = 7%, Quality = 6%, Legal = 6%, IT = 3%, Logistics = 3%, and Risk = 3%). Only 17% of firms had a specific budget to address supply chain issues, with other firms reporting that budget for managing supply chain risks came from other specific department (57%) or general operations (26%). It seems that while spending intentions for managing supply chain risks are moderate, funding is poorly targeted and ownership is not centered within the SCM discipline. Managing risks is just now reaching the core of traditional and mature SCM applications.

Organization: Respondents indicated that they have no intention to outsource risk management. Currently, however, the supply chain function lacks the appropriate knowledge and structure (e.g., no supply risk managers linked with corporate risk managers) to most effectively mitigate supply risks. It would appear that the corporate function is involved with risk management but does not necessarily coordinate risk management activities in the whole group.

Event Identification and Risk Assessment

Table 3.9 suggests that although specific risk issues (e.g., moving facilities overseas) may be carefully evaluated, only about half of the firms indicated that a key part of SCM is documenting the likelihood and impact of risks. Further, only half of the firms exploited risks to an advantage. This fact is not surprising given that few firms have an integrated risk strategy and appropriate supply chain risk management skills as previously discussed.

Respondents saw a broad set of risk factors that could pose a disruption to their supply chains (Table 3.10). These risks did not vary much by industry. Supplier failure/reliability was the top risk factor, with bankruptcies of suppliers, logistics failure, commodity cost volatility, natural disasters, and strikes/labor disputes as distant seconds. The non-manufacturing respondents were more inclined to place a higher priority on logistics failure, which is not surprising since they were mostly made up of distributors and a retailer. Respondents were asked if each firm's supply chain risks would increase, stay the same, or decrease in the next 1 to 2 years (Table 3.11).

While supplier failure is a high risk factor for all of the firms and will increase in risk for several of the firms, 13 firms did say that they expected

TABLE 3.9

Event Identification and Risk Assessment

	Mean	SD
Risks of moving manufacturing facilities overseas are carefully evaluated.	5.65	1.15
Supplier reliability and continuous supply is the top risk factor for our supply chain.	5.35	1.34
Risks of not being able to fulfill a spike in consumer demand are carefully evaluated.	5.22	1.25
Key metrics are in place to measure the risk associated with key suppliers.	4.65	1.68
We apply high levels of analytical rigor to assess our supply chain practices.	4.37	1.53
A key part of our supply chain management is documenting the likelihood and impact of risks.	4.20	1.67
We can actually exploit risk to an advantage by taking calculated risks in the supply chain.	4.02	1.63
Taxes such as excise and VAT impact our supply chain decisions.	3.86	1.69

TABLE 3.10

Current Supply Chain Risks

Risk Factor	Frequency
Supplier failure/reliability	41
Bankruptcy, ruin, or default of suppliers, shippers, etc.	22
Logistics failure	20
Commodity cost volatility	18
Natural disasters or accidents (tsunamis, hurricanes, fires, etc.)	15
Strikes—labor, buyers, and suppliers	15
Diminishing capacities (financial, production, structural, etc.)	10
Government regulations (SOX, SEC, Clean Air Act, OSHA, EU)	9
Customer-related (demand change, system failure, payment delay)	8
Attracting and retaining skilled labor	8
Intellectual property infringement	7
Lack of trust with partners	7
Currency exchange, interest, and/or inflation rate fluctuations	7
Geopolitical events (terrorism, war, etc.)	6
Energy/raw material shortages and power outages	6
Information delays, scarcity, sharing, and infrastructure breakdown	5
Legal liabilities and issues	5
Contract failure	4
Contamination exposure—food, germs, infections	3

TABLE 3.11

Projected Change in Supply Chain Risks

	Frequency		
Risk Category	Less	Same	More
Currency exchange, interest, and/or inflation rate fluctuations	0	7	36
Commodity cost volatility	2	9	33
Bankruptcy, ruin, or default of suppliers, shippers, etc.	2	13	29
Banking regulations and tighter financing conditions	1	16	28
Supplier failure/reliability	13	7	24
Customer-related (demand change, system failure, payment delay)	3	22	19
Intellectual property infringement	3	23	18
Diminishing capacities (financial, production, structural, etc.)	5	22	17
Legal liabilities and issues	2	26	17
Government regulations (SOX, SEC, Clean Air Act, OSHA, EU)	0	28	16
Customs Acts/Trade restrictions and protectionism	2	27	16
Attracting and retaining skilled labor	12	15	16
Geopolitical events (terrorism, war, etc.)	0	29	15
Energy/raw material shortages and power outages	3	26	15
Language and educational barriers	8	21	15
Insurance coverage	1	29	14
Strikes—labor, buyers, and suppliers	4	26	14
Port/cargo security (information, freight, vandalism, sabotage, etc.)	3	29	13
Natural disasters or accidents (tsunamis, hurricanes, fires, etc.)	2	34	12
Logistics failure	8	27	9
Return policy and product recall requirements	5	29	9
Tax issues (VAT, transfer pricing, excise, etc.)	3	32	9
Weaknesses in the local infrastructures	9	27	8
Information delays, scarcity, sharing, and infrastructure breakdown	18	18	8
Contract failure	5	32	7
Ethical issues (working practices, health, safety, etc.)	8	30	7
Measuring tools—metrics translate differently	10	27	7
Lack of trust with partners	13	24	7
Fraud or scandal	3	34	7
Property development—local codes and requirements	4	35	6
Degree of control over operations	8	30	6
Internal and external theft	4	36	5
Unfamiliar business and property laws	6	36	3
Obtaining proper bonds and licenses	6	35	3
Contamination exposure—food, germs, infections	5	37	2

supplier failure to be less of a risk in the future. A close assessment of these 13 firms reveals that they have done the most to build risk considerations into as many SCM applications as possible.

Some of the top risk factors are to a large extent beyond the control of buying organizations (e.g., natural disasters, default or ruin of supplier, geopolitical events, or perhaps even supplier failure). Managers insisted that while preventing these will not always be possible, reacting to them quickly is an option through contingency planning.

Risk Response

Table 3.12 suggests that companies use a wide range of response options by accepting, reducing, or sharing risks. Inventory management in particular

TABLE 3.12

Risk Response

	Mean	SD
Acceptance		
Inventory management (buffers, safety stock levels, optimal order, and production quantity)	4.96	1.69
We have placed an increased focus on inventory management to deal with supply risks	4.80	1.34
Our suppliers are required to have secure sourcing, business continuity, and contingency plans	4.62	1.71
Contingency planning (jointly with suppliers)	4.22	1.25
We are prepared to minimize the effects of disruptions (terrorism, weather, theft, etc.)	3.70	1.31
Reduction		
Using an approved list of suppliers	5.78	1.18
Multiple sourcing (rather than sole sourcing)	4.04	1.36
Increasing product differentiation	3.91	1.50
Postponement (delaying the actual commitment of resources to maintain flexibility)	3.70	1.35
Sharing		
Partnership formation and long-term agreements	5.11	1.08
Supplier development initiatives	4.83	1.37
Speculation (forward placement of inventory, forward buying of raw material, etc.)	4.07	1.69
We are hedging our raw material exposure to reduce input cost volatility.	3.78	1.49
Hedging strategies (to protect against commodity price swings)	3.61	1.63
Joint technology development initiatives	3.59	1.47

was a critical SCM application used to buffer risk and serve as a de-coupler between echelons of the supply chain when risk was accepted. The table also suggests that although contingency plans may be in place, there will always be some disruptions that ultimately will impact a firm.

Reduction activities focused on the standard SCM practice of identifying qualified suppliers. Very few firms used postponement or product differentiation approaches, which is somewhat surprising given the discussion of "mass customization" and "portfolio management" over the last decades. Risk sharing appears to be focused on development of strong supplier relationships. Few firms seemed to be taking advantage of hedging and speculation approaches, particularly given the recognized volatility of global markets. Even fewer firms seemed to be engaged in joint technology development, which is where lifecycle risks might be most effectively addressed.

Control Activities

Table 3.13 suggests that firms are not using training or network optimization tools to ensure that risk management practices are properly executed. However, other performance analysis tools (e.g., spending analysis, business process management) seemed to be in place, although it is unclear if such tools are integrated to optimize the entire value chain performance.

Information and Communications

Table 3.14 suggests that information systems and communications channels are relatively well established to support supply activities. However,

TABLE 3.13

Control Activities

	Mean	SD
Spend management and analysis	4.85	1.53
Inventory optimization tools	4.78	1.66
Business process management	4.65	1.37
Credit and financial data analysis	4.54	1.60
Contract mgmt (e.g., leverage tools to monitor performance against commitments)	4.48	1.64
We use network design and optimization tools to cope with uncertainty in the supply chain	3.66	1.85
Training programs	3.54	1.59

TABLE 3.14

Information and Communication

	Mean	SD
Information gathering	5.67	1.21
Establishing good communications with suppliers	5.65	1.04
Our company uses real-time inventory information and analytics in managing the supply chain.	4.76	1.52
Forecasting techniques (e.g., to pre-build and carry additional inventory of critical items)	4.61	1.57
Visibility (detailed knowledge of what goes on in other parts of the supply chain, e.g., finished goods inventory, material inventory, work in progress, pipeline inventory, actual demands and forecasts, production plans, capacity, yields, and order status)	4.26	1.29
Data warehousing	4.09	1.76
Supply chain risk information is accurate and readily available to key decision makers.	3.87	1.57
Demand signal repositories	3.42	1.85
Network design analysis programs	3.25	1.94

overall visibility is only modest and supply chain risk information accuracy and availability is less than optimal. The information that is communicated can certainly help manage risks, but without communication of risk factors overall ERM effectiveness may be limited.

Most firms in this study did not use their information technology to evaluate their supply chain networks and risks. A few firms did leverage their technology to periodically assess strategic decisions about where to locate distribution centers and manufacturing capacity, and to determine how to service customer demand at the lowest cost and risk. None of them, however, were using network design tools in innovative ways such as modeling risks or modeling the networks of their key competitors to test various scenarios and to perform "what-if" analyses.

Monitoring

Table 3.15 indicates that firms are monitoring supply chain performance using traditional processes (e.g., supplier visits and assessment systems) but relatively few assess their risk management processes relative to best in class.

Table 3.16 suggests that most firms are relatively satisfied with key SCM performance outcomes. However, 65% of the respondents indicated that

TABLE 3.15

Monitoring

	Mean	SD
Supplier performance measurement systems	5.35	1.61
Visiting supplier operations	5.04	1.32
Consistent monitoring and auditing of a supplier's processes	4.59	1.72
Benchmarking (internal, external, industry-wide, etc.)	4.59	1.54
We have placed an emphasis on incident reporting to decrease the effects of disruptions	4.50	1.43
We actively benchmark our supply chain risk processes against competitors	3.57	1.68

TABLE 3.16

Satisfaction with Performance

	Mean	SD
Damage-free and defect-free delivery	5.41	0.83
Meeting customer service levels	5.07	1.20
Logistics and delivery reliability	4.96	1.01
Order completeness and correctness	4.96	1.11
Supplier reliability and continuous supply	4.85	0.99
Reduced disruptions in the supply chain	4.59	1.15
After sales service performance	4.57	1.29
Inventory management	4.52	1.22
Lower commodity prices	3.98	1.27
Reduced material price volatility	3.80	1.51

they have had supply disruptions that have caused financial hardships in the past 24 months.

DISCUSSION AND CONCLUSION

Risk management professionals and organizations (including COSO) prescribe that risk management should be led by senior management, and that ERM is a continuous process embedded throughout the organization's culture, strategy, and processes, and that is integrated across all levels of the firm. ERM should translate strategy into tactical and operational objectives, assigning ownership throughout the organization with each manager and employee responsible for the management of risk as part of their job description. It must support accountability, performance metrics, and rewards, thus promoting operational efficiency at all levels, including SCM. However, most of the supply risk management strategies in this study appear to be fragmented (e.g., one group buys insurance, another administers claims, another handles everything related to safety or security, another selects dual sources, etc.).

SCM focuses primarily on the input part of the value chain, though it has at least some type of support role throughout the value chain. An effective strategy for managing risks in the supply chain requires a closely aligned strategy and relationship between risk managers and others in the organization. Only a corporate risk management group can address risks for the entire supply chain and lifecycle of a program. There has been an increased recognition of the "chief risk officer" position to take on such responsibilities. Though not an absolute requirement, having somebody in charge of ERM enables integrated risk management. The supply chain risk manager would work closely with corporate risk management, as well as with the supply chain managers. In this study, a gap was suggested as firms failed to use supply chain managers who worked closely with corporate risk management, and managers did not fully understand the activities being performed by their risk management groups.

Gaining management support is often the most challenging part of implementing a proactive system for managing risks in the supply chain. It is necessary for the SCM leader to emphasize the importance of supply chain risk management to senior management in order to get the properly targeted resources necessary to implement such a system, rather than the poorly targeted budgets seen in this study. The firms in this study recognized the need for risk management and had at least moderate top management support for such initiatives. This suggests the strong potential for proactive risk management, yet few firms seem to have such an approach.

Managers agreed that without a systematic analysis technique to assess risk, much can go wrong in a supply chain (i.e., unexpected cost, extended lead times, poor quality, or numerous other negative performance variables). Analyzing the risk associated with SCM is a relatively new subject, and little has been done to assist managers with this process. It would seem a key first step is to document and analyze risk.

The method for analyzing supply chain risk must be a cross-functional process that involves senior management as well as key stakeholders from finance, operations, internal audit, and risk management. This could make roles unclear, so responsibilities need to be defined. In general, the companies in this study have not adopted such boundary-spanning processes for risk management. Instead, they have managed risks within functional silos.

In the absence of cross-functional processes and the lack of risk management applications, the supply chain managers in this study are building risk considerations into existing traditional SCM applications (e.g., spend, contract and inventory management, demand planning, benchmarking, etc.). This study suggests that supply chain managers generally run and coordinate the work to maintain an optimal balance between risk exposures and costs for damages versus protection activities.

Supply chain risk management goes beyond documenting the likelihood and impact of risks. It also requires visibility to risks when they occur and translating that risk information to key decision makers so that they can evaluate and act on information. This study suggests that throughout the supply chain, key operational data and information such as inventory, demand, forecasts, production and shipment plans, work in progress, yields, capacities, and backlogs was accessible to key members of the supply chains. However, this study also showed that documenting the likelihood and impact of risks was not always a key part of SCM and that supply chain risk information was not readily available to key decision makers. Perhaps because of this risk information shortcoming, very few of the firms are actually able to exploit risk to an advantage by taking calculated risks in the supply chain and even fewer were prepared to minimize the effects of disruptions. Thus, it is important that data and information be tightly managed and that any updates be made in as timely a manner as possible. The accuracy of the data should be a source of confidence to the parties using the data.

The role of supply network design and optimization tools for risk management is still evolving on the SCM side. Some of the firms in this study make use of network design tools for infrequent, long-range decision making, such as manufacturing location or distribution capacity given long-term demand expectations. However, there was no indication that there are new cases of usage, such as helping companies understand, model, and cope with increasing levels of uncertainty in the supply chain or network.

Some companies have adopted software tools to address multi-echelon inventory optimization. Firms are using these tools to apply probabilistic forecasting techniques to make inventory policy and configuration decisions and to evaluate different inventory strategies, though none of them used the tools to evaluate postponement strategies. Used effectively, these tools can help companies improve customer service levels and fill rates, dampen the impact of supply disruptions, reduce risk, and yield better trade-off decisions between customer service levels and required inventory investment.

All of the firms in this study have developed and monitor a set of performance metrics to maintain a risk profile for their supply chains. They do so by using an assortment of tools and techniques such as: initial supplier evaluations, QS audits, industry benchmarking, supplier questionnaires, report cards, capacity planning, lead-time analysis, financial risk assessment, business continuity plans, risk analysis based on accounts payable performance, historical data, technical capability assessment, on-site capability reviews, forecasting techniques and analysis, data tracking with customers to identify demand trends, supplier performance measurement, and so on. Some also used supplier risk rankings, similar to credit scores used in the financial industry, to measure suppliers on stability, contingency planning, and on-target delivery performance. Firms tracked this type of performance through supplier scorecards to monitor leading indicators that impact risk. However, no firm had an ongoing risk-review process to ensure that they keep their risk profile within an optimal range of economic impact. In general, the development of proactive risk management performance metrics in the supply chain was lacking in this study. The supplier scorecards were not balanced or optimal, and supported reactive decision making.

Several of the firms used financial reports and questionnaires during supplier approval to compare supply candidates to the business requirements of the buyers or project teams. When justified by a perceived level of risk, a few of the firms went one step further and had candidate comparison matrices (e.g., supplier profiling form and supply Chain PFMEA). Additionally, most had formal processes for supplier visits (e.g., rapid plant assessment, site verification of the supplier questionnaire, etc.). Some firms actually used lifecycle management with supplier report cards and their buyers would conduct periodic supply chain reviews. In one firm, sourcing was assigned risk ownership and they used PFMEA principles to evaluate risk impact. For each risk, they would assess what the financial impact would be in the event of a disruption. They then assigned a probability to each risk area and then they prioritized by multiplying the financial impact by the risk probability.

This study also demonstrates that the measurement of risk factors does not necessarily require a new or unique set of performance measures. For example, one firm used average on-time delivery as a measure of supplier performance and chose to look more closely at the peaks and valleys of this indicator to determine the supplier's risk impact on its own delivery performance. In another example, key metrics were established to measure the risk associated with key suppliers and their performance against service level agreements. Supplier agreements were then aligned with the established levels negotiated with the company's key customer agreements.

Firms face a variety of risks and are unlikely to be able to cost-effectively identify and respond to all risks. Firms should conduct a Pareto analysis to determine where to focus their SCM risk management efforts. The most common current risk identified by respondents was supplier failure. Though some firms indicated that in the future such risk would decrease, more firms indicated that the risk would increase. This provides support for the suggestion that current ad hoc approaches by the firm and SCM are largely ineffective in the long term.

Commodity cost volatility was also a growing concern, but with limited amounts of systems to manage its risk. For example, the majority of the firms strongly disagreed that they were using hedging strategies (to protect against commodity price swings) and speculation (forward placement of inventory, forward buying of raw materials, etc.) for managing supply chain risks (and yet it was identified as one of the top risk factors). Not surprisingly, firms were very disappointed with their supply chain's performance on lower commodity prices and reduced material price volatility. Only one firm in the entire sample had a system in place to proactively manage commodity prices. This firm had a dedicated staff that used a price sliding system on key commodities, which were tied to market indices (e.g., plastics, metals, rubbers, etc.).

Some firms in this study used management scorecards that can identify some trends in advance. They often referred to them as dashboards, reviews, audits, and so on, and they allowed managers to view the progress of their supply chains according to a collection of performance indicators. In this manner, they do get some early warning signs if suppliers or carriers are underperforming. However, they fall short on having systems with event-based alerts that let them know when their supply chains are at risk. Until that happens, managers will not take appropriate and well-managed risks. Instead, they will outsource to low cost regions to meet their cost savings goals and not stay within an optimal range on the risk management side.

In general, no one was compensated or incentivized in their day-to-day job to look at and evaluate the risks within an optimal range of economic impact. For example, a typical offshore target for several supply chain managers was to achieve x million dollars of component off shore in y years. Such situations forced managers to inevitably compromise on risk issues as they focused on achieving cost efficiency. None of the firms have developed some sort of on-demand platform that helps them predict supplier failures before they occur.

If the reward system only rewards those who achieve their objectives irrespective of due attention to risks, then managers will strive to achieve objectives at the cost of disproportionate risks. In most of the firms in this study, the major objectives were to reduce inventory, improve in-stock availability, and cut costs. Most of these firms had specific targets for off-shore sourcing that forced managers to inevitably compromise on risk issues. Managing risks in the supply chain was perceived as something that contradicts the process of achieving these company objectives.

Responses to supply risk included acceptance, reduction, and sharing. Though firms used a variety of techniques, unfortunately this research did not determine if the techniques were used based on sound risk management principles or because it was the only technique the firm was able to implement. Perhaps the old adage that "if the only tool you have is a hammer, then everything looks like a nail" applies.

ERM frameworks, including the COSO ERM framework, seem complex. However, in many respects such frameworks are similar to other process management and improvement frameworks such as Six Sigma's DMAIC (define, measure, analyze, improve, and control). Most ERM implementation frameworks include planning, identification, analysis, handling, and monitoring. SCM risk management should be an extension of corporate ERM, and should follow a similar implementation process. The challenge, of course, is not in understanding the framework or concepts, but in making ERM happen.

REFERENCES

Armstrong, J.S. & Overton, T.S. 1977. Estimating Nonresponse Bias in Mail Surveys. *Journal of Marketing Research*, 14(3): 396–402.

Ballou, B. & Heitger, D. 2005. A Building Block Approach for Implementing COSO's Enterprise Risk Management—Integrated Framework. *Management Accounting Quarterly*, 6(2): 1–10.

Beasley, M., Clune, R., & Hermanson, D. 2005. ERM: A Status Report. *The Internal Auditor*, 62(1): 67–72.

Black, S. & Porter, L. 1996. Identification of the Critical Factors of TQM. *Decision Sciences Journal*, 27(1): 1–21.

Blackhurst, J., Wu, T., & O'Grady, P. 2005. PDCM: A Decision Support Modeling Methodology for Supply Chain, Product and Process Design Decisions. *Journal of Operations Management*, 23(3–4): 325–343.

Bowling, D. & Rieger, L. 2005. Making Sense of COSO's New Framework for Enterprise Risk Management. *Bank Accounting & Finance*, February/March: 35–40.

Capon, N., Kaye, M., & Wood, M. 1994. Measuring the Success of a TQM Programme. *International Journal of Quality and Reliability Management*, 12(8): 8–22.

Chapman, C. 2003. Bringing ERM into Focus. *The Internal Auditor*, 60(3): 30–35.

Chiang, C.Y., Kocabasoglu-Hillmer, C., & Suresh, N. 2012. An Empirical Investigation of the Impact of Strategic Sourcing and Flexibility on Firms' Supply Chain Agility. *International Journal of Operations and Production Management*, 32(1): 49–78.

COSO. 2004. Enterprise Risk Management—Integrated Framework. *Committee of Sponsoring Organizations of the Treadway Commission.*

COSO. 2010. Current State of Enterprise Risk Oversight and Market Perceptions of COSO's ERM Framework. *Committee of Sponsoring Organizations of the Treadway Commission.*

Curkovic, S., Melnyk, S., Calantone, R., & Handfield, R. 2000. Validating the Malcolm Baldrige National Quality Framework through Structural Equation Modeling. *International Journal of Production Research*, 38(4): 765–791.

Dean, J. & Bowen, D. 1994. Management Theory and Total Quality: Improving Research and Practice through Theory Development. *Academy of Management Journal*, 19(3): 392–418.

Eisenhardt, K. 1989. Building Theories from Case Study Research. *The Academy of Management Review*, 14(4): 532–550.

Flynn, B., Schroeder, R., & Sakakibara, S. 1994. A Framework for Quality Management Research and an Associated Instrument. *Journal of Operations Management*, 11(4): 339–366.

Giannakis, M. & Louis, M. 2001. A Multi-Agent Based Framework for Supply Chain Risk Management. *Journal of Purchasing and Supply Management*, 17(1): 23–31.

Hallikas, J., Karvonen, I., Pulkkinen, U., Virolainen, V.M., & Tuominem, M. 2004. Risk Management Processes in Supplier Networks. *International Journal of Production Economics*, 90(1): 47–58.

Holschbach, E. & Hofmann, E. 2011. Exploring Quality Management for Business Services from a Buyer's Perspective Using Multiple Case Study Evidence. *International Journal of Operations & Production Management*, 31(6): 648–685.

Hoyt, R. & Liebenberg, A. 2011. The Value of Enterprise Risk Management. *Journal of Risk and Insurance*, 78(4): 795–822.

Inderfurth, K. & Kelle, P. 2011. Capacity Reservation Under Spot Market Price Uncertainty. *International Journal of Production Economics*, 133(1): 272–279.

Kern, D., Moser, R., Hartman, E., & Moder, M. 2012. Supply Risk Management: Model Development and Empirical Analysis. *International Journal of Physical Distribution & Logistics Management*, 42(1): 60–82.

Khan, O. & Burnes, B. 2007. Risk and Supply Chain Management: A Research Agenda. *The International Journal of Logistics Management*, 18(2): 197–216.

Kleindorfer, P.R., & Saad, G.H. 2005. Managing Disruptions in Supply Chains. *Production and Operations Management*, 14(1): 53–68.

Kumar, S. & Verruso, J. 2008. Risk Assessment of the Security of Inbound Containers at U.S. Ports: A Failure, Mode, Effects, and Criticality Analysis Approach. *Transportation Journal*, 47(4): 26–41.

Laeequddin, M., Sardana, G.D., Sahay, B.S., Abdul Waheed, K., & Sahay, V. 2009. Supply Chain Partners Trust Building Process through Risk Evaluation: The Perspectives of UAE Packaged Food Industry. *Supply Chain Management*, 14(4): 280–290.

Landsittel, D. & Rittenberg, L. 2010. COSO: Working with the Academic Community. *Accounting Horizons*, 24(3): 455–469.

Liu, Z. & Cruz, J. 2012. Supply Chain Networks with Corporate Financial Risks and Trade Credits under Economic Uncertainty. *International Journal of Production Economics*, 137(1): 55–67.

Manuj, I. & Mentzer, J.T. 2008. Global Supply Chain Risk Management. *Journal of Business Logistics*, 29(1): 133–156.

Martin, C., Mena, C., Khan, O., & Yurt, O. 2011. Approaches to Managing Global Sourcing Risk. *Supply Chain Management*, 16(2): 67–81.

Matook, S., Lasch, R., & Tamaschke, R. 2009. Supplier Development with Benchmarking as Part of a Comprehensive Supplier Risk Management Framework. *International Journal of Operations and Production Management*, 29(3): 241–267.

Miles, M. & Huberman, A. 1994. *Qualitative Data Analysis: A Sourcebook of New Methods*. Newbury Park, CA: Sage Publications.

Nocco, B. & Stulz, R. 2006. Enterprise Risk Management: Theory and Practice. *Journal of Applied Corporate Finance*, 18(4): 8–20.

Samad-Khan, A. 2005. Why COSO Is Flawed. *Operational Risk*, 6(1): 24–28.

Saraph, V., Benson, P., & Schroeder, R. 1989. An Instrument for Measuring the Critical Factors of Quality Management. *Decision Sciences*, 200(4): 810–829.

Smithson, C. & Simkins, B. 2005. Does Risk Management Add Value? A Survey of the Evidence. *Journal of Applied Corporate Finance*, 17(3): 8–17.

Sobel, P. 2006. Building on Section 404: Investments in Sarbanes-Oxley Compliance can Provide a Solid Foundation for Enterprise Risk Management Projects. *The Internal Auditor*, 63(2): 38–44.

Sodhi, M.S., Son, B.G., & Tang, C.S. 2012. Researcher's Perspective on Supply Risk Management. *Productions and Operations Management*, 21(1): 1–13.

Tang, C.S. 2006. Perspectives in Supply Chain Risk Management. *International Journal of Production Economics*, 103(2): 451–488.

Tummala, R. & Schoenherr, T. 2011. Assessing and Managing Risks Using the Supply Chain Risk Management Process (SCRMP). *Supply Chain Management*, 16(6): 474–483.

Zsidisin, G., Ellram, L., Carter, J., & Cavinato, J. 2004. An Analysis of Supply Risk Assessment Techniques. *International Journal of Physical Distribution & Logistics Management*, 34(5): 397–413.

Zsidisin, G. & Hartley, J. 2012. A Strategy for Managing Commodity Price Risk. *Supply Chain Management Review*, March/April(2): 46–53.

Zsidisin, G. & Wagner, S. 2010. Do Perceptions become Reality? The Moderating Role of Supply Chain Resiliency on Disruption Occurence. *Journal of Business Logistics*, 31(2): 1–20.

4

Integration of ISO 31000:2009 and Supply Chain Risk Management

INTRODUCTION

Enterprise risk management (ERM) is a critical component of business strategy (Hoyt & Liebenberg 2011). Despite ERM's importance, ERM implementation is limited (Beasley, Clune, & Hermanson 2005). The International Organization for Standardization (ISO) released ISO 31000:2009 Risk Management Principles to provide ERM implementation guidance (ISO 2009).

A key component of ERM is supply chain risk management (SCRM) (Hauser 2003; VanderBok, Sauter, Bryan, & Horan 2007). A well-designed, risk-oriented supply chain provides a strong competitive position and reliable long-term benefits to all stakeholders. For SCRM to be most effective, it should be integrated with ERM. However, SCRM is often implemented in an ad hoc manner.

SCRM research is in its infancy stage (Richey 2009). SCRM research might advance more readily if research is linked to practitioner needs, and if a standard SCRM framework is developed (Teuscher, Gruninger, & Ferdinand 2006). This research has two primary goals: (1) determine whether ISO 31000 provides the framework to reach consensus on SCRM scope and definition, which in turn could accelerate SCRM research, and (2) determine whether ISO 31000 provides the foundation for planning and executing SCRM.

To pursue these goals, survey data and follow-up interviews were used. Findings suggest that ISO 31000 provides researchers with a framework for developing a consensus on SCRM terms and scope, and provides practitioners with a foundation for linking ERM and SCRM, and then planning and executing SCRM. The findings also suggest that though companies recognize the importance of SCRM, SCRM is not generally linked to ERM and that key SCRM skills are lacking.

LITERATURE REVIEW

SCRM research gaps include a lack of agreement regarding SCRM scope and definition, and a lack of empirical research focused on current practices (Teuscher, Gruninger, & Ferdinand 2006). This research accepts the perspective that empirical research focused on developing frameworks may advance research. The total quality management (TQM) discipline provides an example. TQM research advancements were supported by operational definitions and standardized frameworks, which provided a foundation for theory building and testing (Black & Porter 1996; Capon, Kaye, & Wood 1994; Curkovic, Melnyk, Calantone, & Handfield 2000; Dean & Bowen 1994; Flynn, Schroeder, & Sakakibara 1994).

While TQM research has reached a "mature" stage, SCRM research is in an "early" stage. For example, Richey (2009) suggested that SCRM research regarding crisis situations was in its "infancy" stage, then examined the literature and conducted interviews to develop a theoretically grounded framework for examining supply crisis management. Driven by the suggestions that SCRM research is in an early stage, that a standard SCRM framework may advance research, and that SCRM is a subset of ERM, this exploratory research examines SCRM relative to the ISO 31000 framework.

ISO 31000:2009

ERM has received attention as a way to gain competitive advantage, yet it has not gained much traction (Moody 2010). The International Organization for Standardization (ISO) published ISO 31000:2009 Risk Management Principles and Guidelines (ISO 2009) to provide a foundation for ERM implementation. It is anticipated that ISO 31000 will become

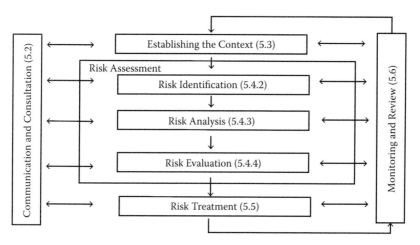

FIGURE 4.1
ISO 31000:2009 Clause 5 Process for managing risk.

an international norm for ERM (Gjerdrum & Salen 2010). This research focuses on ISO 31000, Clause 5 Risk Management Process, which consists of five integrated segments (Purdy 2010) (Figure 4.1).

Communication and Consultation (Clause 5.2) requires engagement of stakeholders to determine objectives, secure involvement, and to disseminate risk information. Establishing the Context (Clause 5.3) sets objectives, identifies factors that influence success, appraises stakeholder relationships, and identifies the risk management environment. This essential step precedes risk assessment.

Risk Assessment (Clause 5.4) consists of three interrelated steps. Risk Identification defines risks, and identifies risk drivers and risk categories. Risk Analysis evaluates risk, including potential business consequences and occurrence likelihood. Risk Evaluation prioritizes risks from acceptable to unacceptable, and identifies which risks require treatment.

Risk Treatment (Clause 5.5) identifies options for treating risks, including: accepting risk to achieve competitive advantage; avoiding risk; reducing or removing the likelihood or consequence of risk; and sharing or transferring risk. Monitoring and Review (Clause 5.6) analyzes changes in risks and the emergence of new risks that result from changes in the external environment, risk treatment, or corporate objectives. It also assesses the success of risk treatments.

SCRM FRAMEWORKS

SCRM frameworks (Hallikas, Karvonen, Pulkkinen, Virolainen, & Tuominem 2004; Kleindorfer & Saad 2005; Manuj & Mentzer 2008) share common elements with each other and with ISO 31000. However, Table 4.1 identifies a lack of consensus regarding what constitutes SCRM, and indicates that ISO 31000 is more comprehensive than SCRM frameworks. ISO 31000 emphasizes that the first critical step for enabling holistic risk management is establishing the context. It also explicitly recognizes the need for stakeholder engagement and communication, and emphasizes continuous monitoring, review, and improvement.

SUPPLY RISKS AND RESPONSES

The research identifies many supply risks, including but not limited to order fulfillment problems, information delays, labor tensions, natural disasters, capacity fluctuations, bankruptcy, exchange rates, government regulations, security, and opportunism (Blackhurst, Wu, & O'Grady 2005; Manuj & Mentzer 2008; Spekman & Davis 2004; Tummala & Schoenherr 2011). Risk treatments might include dual-sourcing (Khan & Burnes 2007), credit analysis (Kern, Moser, Hartmann, & Moder 2012), use of capable suppliers (Manuj & Mentzer 2008), building structural flexibility into supply chain designs, supply chain modeling (Giannakis & Louis 2001), inventory buffers (Zsidin & Hartley 2012), trust development (Giannakis & Louis 2001), or contingency planning (Skipper & Hanna 2009; Tang 2006), for example.

RESEARCH METHOD

This exploratory research selected a purposeful sample to pursue the research objectives (Miles & Huberman 1982). Targeted participants were known to support supply research and education, and were active in professional supply associations. The survey was sent to 58 firms. A 66% response rate was achieved. Early-to-late respondent survey comparisons

TABLE 4.1

ISO 31000:2009 and SCRM Frameworks

ISO 31000:2009	5.2 Communication and Consultation	5.3 Establishing the Context	5.4.2 Risk Identification	5.4.3 Risk Analysis	5.4.4 Risk Evaluation	5.5 Risk Treatment	5.6 Monitoring and Review
Hallikas, Karvonen, Pulkkinen et. al. 2004			Risk identification	Risk assessment		Decision and implementation of risk management actions	Risk monitoring
Kleindorfer & Saad 2005			Specifying sources of risks and vulnerabilities	Assessment		Mitigation	
Manuj & Mentzer 2008			Risk identification	Risk assessment and evaluation		Selection of appropriate risk management strategies Implementation of supply chain risk management strategies. Mitigation supply chain risks	
Tummala & Schoenherr 2011		Risk measurement	Risk identification	Risk assessment	Risk evaluation	Risk mitigation and contingency plans	Risk control and monitoring

TABLE 4.2

Industry Profile

Industry	Count
Manufacturing	11
Automotive	10
Aerospace/Defense	4
Consumer Products	3
Health Care	2
Construction	2
Other	6

TABLE 4.3

Sales

Sales ($)	Count
10M–49M	1
50M–99M	3
100M–499M	2
500M–999M	4
1B–9B	7
10B–49B	15
50B–99B	3
Over 100B	3

TABLE 4.4

Employment

Employees	Count
50–99	1
100–499	3
500–999	2
1,000–4,999	6
5,000–9,999	3
Over 10,000	23

TABLE 4.5

Respondent Titles

Titles	Percent
Supply Chain Leader/Manager/Buyer	54%
Production/Operations/Materials Manager	29%
Analyst	17%

were made to analyze potential non-response bias (Armstrong & Overton 1977). No statistically significant differences were found. The majority of responses were from manufacturing firms (Table 4.2). Sales volume, number of employees, and respondent titles are shown in Tables 4.3, 4.4, and 4.5, respectively.

DATA ANALYSIS

Results are categorized relative to the segments of ISO 31000:2009. In all tables, the "agree/disagree" questions are scaled from "1 = strongly disagree" to "7 = strongly agree," and the "extent of use" questions are scaled from "1 = not used" to "7 = extensively used."

Communication and Consultation (Clause 5.2): Table 4.6 suggests that firms attempt to create communication channels supported by extensive information gathering. Although information visibility was relatively high, there are concerns regarding information reliability and timeliness.

TABLE 4.6

Communication and Consultation

Item	Mean	SD
Establishing good communications with suppliers	5.81	1.05
Information gathering	5.51	1.54
Forecasting techniques (e.g., to pre-build and carry additional inventory of critical items)	4.79	1.56
Our company uses real-time inventory information and analytics in managing the supply chain	4.61	1.66
Data warehousing	4.59	1.54
Visibility (detailed knowledge of what goes on in other parts of the supply chain, e.g., finished goods inventory, material inventory, WIP, pipeline inventory, actual demands and forecasts, production plans, capacity, yields, and order status)	4.24	1.46
Demand signal repositories	3.95	1.68
Supply chain risk information is accurate and readily available to key decision makers	3.81	1.68
Network design analysis programs	3.41	1.40

Establishing the Context (Clause 5.3): Contextual factors were categorized as needed—approach, budget, and organization (Table 4.7). Although SCRM is strategic, there is a challenge to implementing SCRM, because no single set of tools exists for managing all risks. SCRM personnel lack insight into ERM efforts and may lack the critical skills needed for managing global risk. Organizational structures and capabilities, as well as the allocation of resources and budgets, appear to be misaligned with strategic objectives.

Risk Assessment (Clause 5.4): Risk assessment consists of the interrelated steps of identification, analysis, and evaluation. Specific risk factors (e.g., supplier reliability) are carefully evaluated (Table 4.8). However, few firms extensively document the likelihood and impact of risks, and SCRM tends to focus on "negative risks" rather than exploiting "positive risks."

Firms face a wide range of supply risks (Table 4.9). Supplier failure/reliability was the top risk, followed by supplier bankruptcies, natural disasters, commodity cost volatility, and logistics failure. Table 4.10 summarizes responses regarding whether supply risks would increase, stay the same, or decrease in the next one to two years. Many of the risk factors identified as increasing (e.g., currency exchange, government regulations) highlight that many risks are outside of supply's direct control, suggesting that successful treatment of such risks will require integrated SCRM and ERM.

TABLE 4.7

Establishing the Context

	Mean	SD
Need		
Without a systematic analysis technique to assess risk, much can go wrong in a supply chain.	6.19	0.97
Managing supply chain risk is an increasingly important initiative for our operations.	5.92	1.19
It is critical for us to have an easily understood method to identify and manage supply chain risk.	5.27	1.52
My workplace plans on evaluating or implementing supply chain risk tools and technologies.	5.08	1.91
We are very concerned about our supply chain resiliency, and the failure implications.	4.81	1.65
Approach		
There is no single set of tools or technologies on the market for managing supply chain risks.	5.50	1.34
We are currently using some form of supply chain risk management tools and services.	5.03	1.83
Managing supply chain risks is driven by reactions to failures rather than being proactively driven.	4.19	1.67
Proactive risk mitigation efforts applied to the supply chain is common practice for us.	4.19	1.76
Supply chain risk initiatives are driven from the bottom up rather than top down.	3.70	1.75
Budget		
We do plan on investing nontrivial amounts in managing supply chain risks.	4.17	1.46
We have a dedicated budget for activities associated with managing supply chain risks.	3.89	2.27
Funding for managing supply chain risks will come from a general operations budget.	3.81	2.03
Our spending intentions for managing supply chain risks are very high.	3.08	1.54
Organization		
Supply chain employees understand government legislation and geopolitical issues.	3.73	1.61
I fully understand the activities being performed by our risk management group.	3.70	1.54
My workplace uses supply chain risk managers who work closely with corporate risk management.	2.64	1.81
We are planning to outsource all or some of our risk management functions.	2.14	1.22

TABLE 4.8

Clause 5.4: Risk Assessment

Item	Mean	SD
Supplier reliability and continuous supply is the top risk factor for our supply chain.	5.68	1.43
Risks of moving manufacturing facilities overseas are carefully evaluated.	5.30	1.63
Risks of not being able to fulfill a spike in consumer demand are carefully evaluated.	5.11	1.49
Key metrics are in place to measure the risk associated with key suppliers.	4.68	1.60
We apply high levels of analytical rigor to assess our supply chain practices.	4.38	1.78
A key part of our supply chain management is documenting the likelihood and impact of risks.	4.19	1.60
Taxes such as excise and VAT impact our supply chain decisions.	4.05	1.73
We can actually exploit risk to an advantage by taking calculated risks in the supply chain.	3.97	1.64

TABLE 4.9

Current Supply Chain Risks

Risk Factor	Rank					Count	Weighted Points	Average Weight
	1	2	3	4	5			
Supplier failure/reliability	14	10	6	2	1	33	133	4.03
Bankruptcy, ruin, or default of suppliers, shippers, etc.	8	2	6	2	1	19	71	3.74
Commodity cost volatility	3	3	4	3	2	15	47	3.13
Natural disasters or accidents (tsunamis, hurricanes, fires, etc.)	4	3	4	2	1	14	49	3.50
Logistics failure	2	4	1		5	12	34	2.83
Geopolitical events (terrorism, war, etc.)		1	2	6	1	10	23	2.30
Contract failure	1	2	1		4	8	20	2.50
Strikes—labor, buyers, and suppliers		2	3	1	2	8	21	2.63

Continued

TABLE 4.9 *(Continued)*

Current Supply Chain Risks

Risk Factor	Rank					Count	Weighted Points	Average Weight
	1	2	3	4	5			
Customer-related (demand change, system failure, payment delay)	1	3	1	2	1	8	25	3.13
Energy/raw material shortages and power outages		2	1	4	1	8	20	2.50
Information delays, scarcity, sharing, and infrastructure breakdown		1	1	2	2	6	13	2.17
Government regulations (SOX, SEC, Clean Air Act, OSHA, EU)	1		2	2		5	15	3.00
Intellectual property infringement	1	1		1	2	5	13	2.60
Lack of trust with partners				2	3	5	7	1.40
Diminishing capacities (financial, production, structural, etc.)	1			2	2	5	11	2.20
Contamination exposure—food, germs, infections	2	1		2		5	18	3.60
Legal liabilities and issues			3		1	4	10	2.50
Return policy and product recall requirements				2	2	4	6	1.50
Attracting and retaining skilled labor			1	2	1	4	8	2.00
Currency exchange, interest, and/or inflation rate fluctuations		3			1	4	13	3.25

TABLE 4.10

Projected Change in Supply Chain Risks

Risk	Decrease	Same	Increase
Currency exchange, interest, and/or inflation rate fluctuations	1	3	34
Commodity cost volatility	4	6	28
Banking regulations and tighter financing conditions	2	9	27
Government regulations (SOX, SEC, Clean Air Act, OSHA, EU)	0	14	24
Supplier failure/reliability	7	14	17
Geopolitical events (e.g., terrorism, war)	0	22	16
Energy/raw material shortages and power outages	1	21	16
Customs acts/trade restrictions and protectionism	3	19	16
Logistics failure	5	17	16
Bankruptcy, ruin, or default of suppliers, shippers, etc.	6	16	16
Customer related (demand change, system failure, payment delay)	2	21	15
Diminishing capacities (financial, production, structural, etc.)	5	18	15
Return policy and product recall requirements	1	23	14
Port/cargo security (information, freight, vandalism, sabotage, etc.)	1	24	13
Legal liabilities and issues	1	24	13
Insurance coverage	0	26	12
Tax issues (VAT, transfer pricing, excise, etc.)	0	27	11
Natural disasters or accidents (tsunamis, hurricanes, fires, etc.)	1	26	11
Intellectual property infringement	1	28	9
Attracting and retaining skilled labor	7	22	9
Language and educational barriers	11	18	9
Strikes (labor, buyers, or suppliers)	4	26	8
Property development (local codes and requirements)	1	30	7
Unfamiliar business and property laws	2	29	7
Weaknesses in the local infrastructures	5	26	7
Contract failure	6	25	7
Contamination exposure (food, germs, infections)	3	29	6
Ethical issues (working practices, health, safety, etc.)	5	27	6

TABLE 4.11

Risk Treatment

	Mean	SD
Acceptance		
Inventory management (buffers, safety stock levels, optimal order, and production quantity)	5.42	1.08
Contingency planning (jointly with suppliers)	4.63	1.50
We have placed an increased focus on inventory management to deal with supply risks	4.56	1.46
Our suppliers are required to have secure sourcing, business continuity, and contingency plans	4.54	1.86
We are prepared to minimize the effects of disruptions (terrorism, weather, theft, etc.)	3.86	1.87
Reduction		
Using an approved list of suppliers	6.11	1.11
Multiple sourcing (rather than sole sourcing)	4.47	1.72
Increasing product differentiation	4.24	1.46
Postponement (delaying the actual commitment of resources to maintain flexibility)	3.97	1.30
Sharing		
Partnership formation and long-term agreements	5.24	1.15
Supplier development initiatives	5.18	1.41
Speculation (forward placement of inventory, forward buying of raw material, etc.)	4.08	1.38
Hedging strategies (to protect against commodity price swings)	3.92	1.62
We are hedging our raw material exposure to reduce input cost volatility	3.65	1.69
Joint technology development initiatives	3.47	1.89

Risk Treatment (Clause 5.5): Risk treatment options include acceptance, reduction, and sharing (Table 4.11). Inventory buffering remains a key acceptance option. Qualifying suppliers to reduce risk and partnering with suppliers to share risk are also used extensively.

Monitoring and Review (Clause 5.6): Firms use a range of processes to monitor outcomes (Table 4.12). However, few firms benchmark SCRM relative to best practices, or use training and design optimization tools to monitor and review SCRM processes. Firms are generally satisfied with key supply performance outcomes (Table 4.13), though there is room for improvement, particularly in terms of managing commodity and material price volatility.

TABLE 4.12

Monitoring and Review

Item	Mean	SD
Supplier performance measurement systems	5.71	1.64
Credit and financial data analysis	5.37	1.34
Visiting supplier operations	5.34	1.24
Business process management	5.11	1.27
Consistent monitoring and auditing of a supplier's processes	5.03	1.68
Spend management and analysis	5.03	1.70
Contract management (e.g., leverage tools to monitor performance against commitments)	5.00	1.52
Benchmarking (internal, external, industry-wide, etc.)	4.68	1.51
We have placed an emphasis on incident reporting to decrease the effects of disruptions	4.49	1.76
Inventory optimization tools	4.49	1.68
Training programs	3.79	1.66
We use network design and optimization tools to cope with uncertainty in the supply chain	3.67	1.64
We actively benchmark our supply chain risk processes against competitors	3.39	2.02

TABLE 4.13

Performance Satisfaction

Outcome	Mean	SD
Logistics and delivery reliability	5.32	1.25
Meeting customer service levels	5.19	1.17
Supplier reliability and continuous supply	5.03	1.12
Damage-free and defect-free delivery	5.00	0.94
Order completeness and correctness	4.86	1.29
After sales service performance	4.86	1.09
Inventory management	4.84	1.32
Reduced disruptions in the supply chain	4.54	1.07
Reduced material price volatility	4.32	1.06
Lower commodity prices	4.05	1.20

DISCUSSION

Communication and Consultation

Communication and consultation provide visibility so that supply chain members can access reliable information. Specific operations information, such as inventory and quality, was generally available. However, data centralization seemed lacking, causing visibility and accuracy problems. One manager stated that inadequate information flow was a significant supply risk: "Demand variation, extending supply chains, and *information speed* that is too reactive, will all continue to be major failure modes." Perhaps limited information visibility and timeliness reinforces the practice of mitigating negative risks, rather than enabling proactive exploitation of positive risk opportunities.

For some firms, there was a lack of information technology (IT) integration throughout the value chain. One manager commented that the most significant failure mode he faced was "companies failing to use up-to-date MRP systems, and not accepting change. By relying on old procedures, companies are missing a lot of information that can be accurate and readily available." As companies continue to use new and global suppliers, IT integration can become a significant challenge.

Establishing the Context

Respondents use many of the individual processes suggested by ISO 31000, but it appears that integration is limited and that SCRM approaches are ad hoc rather than systematic. One manager commented, "We currently do not possess or utilize any tools to identify and analyze risk within the supply chain. All activities currently practiced are from the working knowledge of the buyers." This was not universally true, as one manager indicated: "Top management at my company recognizes supply risk by investing capital into our systems, training, and people. Our stock price is a direct correlation to our supply chain success, thus it has a very high level of visibility."

Leaders have a responsibility for establishing the context from which supply risk will be managed and for defining the responsibilities and scope of risk management processes. Despite recognizing a need for integrated SCRM, many firms did not establish a supportive organizational context for SCRM. One manager stated: "What is lacking is clear ownership of the supply chain at an executive level. The supply chain group of 200 employees has belonged to the CEO, the head of operations, and the head of purchasing at different times."

Supply chain managers need to present a business case in order to "get a seat at the table" and to secure requisite SCRM resources. Another manager stated: "As managers, you are the voice for your associates and those who may not get the face time with the people who can affect change. The metrics speak for themselves, so managers need to be able to relate the needed resources to areas in the supply chain that need improvement."

If persuasion does not work, it may take a catastrophe for firms to realize SCRM's importance. One manager commented: "We did not have anyone devoted to risk management in the past, but due to the Japan earthquake, tsunamis, Thailand floods, and other large-scale issues, risk management has now become very important. We now have someone dedicated to mitigate risk on all fronts for purchasing due to risks globally."

Despite evidence that supply personnel lack some of the necessary risk management skills, and that supply managers have limited linkage to corporate risk managers, few firms intend to outsource SCRM (though components of SCRM may be outsourced). One manager commented: "Most of our risk management resources are from within. We rely on the supply chain professionals at a working level to meet with the global supply chain group, as well as plant management. We do outsource some of our financial analysis of our suppliers, where they do an in-depth financial analysis and come back with a letter grade and summary."

Risk Assessment

Respondents agreed that many things can go wrong in a supply chain without a systematic process for assessing risk, and that they lack a comprehensive supply risk assessment process. One manager commented: "The biggest challenge is that most of the risk assessment relates to financial performance and standing. It does not take into account really the key operational risk issues at the supplier, which impact supplier performance. That really then falls on the supply chain team as part of their vendor selection and ongoing performance evaluations." Most companies reported a high level of activity devoted to supplier measurement, visiting supplier operations, and consistent monitoring of a supplier's processes. Only a few firms used dashboards or scorecards to predict risk trends in advance.

Most firms prioritize risks, and then allocate resources to manage the most significant risks. Though a Pareto approach is common, one manager cautioned that firms may lose sight of seemingly "minor" risks and the interaction of those risks: "We need additional sustained allocation of resources to address individual items further down the Pareto that have a lower amount of impact as an individual issue, but can have significant impact when all individual items are combined."

Increasing government regulations were a concern across many industries. Companies recognize the value of complying with regulations, though there is concern that compliance with so many regulations consumes resources that might be better allocated to risk efforts. One manager noted:

> Compliance risk management activity is taking precedence over an overall supplier risk approach. This challenge is created by regulatory agencies and pushing resources toward certain areas of risk mitigation such as FDA, DOJ, AdvaMED, Sarbanes-Oxley, etc. Without some of these distractions, we would be able to free up additional resources to develop and deploy updated supplier risk processes that would allow for future risk mitigation and support further growth.

Risk Treatment

Many of the highest-rated current and future risk factors (e.g., natural disasters) are not directly controlled by the supply organization, so reacting quickly through contingency planning is required. One manager commented: "I believe there is no clear solution for every situation. Having thorough contingency plans for each part is a must, and based from that assessment, a decision needs to be made by management. Having a budget for supply security is a must even though you may never use it." One respondent indicated that his firm now requires key suppliers to develop contingency plans for their own supply chains as well.

Inventory buffering was a commonly used treatment when companies accepted supply risks. Inventory carrying costs must be assessed relative to the benefits, as one manager stated:

> Pursuit of a long-distance supply chain to leverage low-cost country suppliers necessarily results in higher localized inventory storage near production sites to buffer long lead time demand variation risk. This creates higher inventories, and longer overall supply chain lead times, but achieves overriding delivered material cost savings to the organization.

Risk reduction efforts emphasized qualification of preferred suppliers. However, one manager pointed out that many of the supplier assessment measures are generic and are not linked with a specific sourcing situation or risk condition. Thus, though a supplier may be approved, the specific needs and risks of each sourcing project should be assessed prior to defaulting to an approved supplier.

Development of strong buyer/supplier relationships was a common way to share risk. Some managers expressed concerns that developing relationships on a "personal" basis is increasingly difficult. Challenges for developing "personal" ties included physical distance, limited budget for travel, and the constant switching to the lowest cost suppliers, for example.

Few firms extensively used joint technology development to share risk, which is surprising given that lifecycle risks are addressed most effectively at the early stage design. One manager suggested why early supplier involvement may be limited:

> The supply chain group is taking too long in the analysis of the supply chain decisions, thus risking product development/sourcing lead-time. This is created when supply chain cannot finalize supplier analysis in the 3–4 weeks that are provided. Eventually the company will move without supply chain because product development needs to continue. This can be resolved by hiring efficient people and also measuring supply chain employees on turning around analysis in less than two weeks.

Monitoring and Review

Many firms were satisfied with specific supply chain performance outcomes, though such positive outcomes are not universal and there is room for improvement. It is not clear if these outcomes are achieved more directly through proactive risk management processes or through reactively battling problems. One manager suggested it was the latter: "Results are achieved through daily firefighting instead of continuous improvement due to shortage of resources, inaccurate focus of efforts, and inadequate long-term planning."

It is difficult to directly assess risk management's impacts through anything other than final supply performance, as one manager commented: "In the end, you only know if you made the right decision if you are maintaining the level of supply you need to service your customers." Regardless, firms monitor supply chain performance and risks through supplier visits and assessment systems, ongoing supplier scorecards, and financial risk analysis, for example. Few firms benchmark risk management processes relative to external competitive levels. One respondent suggested that being able to specifically measure "risk management success" was not critical: "Our only measure is whether or not our assembly lines were impacted. If not, our contingency plans were successful. I believe that measuring the success of the plan isn't as important as the thought and ideas generated by having a plan."

Managerial Implications

Managerial implications were suggested throughout the discussion section above. Supply managers are putting effort into SCRM, yet few managers integrate SCRM with ERM. ISO 31000 provides a foundation for supply managers to make the business case for linking SCRM and ERM, and to secure the resources needed to implement SCRM.

Companies often focus on frequently occurring risks or the rare but catastrophic risks. Managers should not lose sight of less frequently occurring risks that perhaps in combination drive significant supply problems. Multiple respondents suggested that complex sourcing systems require advanced SCRM approaches, such as process failure mode and effects analysis and design of experiments for risk. Supply personnel would require training to use such tools effectively.

Information technology continues to advance and become ubiquitous. Companies should proactively develop strategies and plans for using IT to identify and manage supply risks. They should also consider how IT usage impacts the development of "personal" supply relationships. Perhaps new methods of developing supply "relationships" will be required, and the skill set of supply personnel will need to expand.

As companies expand their global reach, supply personnel will need to develop a better understanding of corporate strategy, ERM practices, and financial techniques to manage risks. Such understanding and skills are currently lacking.

Supply risks might be most effectively addressed at early-stage product design. However, compressed development times limit the time allowed for supply risk assessment. Supply managers may consider adopting rapid risk assessment techniques to provide support during early stage design. Companies should also examine the extent to which supplier qualification processes explicitly examine a supplier's SCRM capabilities. Standard qualification measures provide some indication of risk management, but fail to explicitly explore if risk management or contingency plans are in place.

Future Research Questions

The following future research questions were developed based on the interviews and survey data:

1. Over the long term, does a formal integrated strategy and structure for SCRM and/or ERM provide appropriate returns? Perhaps SCRM programs that only use contingency budgets provide better returns, even when in the short term they might recover more slowly from rare major disruptions. Situational factors have already been proposed that influence the level of investment in risk management systems (Giunipero & Eltantawy 2004).

2. Should SCRM adopt a standard ERM framework in future SCRM research? This research identified that ISO 31000:2009 provides a comprehensive framework for examining SCRM. Has it reached the point that researchers should agree to a common framework such as ISO 31000:2009? Will practitioners also find the adoption of ISO 31000 useful?

3. How can IT better support SCRM? Though respondents used IT to support risk management, there was limited use of IT to model and manage supply risks. IT applications, such as Internet-based systems, cloud computing, and mobile devices are becoming more secure and ubiquitous. Research questions might include: What are the most effective tools and how can they most efficiently be adopted in a value chain? What are the barriers to adoption and how can firms overcome the barriers?

4. What is the most effective SCRM organizational structure? Six Sigma requires that quality is everybody's business, yet establishes different levels of expertise. Lean systems also establish a hierarchy of responsibility. Would it be more effective to have people manage risk as part of their everyday responsibility, or would a hierarchy of "risk experts" prove more effective? Further, would it be more effective for firms to focus on their core competencies and to outsource SCRM?

5. Should companies include "design for supply risk management" in product design processes? Most new product development processes already assess risk, though it is not clear if longer-term supply risks are considered. Research suggests that addressing supply risk during new product development has a positive impact (Khan, Christopher, & Burnes 2008). Perhaps "rapid supply risk assessment" techniques similar to "rapid plant assessment" (Goodson 2002) techniques will prove effective.

REFERENCES

Armstrong, J.S. & Overton, T.S. 1977. Estimating Nonresponse Bias in Mail Survey. *Journal of Marketing Research*, 14(3): 396–402. http://dx.doi.org/10.2307/3150783.

Beasley, M., Clune, R., & Hermanson, D. 2005. ERM: A Status Report. *The Internal Auditor*, 62(1): 67–72.

Black, S. & Porter, L. 1996. Identification of the Critical Factors of TQM. *Decision Sciences Journal*, 27(1): 1–21. http://dx.doi.org/10.1111/j.1540-5915.1996.tb00841.x.

Blackhurst, J., Wu, T., & O'Grady, P. 2005. PDCM: A Decision Support Modeling Methodology for Supply Chain, Product and Process Design Decisions. *Journal of Operations Management*, 23(3–4): 325–343. http://dx.doi.org/10.1016/j.jom.2004.05.009.

Capon, N., Kaye, M., & Wood, M. 1994. Measuring the Success of a TQM Programme. *International Journal of Quality and Reliability Management*, 12(8): 8–22. http://dx.doi.org/10.1108/02656719510097471.

Christopher, M. & Holweg, M. 2011. Supply Chain 2.0: Managing Supply Chains in the Era of Turbulence. *International Journal of Physical Distribution & Logistics Management*, 41(1): 63–82. http://dx.doi.org/10.1108/09600031111101439.

Curkovic, S., Melnyk, S., Calantone, R., & Handfield, R. 2000. Validating the Malcolm Baldrige National Quality Framework through Structural Equation Modelling. *International Journal of Production Research*, 38(4): 765–791. http://dx.doi.org/10.1080/002075400189149.

Dean, J. & Bowen, D. 1994. Management Theory and Total Quality: Improving Research and Practice through Theory Development. *Academy of Management Journal*, 19(3): 392–418.

Flynn, B., Schroeder, R. & Sakakibara, S. 1994. A Framework for Quality Management Research and an Associated Instrument. *Journal of Operations Management*, 11(4): 339–366. http://dx.doi.org/10.1016/S0272-6963(97)90004-8.

Giannakis, M. & Louis, M.A. 2001. Multi-Agent Based Framework for Supply Chain Risk Management. *Journal of Purchasing and Supply Management*, 17(1): 23–31. http://dx.doi.org/10.1016/j.pursup.2010.05.001.

Giunipero, L. & Eltantawy, R. 2004. Securing the Upstream Supply Chain: A Risk Management Approach. *International Journal of Physical Distribution & Logistics Management*, 34(9): 698–713. http://dx.doi.org/10.1108/09600030410567478.

Gjerdrum, D. & Salen, W. 2002. The New ERM Gold Standard: ISO 31000:2009. *Professional Safety*, 55(8): 2010: 43–44.

Goodson, R.E. 2002. Read a Plant—Fast. *Harvard Business Review*, 80(5): 105–113.

Hallikas, J., Karvonen, I., Pulkkinen, U., Virolainen, V.M., & Tuominem, M. 2004. Risk Management Processes in Supplier Networks. *International Journal of Production Economics*, 90(1): 47–58. http://dx.doi.org/10.1016/j.ijpe.2004.02.007.

Hauser, L. 2003. Risk Adjusted Supply Chain Management. *Supply Chain Management Review*, 7(6): 64–71.

Hoyt, R. & Liebenberg, A. 2011. The Value of Enterprise Risk Management. *Journal of Risk and Insurance*, 78(4): 795–822. http://dx.doi.org/10.1111/j.1539-6975.2011.01413.x.

ISO. 2009. ISO 31000:2009, Risk Management—Principles and Guidelines. Geneva: International Standards Organization.

Kern, D., Moser, R., Hartmann, E., & Moder, M. 2012. Supply Risk Management: Model Development and Empirical Analysis. *International Journal of Physical Distribution & Logistics Management*, 42(1): 60–82. http://dx.doi.org/10.1108/09600031211202472.

Khan, O. & Burnes, B. 2007. Risk and Supply Chain Management: A Research Agenda. *The International Journal of Logistics Management*, 18(2): 197–216. http://dx.doi.org/10.1108/09574090710816931.

Khan, O., Christopher, M., & Burnes, B. 2008. The Impact of Product Design on Supply Chain Risk: A Case Study. *International Journal of Physical Distribution & Logistics Management*, 38(5): 412–432. http://dx.doi.org/10.1108/09600030810882834.

Kleindorfer, P.R. & Saad, G.H. 2005. Managing Disruptions in Supply Chains. *Production and Operations Management*, 14(1): 53–68. http://dx.doi.org/10.1111/j.1937-5956.2005.tb00009.x.

Manuj, I. & Mentzer, J.T. 2008. Global Supply Chain Risk Management. *Journal of Business Logistics*, 29(1): 133–156. http://dx.doi.org/10.1002/j.2158-1592.2008.tb00072.x.

Miles, M. & Huberman, A. 1982. *Qualitative Data Analysis: A Sourcebook of New Methods*. Newbury Park, CA: Sage Publications.

Moody, M. 2010. ERM & ISO 31000. *Rough Notes*, 153(3): 80–81.

Purdy, G. 2010. ISO 31000:2009—Setting a New Standard for Risk Management. *Risk Analysis*, 30(6): 881–886. http://dx.doi.org/10.1111/j.1539-6924.2010.01442. xPMid:20636915.

Richey, R.G. 2009. The Supply Chain Crisis and Disaster Pyramid: A Theoretical Framework for Understanding Preparedness and Recovery. *International Journal of Physical Distribution & Logistics Management*, 39(7): 619–628. http://dx.doi.org/10.1108/09600030910996288.

Skipper, J. & Hanna, J. 2009. Minimizing Supply Chain Disruption Risk through Enhanced Flexibility. *International Journal of Physical Distribution & Logistics Management*, 39(5): 404–427. http://dx.doi.org/10.1108/09600030910973742.

Sodhi, M.S., Son, B.G., & Tang, C.S. 2012. Researcher's Perspective on Supply Risk Management. *Productions and Operations Management*, 21(1): 1–13. http://dx.doi.org/10.1111/j.1937-5956.2011.01251.x.

Spekman, R. & Davis, E. 2004. Risky Business: Expanding the Discussion on Risk and Extended Enterprise. *International Journal of Physical Distribution & Logistics Management*, 34(5): 414–433. http://dx.doi.org/10.1108/09600030410545454.

Tang, C.S. 2006. Perspectives in Supply Chain Risk Management. *International Journal of Production Economics*, 103(2): 451–488. http://dx.doi.org/10.1016/j.ijpe.2005.12.006.

Teuscher, P., Gruninger, B., & Ferdinand, N. 2006. Risk Management in Sustainable Supply Chain Management (SSCM): Lessons Learnt from the Case of GMO-Free Soybeans. *Corporate Social Responsibility and Environmental Management*, 13(1): 1–10. http://dx.doi.org/10.1002/csr.81.

Tummala, R. & Schoenherr, T. 2011. Assessing and Managing Risks Using the Supply Chain Risk Management Process (SCRMP). *Supply Chain Management*, 16(6): 474–483. http://dx.doi.org/10.1108/13598541111171165.

VanderBok, R., Sauter, J., Bryan, C., & Horan, J. 2007. Manage Your Supply Chain Risk, *Manufacturing Engineering*, 138(3): 153–161.

Zsidisin, G. & Hartley, J.A. 2012. Strategy for Managing Commodity Price Risk. *Supply Chain Management Review*, March/April(2): 46–53.

5

ISO 31000:2009 Enterprise and Supply Chain Risk Management: A Longitudinal Study

INTRODUCTION

Enterprise risk management (ERM) has been identified as a key strategic issue for business (Wu et al. 2011). ERM presents a systematic approach for managing corporate risks and is a driver of company success (Hoyt & Liebenberg 2011; Smithson & Simkins 2005). However, adoption of ERM is not widespread (Beasley et al. 2005). ISO 31000:2009 is intended to support firms in their development and implementation of ERM strategy, structure, and process. Supply chain risk management (SCRM) has also taken on an increased importance for firms, particularly as global sourcing has increased, companies have "leaned out" their supply chains, and product cycle times have become shorter. ERM is supported by SCRM by positively impacting customer satisfaction, costs, delivery, and quality performance (Hauser 2003; Sodhi et al. 2012; Tummala & Schoenherr 2011; VanderBok et al. 2007).

It has been suggested that despite the increasing literature focused on ERM, the broad topic of ERM research is underdeveloped (Wu et al. 2011). It has also been suggested that despite more research into SCRM, there are still gaps in SCRM research (Tang & Musa 2011). This research was motivated by the idea that SCRM research would advance more effectively if there was a consensus on what constitutes SCRM and the assessment that there is a lack of empirical SCRM research (Sodhi et al. 2012). Two primary research questions were explored: (1) How do the current SCRM frameworks proposed by researchers map to the ISO 31000:2009 ERM standard? (2) What are the past, current, and future risks and risk management strategies reported by firms, and how do they map to ISO 31000:2009? Longitudinal data are analyzed to address the questions. Managerial implications and future research suggestions were developed based on the responses.

The findings indicate that despite firms reporting an increased recognition of SCRM importance, SCRM approaches tend to be ad hoc rather than integrated. It was also found that actual SCRM practices and proposed SCRM frameworks all map well to ISO 31000. Thus, for practitioners, ISO 31000 provides a foundation for linking SCRM to ERM, and for developing SCRM strategies and processes. For researchers, ISO 31000 provides a reasonable framework that could accelerate the understanding of SCRM.

In the next section, the literature review discusses gaps in SCRM research, explores the ISO 31000 ERM standard, compares existing SCRM frameworks with ISO 31000, and briefly identifies supply risks and SCRM practices. The methodology is then presented and the survey data results are summarized. Finally, the results are interpreted and discussed, using qualitative feedback from practitioners to support the discussion.

LITERATURE REVIEW

SCRM Research Gaps

The advancement of any field or strategic initiative (e.g., total quality management [TQM], mass customization, just-in-time manufacturing, supply chain risk management) requires empirically based research whose thrust is the development and validation of frameworks, concepts, and measurement instruments. For example, the TQM discipline required that an operational definition and standardized framework be developed and validated in order for theory building to advance (see, for example, Black & Porter 1996; Capon et al. 1994; Curkovic et al. 2000; Dean & Bowen 1994; Flynn et al. 1994; Saraph et al. 1989). By doing so, the TQM discipline moved from the important contributions of anecdotes and case studies (the current state of SCRM research) to testable models and specific research hypotheses, linking the theoretical concept of TQM to empirical indicants. Operational definitions and standardized frameworks have contributed to TQM theory building by identifying the constructs associated with TQM, developing scales for measuring these constructs, and empirically validating the scales. The SCRM research is in its infancy stages and requires the same type of research.

Global competitive landscapes and increasingly complex supply chain processes and partnerships, coupled with increased requirements to comply with regulations, laws, and industry guidelines has heightened awareness that firms may benefit from a systematic approach to risk management. SCRM has garnered significant academic, consultant, and practitioner interest over the last decade as a way to not only mitigate risk but to take advantage of risk opportunities (Hoyt & Liebenberg 2011; Nocco & Stulz 2006). SCRM is a process for identifying, analyzing, and proactively planning responses to a portfolio of risks (Bowling & Rieger 2005; Chapman 2003).

Even though effective SCRM can provide significant benefits for a firm (Hoyt & Liebenberg 2011; Smithson & Simkins 2005), a relatively small percentage of firms have a detailed understanding of this integrated process and the adoption of SCRM is rather limited (Chapman 2003). Ad hoc approaches to risk management by various "silos" in an organization lead to a duplication of resources, uncoordinated planning, and less efficient and effective risk management processes (Hoyt & Liebenberg 2011). Varying frameworks have been proposed to support and standardize the implementation of systematic SCRM. Sample frameworks include the Joint Australia/New Zealand AS/NZ 4360-2004, the Turnbull Guidance, and the ISO 31000 standards for risk management.

SCRM and related frameworks are not without detractors. There is a lack of empirical research into the effectiveness of SCRM in general (Hoyt & Liebenberg 2011) and the specific frameworks in particular. Other detractors note that implementing SCRM requires a substantial commitment of resources (time, personnel, money) that are not likely to be available during lean times, and a cultural shift of the entire organization (Ballou & Heitger 2005) without an appropriate return on such efforts (Samad-Khan 2005). However, with appropriate planning and execution, SCRM frameworks may be implemented by any organization, from large to small firms (Ballou & Heitger 2005; Chapman 2003). Other SCRM frameworks have also been proposed (Hallikas et al. 2004; Kleindorfer & Saad 2005; Manuj & Mentzer 2008; Tummala & Schoenherr 2011). There are many similarities in these frameworks, though there is no consensus on the scope of SCRM (Sodhi et al. 2012). In some cases, the concepts are the same, but the terms used are slightly different (e.g., risk assessment versus risk evaluation) and some frameworks do not explicitly identify key processes (e.g., monitoring and review).

Sodhi, Son, and Tang (2012) identified multiple SCRM research gaps and recommended ways to close the gaps. One gap they identified is a lack of consensus regarding the definition and scope of SCRM. They suggested that there is a great need to reach a consensus on such issues in order to better communicate with company executives and practitioners, and to more quickly advance SCRM research. They also suggest that SCRM is a subset or extension of ERM (Sodhi et al. 2012). Given their suggestions, the ISO 31000 ERM framework, developed by and for practitioners, was identified as a potential consensus framework for SCRM that could fill the research gap. Another gap identified by Sodhi, Son, and Tang (2012), was a lack of empirical SCRM research, particularly with regard to understanding current practices. This empirical research focuses on current practices and is one important first step toward filling the empirical research gap.

ERM, ISO 31000:2009, and SCRM Frameworks

Enterprise risk management (ERM) is a holistic approach to identify and manage corporate-wide risks to achieve long-term success (Smithson & Simkins 2005). Though ERM is an increasingly important topic for practitioners and researchers (Hoyt & Liebenberg 2011), it is not widely adopted (Moody 2010). ISO 31000 "Risk Management Principles," released by the International Organization for Standardization (ISO), presents a set of principles, frameworks, and processes for achieving ERM (ISO 2009a). Given the clout and impact of prior ISO standards, ISO 31000 will likely become a globally adopted format for ERM (Gjerdrum & Salen 2010). ISO 31000 was built upon the foundation established by the AS/NZS 4360 process (AS/NZS 2004), which has been used and tested over time. ISO 31000 intends to support risk management across all functions of an organization, including supply, finance, and operations, for example. The ISO Guide 73:2009 (ISO 2009b) provides definitions to support understanding and implementation of ISO 31000.

ISO 31000 identifies 11 principles for effective ERM: create value; be an integral part of all processes; be integrated with decision making; explicitly examine uncertainty; be systematic, structured, and timely; rely on best available information; be tailored to specific needs; account for human and cultural factors; be transparent and inclusive; be responsive to change; and facilitate continual improvement (ISO 2009a). The ISO 31000 framework emphasizes integration of risk management practices throughout the value chain to support corporate decision making (ISO 2009a).

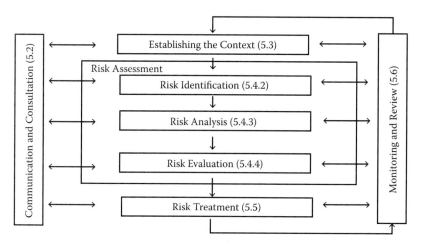

FIGURE 5.1
ISO 31000:2009 Clause 5 Process for managing risk.

ISO 39000:2009 Risk Management Process (Clause 5) is the focus of this research. The process consists of five integrated segments (Figure 5.1). There is a high level of integration and iteration between the risk management processes (Purdy 2010). Communication and Consultation (Clause 5.2) calls for continuous risk information collection and dissemination by involving all stakeholders. Establishing the Context (Clause 5.3) develops objectives and sets the foundation (e.g., culture, organization, resources, responsibilities, etc.) for achieving those objectives.

Risk Assessment (Clause 5.4) presents three interdependent activities: identifying risks; analyzing risks; and evaluating risks. Risk Identification (Clause 5.4.2) is a systematic process to understand and categorize risk, and to identify risk drivers. Risk Analysis (Clause 5.4.3) involves evaluation of risk impacts and likelihood of occurrence. Risk Evaluation (Clause 5.4.4) prioritizes risks and identifies which risks may require treatment. Some risks may be acceptable while others are not. An "acceptable risk" is one for which the perceived benefits outweigh the costs of a possible treatment.

Risk Treatment (Clause 5.5) selects the appropriate options for treating or modifying risks. Such options include: acceptance of risk to realize competitive advantages; avoidance of risk by not engaging in the activity; reduction or removal of the impact or probability of the risk; or distribution of risk by sharing or transferring the risk. Monitoring and Review (Clause 5.6) involves an ongoing analysis of the risks encountered, and an assessment of risk treatment effectiveness.

SCRM frameworks have also been proposed (Hallikas et al. 2004; Kleindorfer & Saad 2005; Manuj & Mentzer 2008; Tummala & Schoenherr 2011). There are many similarities in these frameworks, though there is no consensus on the scope of SCRM (Sodhi et al. 2012). In some cases, the concepts are the same, but the terms used are slightly different (e.g., risk assessment versus risk evaluation) and some frameworks do not explicitly identify key processes (e.g., monitoring and review). Table 5.1 compares four SCRM frameworks with the ISO 31000:2009 standard.

TABLE 5.1

Comparison of Proposed SCRM Frameworks to ISO 31000:2009

ISO 31000:2009	Hallikas, Karvonen, Pulkkinen et al. 2004	Kleindorfer & Saad 2005	Manuj & Mentzer 2008	Tummala & Schoenherr 2011
5.2 Communication and Consultation				
5.3 Establishing the Context				
5.4.2 Risk Identification	Risk identification	Specifying sources of risks and vulnerabilities	Risk identification	Risk identification Risk measurement[a]
5.4.3 Risk Analysis	Risk assessment	Assessment	Risk assessment and evaluation	Risk assessment
5.4.4 Risk Evaluation				Risk evaluation
5.5 Risk Treatment	Decision and implementation of risk management actions	Mitigation	Selection of appropriate risk management strategies Implementation of supply chain risk management strategies Mitigation of supply chain risks	Risk mitigation and contingency plans
5.6 Monitoring and Review	Risk monitoring			Risk control and monitoring

[a] Covered in ISO 31000:2009 in Section 5.3.5 "Risk Criteria."

Though SCRM frameworks and ISO 31000 share overlapping concepts, the ISO 31000 standard provides a more comprehensive framework. It requires an "establishment of the context," a critical step for holistic risk management and for linking SCRM with ERM. ISO 31000 also emphasizes "monitoring and review" to create a closed loop process. ISO 31000 was used in this research to explore SCRM rather than any of the proposed SCRM frameworks because it is more comprehensive and it is expected to become an internationally adopted approach to risk management (Gjerdrum & Salen 2010). Further, Sodhi, Son, and Tang (2012) suggest that SCRM is an integral component of ERM, and that there is a need to reach a consensus regarding the scope of SCRM in order to advance research in this field. ISO 31000 provides the framework for integrating SCRM and ERM, and for driving consensus on the scope of SCRM.

Supply Chain Risks and Practices

Firms face multiple supply risks, whether in combination or isolation, such as supplier reliability/failure, currency exchange, commodity cost volatility, banking and government regulations, bankruptcy, material shortages, logistics failures, demand change, diminishing capacities, return policy, port security, legal liabilities, insurance coverage, tax issues, natural disasters, intellectual property, skilled labor, language, strikes, property laws, infrastructure, contract failure, contamination, fraud, information theft, and so on (Blackhurst et al. 2005; Kumar & Verruso 2008; Liu & Cruz 2012; Manuj & Mentzer 2008; Tummala & Schoenherr 2011; Zsidisin & Hartley 2012). Each risk might require a specific SCRM technique (Zsidisin & Wagner 2010).

There are a variety of definitions for SCRM. In general, SCRM may be defined as managing supply risks through collaboration or coordination with supply partners to achieve sustainable profitability and continuity (Tang 2006). SCRM treatment options include evaluation and trust building (Laeequddin, Sardana, Sahay, Abdul Waheed, & Sahay 2009), use of dual sources (Khan & Burnes 2007), environmental scanning (Zsidisin et al. 2004), combined capacity reservation contracts and spot markets (Inderfurth & Kelle 2011), supply chain modeling and information systems integration (Giannakis & Louis 2001), qualification and use of capable suppliers (Manuj & Mentzer 2008), supplier quality management initiatives (Holschbach & Hofmann 2011), buffer inventory (Tang 2006), contingency plans (Kleindorfer & Saad 2005), credit analysis (Kern et al. 2012), strategic sourcing and flexibility (Chiang et al. 2012), forward buying or hedging (Zsidisin & Hartley 2012), and supplier development (Matook, Lasch, & Tamaschke 2009). Despite the plethora of risks and risk management approaches, few firms have a structured SCRM approach (Martin et al. 2011).

RESEARCH METHOD

The focus of this research is exploratory in nature (rather than confirmatory). Field-based data and survey collection methods were used to ensure that the important variables were identified. It also helped us develop an understanding of why these variables might be important (Eisenhardt 1989; Voss et al. 2002). This research examined how current SCRM research frameworks and actual business practices align with the ERM standard ISO 31000:2009, and identified past, current, and future SCRM experiences of firms. A purposeful sample was used in this exploratory research (Eisenhardt 1989; Miles & Huberman 1994). Key criterion included that the company would agree to identify an informed respondent, reply in a timely manner to a scaled and open-ended survey, and be willing to participate in follow-up questions as needed. All targeted respondents support supply chain management higher education, and are involved with professional supply associations such as the Institute of Supply Management, Association of Operations Management, and Council of Supply Chain Management Professionals. The method followed was similar to the grounded theory development methodology suggested by Glaser and Strauss (1967). In instances where a well-developed set of theories regarding a particular branch of knowledge does not exist, Eisenhardt (1989) and McCutcheon and Meredith (1993) suggest that theory building can best be done through limited sample sizes.

Several industries were chosen for this study to achieve some level of generalizability. The first survey was sent to 67 contacts in 2009, yielding 46 responses (68% response rate). The second survey was distributed two years later in 2011 to 58 contacts, yielding 38 usable responses (66% response rate). Both surveys were nearly identical with regard to format, and all items discussed in this chapter were identical in terms of content. For each survey, the non-respondents suggested that they either: (1) did not have time to fill out the survey within the window of time provided;

or (2) company policy prevented them from fully participating. Early to late respondent survey comparisons were made to analyze potential non-response bias (Armstrong & Overton 1977). The mean values for seven randomly selected questions were compared between the first 25% of responses and the last 25% of responses. No statistically significant differences were found between responses. The majority of non-respondents indicated that either company policy prevented them from participation in this particular survey or that resources were constrained when the survey was distributed.

Similar to much of the research in operations strategy, ideally a single industry would have been chosen. Focusing on a single industry controls for variance due to industry-specific conditions. Industries may also differ in the consensus understanding of the meaning of terms. Controlling for industry effects can compensate for variability between industries, in terms of work force management, general market conditions, degree of unionization, and so on. Controlling for these industry-specific differences through the focus on one industry also means that firm-specific variance is highlighted in subsequent analyses. Restricting the sample permits the control of several variables that often differ between industries, including the scope and complexity of risk management concerns. At the same time, one would have to identify a specific industry where the types of SCRM issues and range of programs used offer sufficient variability for study. This variability within that sample would then provide a basis for external generalizability. However, no single industry was selected because there has not been one that has been a leader in implementing progressive SCRM strategies. Furthermore, no single industry has already been the focus of many empirical studies that address SCRM. Given these circumstances and the infancy stages of this topic area, aggregation of survey results among widely varying industries was justified and the route taken.

DATA ANALYSIS

Four profile characteristics of respondents to each survey were compared using t-tests assuming unequal variances (Table 5.2 through Table 5.5). There were no statistically significant differences in any of the characteristics, suggesting that comparison of other survey data was valid. Table 5.6 lists respondent job titles to each survey.

TABLE 5.2

Industry Profile

Industry	Survey 1	Survey 2
Aerospace/Defense	2	4
Agriculture	1	1
Automotive	14	10
Chemicals	0	1
Consumer Products	2	3
Electronics	1	1
Food	1	1
Fuel, Utilities, and Power	0	1
Health Care	1	2
House Building and Construction	0	2
Manufacturing	16	11
Transportation	1	0
Other	7	1
Total	46	38

Note: t-test ($p = 0.13$).

TABLE 5.3

Sales Profile

Annual Sales ($)	Survey 1	Survey 2
10M–49M	3	1
50M–99M	2	3
100M–499M	6	2
500M–999M	3	4
1B–9B	15	7
10B–49B	12	15
50B–99B	3	3
Over 100B	2	3
Total	46	38

Note: t-test ($p = 0.25$).

SCRM Process

Survey data were grouped according to ISO 31000 Clause 5 process segments. The data tables are sorted by the highest mean score or the highest ranking based on survey 2 data. "Agree/disagree" questions were scaled from "1 = strongly disagree" to "7 = strongly agree." "Extent of use" questions were scaled from "1 = not used" to "7 = extensively used."

TABLE 5.4

Employment Profile

Employees	Survey 1	Survey 2
Under 50	1	0
50–99	1	1
100–499	4	3
500–999	2	2
1,000–4,999	10	6
5,000–9,999	4	3
Over 10,000	24	23
Total	46	38

Note: t-test (p = 0.48).

TABLE 5.5

Ownership

Ownership	Survey 1	Survey 2
Privately owned	13	11
Publicly owned	30	25
Publicly/privately owned	3	2
Total	46	38

Note: t-test (p = 0.87).

TABLE 5.6

Respondent Titles

Title	Survey 1	Survey 2
Supply Chain Leader/Manager/Coordinator/Buyer	66%	54%
Production/Operations/Materials Manager	22%	29%
Analyst	6%	17%
Account/Sales Director	6%	0%

Communication and Consultation (Clause 5.2): There were no statistically significant differences in the communication and consultation practices (Table 5.7). Information gathering and establishing communications with suppliers remained paramount approaches. Concerns existed whether supply risk information is accurate and readily available, however. There may be a somewhat increased use of data warehousing and demand signal repositories, though neither change was statistically significant.

TABLE 5.7

SCRM and Clause 5.2 Communication and Consultation

Item	Survey 1		Survey 2		t-test
	Mean	SD	Mean	SD	p
Establishing good communications with suppliers	5.65	1.04	5.81	1.05	0.49
Information gathering	5.67	1.21	5.51	1.54	0.61
Forecasting techniques (e.g., to pre-build and carry additional inventory of critical items)	4.61	1.57	4.79	1.56	0.60
Our company uses real-time inventory information and analytics in managing the supply chain	4.76	1.52	4.61	1.66	0.68
Data warehousing	4.09	1.76	4.59	1.54	0.16
Visibility (detailed knowledge of what goes on in other parts of the supply chain, e.g., finished goods inventory, material inventory, WIP, pipeline inventory, actual demands and forecasts, production plans, capacity, yields, and order status)	4.26	1.29	4.24	1.46	0.95
Demand signal repositories	3.42	1.85	3.95	1.68	0.18
Supply chain risk information is accurate and readily available to key decision makers	3.87	1.57	3.81	1.68	0.87
Network design analysis programs	3.25	1.94	3.41	1.40	0.68

Establishing the Context (Clause 5.3): Contextual factors were grouped according to need, approach, budget, and organization (Table 5.8), consistent with general guidelines proposed by ISO 31000. There was a statistically significant increase in the recognition that much can go wrong in a supply chain without systematic risk analysis. SCRM is recognized as a strategic issue, but the lack of a single set of tools or technologies makes implementation a challenge. The supply chain organization seems to lack key risk management skills and has a limited understanding of corporate risk management strategy.

SCRM budgets are shown in Table 5.9. The response rate was not 100% for this question due to competitive concerns. There was no significant difference in spending plans between the two data sets. Table 5.10 indicates that most firms will keep SCRM spending at current levels or increase spending in the future. Table 5.11 suggests that purchasing/supply generally takes ownership of SCRM investments, though Table 5.12 suggests the SCRM budget generally does not come from a specific SCRM budget.

TABLE 5.8

SCRM and Clause 5.3 Establishing the Context

	Survey 1		Survey 2		t-test
Item	**Mean**	**SD**	**Mean**	**SD**	**p**
Need					
Without a systematic analysis technique to assess risk, much can go wrong in a supply chain.	5.54	1.03	6.19	0.97	0.00
Managing supply chain risk is an increasingly important initiative for our operations.	5.65	1.30	5.92	1.19	0.33
It is critical for us to have an easily understood method to identify and manage supply chain risk.	5.30	1.23	5.27	1.52	0.91
My workplace plans on evaluating or implementing supply chain risk tools and technologies.	4.98	1.58	5.08	1.91	0.79
We are very concerned about our supply chain resiliency and the failure implications.	4.78	1.59	4.81	1.65	0.94
Approach					
There is no single set of tools or technologies on the market for managing supply chain risks.	5.24	1.49	5.50	1.34	0.41
We are currently using some form of supply chain risk management tools and services.	4.46	1.93	5.03	1.83	0.17
Managing supply chain risks is driven by reactions to failures rather than being proactively driven.	4.39	1.36	4.19	1.67	0.57
Proactive risk mitigation efforts applied to the supply chain is common practice for us.	4.33	1.49	4.19	1.76	0.71
Supply chain risk initiatives are driven from the bottom up rather than top down.	3.67	1.56	3.70	1.75	0.94
Budget					
We do plan on investing nontrivial amounts in managing supply chain risks.	4.30	1.86	4.17	1.46	0.71
We have a dedicated budget for activities associated with managing supply chain risks.	3.65	1.96	3.89	2.27	0.61
Funding for managing supply chain risks will come from a general operations budget.	3.91	1.94	3.81	2.03	0.81
Our spending intentions for managing supply chain risks are very high.	3.37	1.58	3.08	1.54	0.41

Continued

TABLE 5.8 *(Continued)*

SCRM and Clause 5.3 Establishing the Context

	Survey 1		Survey 2		t-test
Item	Mean	SD	Mean	SD	p
Organization					
Supply chain employees understand government legislation and geopolitical issues.	3.70	1.26	3.73	1.61	0.92
I fully understand the activities being performed by our risk management group.	4.00	1.86	3.70	1.54	0.43
My workplace uses supply chain risk managers who work closely with corporate risk management.	2.53	1.74	2.64	1.81	0.79
We are planning to outsource all or some of our risk management functions.	2.25	1.28	2.14	1.22	0.69

TABLE 5.9

SCRM Budget

Spend ($)	Survey 1	Survey 2
Less than 500,000	21	16
500,000–1,000,000	1	1
1,000,000–5,000,000	3	3
More than 5,000,000	3	4
Total	28	24

Note: t-test (p = 0.50).

TABLE 5.10

Projected Change in SCRM Budget

Change	Survey 1	Survey 2
Increase	20	14
Decrease	6	3
No change	17	21
Total	43	38

Note: t-test (p = 0.23).

Risk Assessment (Clause 5.4): There were no statistically significant differences in the risk assessment practices (Table 5.13). Most firms will keep SCRM spending at current levels or increase spending in the future. Table 5.11 suggests that specific risk factors such as supplier reliability, relocating facilities overseas, and filling spikes in demand are carefully

TABLE 5.11

Ownership of SCRM Investments

Department	Survey 1	Survey 2
Risk Management	0	1
Supply Chain/Purchasing	40	33
Legal	0	0
Logistics	1	0
Manufacturing/Operations	2	1
IT	0	1
Accounting/Finance	1	1
Quality	0	0
Other	0	0
Total	44	37

Note: t-test (p = 0.99).

TABLE 5.12

SCRM Funding Source

Source	Survey 1	Survey 2
General operations budget	12	9
General IT budget	1	2
Specific departmental budget	20	14
General finance budget	5	2
Specific budget to address supply chain issues	8	11
Total	46	38

Note: t-test (p = 0.55).

assessed. A relatively small percentage of firms anticipate that they will exploit risk to an advantage by taking calculated supply chain risks.

Respondents identified the top five risks that they face (Table 5.14). The most persistent risks seem to be supplier failure/reliability, supplier bankruptcy, commodity cost volatility, natural disasters, logistic failures, and geopolitical events. Respondents were also asked which risks would decrease, remain the same, or increase during the next two years (Table 5.15). Some of the highest rated risk factors such as currency exchange rates and government regulations require that SCRM be integrated with ERM in order to most effectively treat the risk.

Risk Treatment (Clause 5.5): There were no statistically significant differences in the risk treatment practices (Table 5.16). When risk is accepted, inventory management and buffering is a widely used option.

TABLE 5.13

SCRM and Clause 5.4 Risk Assessment

Risk Assessment Practices and Issues	Survey 1		Survey 2		t-test
	Mean	SD	Mean	SD	p
Supplier reliability and continuous supply is the top risk factor for our supply chain.	5.35	1.34	5.68	1.43	0.29
Risks of moving manufacturing facilities overseas are carefully evaluated.	5.65	1.15	5.30	1.63	0.27
Risks of not being able to fulfill a spike in consumer demand are carefully evaluated.	5.22	1.25	5.11	1.49	0.72
Key metrics are in place to measure the risk associated with key suppliers.	4.65	1.68	4.68	1.60	0.95
We apply high levels of analytical rigor to assess our supply chain practices.	4.37	1.53	4.38	1.78	0.98
A key part of our supply chain management is documenting the likelihood and impact of risks.	4.20	1.67	4.19	1.60	1.00
Taxes such as excise and VAT impact our supply chain decisions.	3.86	1.69	4.05	1.73	0.62
We can actually exploit risk to an advantage by taking calculated risks in the supply chain.	4.02	1.63	3.97	1.64	0.89

Risk reduction emphasized using approved suppliers, while risk sharing emphasized supplier partnering and development.

Monitoring and Review (Clause 5.6): There was a statistically significant increase in the monitoring and review practice of using credit and financial data analysis (Table 5.17). Firms extensively monitor supply chain and SCRM performance using a variety of techniques such as measurement systems, supplier visits, and supplier process monitoring. Relatively few firms benchmark SCRM processes to those of competitors. Firms appear to be somewhat satisfied with supply chain performance (Table 5.18). There was a statistically significant decrease in satisfaction with damage-free and defect-free delivery, and a statistically significant increase in satisfaction with reduced material price volatility.

DISCUSSION

The following research limitations should be kept in mind as the data are interpreted and discussed. The sample size was by a relatively small design

TABLE 5.14

Current Supply Chain Risks

Risk Factor	Frequency	
	Survey 1	**Survey 2**
Supplier failure/reliability	41	33
Bankruptcy, ruin, or default of suppliers, shippers, etc.	22	19
Commodity cost volatility	18	15
Natural disasters or accidents (tsunamis, hurricanes, fires, etc.)	15	14
Logistics failure	20	12
Geopolitical events (terrorism, war, etc.)	6	10
Contract failure	4	8
Strikes—labor, buyers, and suppliers	15	8
Customer-related (demand change, system failure, payment delay)	8	8
Energy/raw material shortages and power outages	6	8
Information delays, scarcity, sharing, and infrastructure breakdown	5	6
Government regulations (SOX, SEC, Clean Air Act, OSHA, EU)	9	5
Intellectual property infringement	7	5
Lack of trust with partners	7	5
Diminishing capacities (financial, production, structural, etc.)	10	5
Contamination exposure—food, germs, infections	3	5
Legal liabilities and issues	5	4
Return policy and product recall requirements	2	4
Attracting and retaining skilled labor	8	4
Currency exchange, interest, and /or inflation rate fluctuations	7	4

to ensure a relatively high response rate and to secure participation in follow-up interviews. Future research should consider a larger sample. The research findings are based on perceptual data, and while common to survey work, future research should include objective measures (e.g., actual risk reduction outcomes, actual budget, etc.). Responses came mostly from manufacturing firms and future research should include a greater number of service firms to increase generalizability.

Also, the decision to obtain ISO 31000 registration is not always straightforward for managers since many issues still surround the ERM standard. Although ISO 31000 addresses several criticisms of previous ERM frameworks (Hallikas et al. 2004; Kleindorfer & Saad 2005; Manuj & Mentzer 2008; Tummala & Schoenherr 2011), it is still met with uncertainty and this uncertainty could have impacted the survey findings. Most of this uncertainty is related to perceived weaknesses with regard to its ability to

TABLE 5.15

Projected Change in Supply Chain Risks

Risk Category	Survey 1			Survey 2		
	Less	Same	More	Less	Same	More
Currency exchange, interest, and /or inflation rate fluctuations	0	7	36	1	3	34
Commodity cost volatility	2	9	33	4	6	28
Banking regulations and tighter financing conditions	1	16	28	2	9	27
Government regulations (SOX, SEC, Clean Air Act, OSHA, EU)	0	28	16	0	14	24
Supplier failure/reliability	13	7	24	7	14	17
Geopolitical events (terrorism, war, etc.)	0	29	15	0	22	16
Energy/raw material shortages and power outages	3	26	15	1	21	16
Customs acts/trade restrictions and protectionism	2	27	16	3	19	16
Logistics failure	8	27	9	5	17	16
Bankruptcy, ruin, or default of suppliers, shippers, etc.	2	13	29	6	16	16
Customer-related (demand change, system failure, payment delay)	3	22	19	2	21	15
Diminishing capacities (financial, production, structural, etc.)	5	22	17	5	18	15
Return policy and product recall requirements	5	29	9	1	23	14
Port/cargo security (information, freight, vandalism, sabotage, etc.)	3	29	13	1	24	13
Legal liabilities and issues	2	26	17	1	24	13
Insurance coverage	1	29	14	0	26	12
Tax issues (VAT, transfer pricing, excise, etc.)	3	32	9	0	27	11
Natural disasters or accidents (tsunamis, hurricanes, fires, etc.)	2	34	12	1	26	11
Intellectual property infringement	3	23	18	1	28	9
Attracting and retaining skilled labor	12	15	16	7	22	9
Language and educational barriers	8	21	15	11	18	9
Strikes—labor, buyers, and suppliers	4	26	14	4	26	8
Property development—local codes and requirements	4	35	6	1	30	7

Continued

TABLE 5.15 *(Continued)*

Projected Change in Supply Chain Risks

Risk Category	Survey 1			Survey 2		
	Less	Same	More	Less	Same	More
Unfamiliar business and property laws	6	36	3	2	29	7
Weaknesses in the local infrastructures	9	27	8	5	26	7
Contract failure	5	32	7	6	25	7
Contamination exposure—food, germs, infections	5	37	2	3	29	6
Ethical issues (working practices, health, safety, etc.)	8	30	7	5	27	6
Obtaining proper bonds and licenses	6	35	3	3	30	5
Degree of control over operations	8	30	6	10	23	5
Measuring tools—metrics translate differently	10	27	7	8	26	4
Lack of trust with partners	13	24	7	10	24	4
Internal and external theft	4	36	5	3	32	3
Fraud or scandal	3	34	7	3	32	3
Information delays, scarcity, sharing, and infrastructure breakdown	18	18	8	15	20	3

deliver real benefits and a continued over-emphasis on bureaucratic processes and documentation. Other criticisms generally concern inappropriate misapplication or extension of its use in companies, and the effect this can have on organizational resources and culture. While the criticism focuses on the standard, the problems typically arise from a failure of organizations to understand the underlying philosophy of the standard and the idea that this is a process-driven systematic approach to ERM.

Longitudinal Data Analysis and SCRM Trends

The primary reason for using longitudinal data was to determine if over time the ISO 31000 framework provided a foundation for both researchers and managers to discuss, examine, and/or implement SCRM strategies and practices. There is a reasonable alignment between proposed SCRM frameworks, actual SCRM practices, and ISO 31000:2009. So, if it is true that adopting a consensus framework for SCRM research will

TABLE 5.16

SCRM and Clause 5.5 Risk Treatment

Treatments	Survey 1		Survey 2		t-test
	Mean	SD	Mean	SD	p
Acceptance					
Inventory management (buffers, safety stock levels, optimal order, and production quantity)	4.96	1.69	5.42	1.08	0.13
Contingency planning (jointly with suppliers)	4.22	1.25	4.63	1.50	0.18
We have placed an increased focus on inventory management to deal with supply risks	4.80	1.34	4.56	1.46	0.43
Our suppliers are required to have secure sourcing, business continuity, and contingency plans	4.62	1.71	4.54	1.86	0.84
We are prepared to minimize the effects of disruptions (terrorism, weather, theft, etc.)	3.70	1.31	3.86	1.87	0.64
Reduction					
Using an approved list of suppliers	5.78	1.18	6.11	1.11	0.20
Multiple sourcing (rather than sole sourcing)	4.04	1.36	4.47	1.72	0.22
Postponement (delaying the actual commitment of resources to maintain flexibility)	3.70	1.35	3.97	1.30	0.34
Sharing					
Partnership formation and long-term agreements	5.11	1.08	5.24	1.15	0.60
Supplier development initiatives	4.83	1.37	5.18	1.41	0.24
Speculation (forward placement of inventory, forward buying of raw materials, etc.)	4.07	1.69	4.08	1.38	0.97
Hedging strategies (to protect against commodity price swings)	3.61	1.63	3.92	1.62	0.38
We are hedging our raw material exposure to reduce input cost volatility	3.78	1.49	3.65	1.69	0.72
Joint technology development initiatives	3.59	1.47	3.47	1.89	0.76

enable better communication between researchers and practitioners, and that such a common framework would enable more efficient and effective research to close research gaps (Sodhi et al. 2012), then ISO 31000:2009 provides a reasonable foundation.

A secondary reason for employing longitudinal data was to identify trends in supply risks, strategies, and practices. There were only four statistically significant changes identified. There was an increase in agreement

TABLE 5.17

SCRM and Clause 5.6: Monitoring and Review

Process	Survey 1		Survey 2		t-test
	Mean	SD	Mean	SD	p
Supplier performance measurement systems	5.35	1.61	5.71	1.64	0.31
Credit and financial data analysis	4.54	1.60	5.37	1.34	0.01
Visiting supplier operations	5.04	1.32	5.34	1.24	0.29
Business process management	4.65	1.37	5.11	1.27	0.12
Consistent monitoring and auditing of a supplier's processes	4.59	1.72	5.03	1.68	0.24
Spend management and analysis	4.85	1.53	5.03	1.70	0.62
Contract management (e.g., leverage tools to monitor performance against commitments)	4.48	1.64	5.00	1.52	0.14
Benchmarking (internal, external, industry-wide, etc.)	4.59	1.54	4.68	1.51	0.77
We have placed an emphasis on incident reporting to decrease the effects of disruptions	4.50	1.43	4.49	1.76	0.97
Inventory optimization tools	4.78	1.66	4.49	1.68	0.43
Training programs	3.54	1.59	3.79	1.66	0.49
We use network design and optimization tools to cope with uncertainty in the supply chain	3.66	1.85	3.67	1.64	0.98
We actively benchmark our supply chain risk processes against competitors	3.57	1.68	3.39	2.02	0.67

TABLE 5.18

Performance Satisfaction

Outcome	Survey 1		Survey 2		t-test
	Mean	SD	Mean	SD	p
Logistics and delivery reliability	4.96	1.01	5.32	1.25	0.15
Meeting customer service levels	5.07	1.20	5.19	1.17	0.64
Supplier reliability and continuous supply	4.85	0.99	5.03	1.12	0.45
Damage-free and defect-free delivery	5.41	0.83	5.00	0.94	0.04
Order completeness and correctness	4.96	1.11	4.86	1.29	0.73
After sales service performance	4.57	1.29	4.86	1.09	0.27
Inventory management	4.52	1.22	4.84	1.32	0.27
Reduced disruptions in the supply chain	4.59	1.15	4.54	1.07	0.85
Reduced material price volatility	3.80	1.51	4.32	1.06	0.07
Lower commodity prices	3.98	1.27	4.05	1.20	0.78

that without a systematic analysis technique to assess risk, much can go wrong in a supply chain. As will be discussed subsequently, it does not appear that this awareness has translated into SCRM being raised to a strategic corporate level through linkages with ERM, or into an increased allocation of resources for SCRM. ISO 31000 may provide a foundation for practitioners to remedy those situations.

There was a statistically significant increase in the use of credit and financial data analysis, likely driven by the high level of supplier failures and bankruptcies over the last decade. Firms reported statistically significant better performance in terms of reducing material price volatility. It is not possible to identify specific drivers of this improved performance without controlling for many broad economic factors. Hedging strategies were not widely used, so this is unlikely a driver. Perhaps the relatively high use of supplier partnering, approved supplier lists, and increased use of supplier financial health assessment helped create some price stability. There was a decrease in satisfaction with damage-free and defect-free delivery performance. Again, the direct causes of this outcome are not readily identifiable. The examination of direct cause and effect relationships was beyond the scope of this research. It was also clear that some of the survey responses were linked to the economic recession conditions of 2008. For example, a major risk and source of supply chain disruption was supplier bankruptcy, for which most buying organizations were not proactively evaluating. Future research should explore such relationships over a period of time that goes beyond the two years covered in this study to see how companies have managed this and other risk issues since.

CRM Practices Relative to ISO 31000 Clauses

Communication and Consultation (Clause 5.2): The importance of reliable and timely information communicated throughout the value chain was evident. One manager highlighted this importance:

> We have a very intricate web of parts supply. It can be very difficult to get accurate information about our suppliers and even our own company overseas. Many times it is difficult to know where to obtain information accurately and reliably. So, even if we have a perfect system or structure in place to manage risk, it depends on the input of reliable data that accurately identifies the risk. The old "garbage in/garbage out" theory applies.

Not only was the ability to find reliable information a challenge for some firms, the ability to share information quickly was also a challenge. One manager noted that the major failure mode was "Information speed that is too reactive versus proactive." Some firms indicated that such challenges can be overcome by matching information research efforts with project needs: "In many cases getting good information can be as simple and cheap as subscribing to a few periodicals, or as complex and expensive as hiring outside consultants. It really depends on the business that you're in and the needs of the company."

Establishing the Context (Clause 5.3): Proposed SCRM frameworks as well as SCRM strategies and practices used by respondents align well with the ISO 31000 process. However, it does not appear that the firms are proactively using ISO 31000 or any other such integrative framework for SCRM. Even at firms with seemingly advanced SCRM practices, the linkage to ERM seems a bit weak. One manager stated,

> Supply risk management is handled at the plant location level and not from the corporate level. This is created by a "we have always done it this way" mentality. It has always worked in the past because changes to production plans have never fluctuated like this before, both up and down. This challenge is preventing us from accurately assessing which suppliers are at risk and why, and assessing this early enough to do something about it.

ISO 31000 states that upper managers need to take the lead in ERM and SCRM to establish the appropriate culture, organization, budget, resources, and processes for managing risks. A few respondents suggested that their firms have recently taken steps in this direction, as exemplified by one manager's comment:

> Resources have been allocated to SCRM as we have increased the amount of Full Time Headcount dedicated to supply chain activities across the company. We have also received IT prioritization for projects that will help us understand exposure related to certain supply relationships and allow us to take action on those. As we continue to broaden our business and create revenue streams generated from 100% supplied product, we have a more direct association of revenue risk with the supply chain.

Such strategic linkage of SCRM to ERM was not universal. When support from upper management was lacking, most respondents suggested that it was up to the supply group to make a solid business case for SCRM, as summarized by one manager:

> As supply managers, we need to have an effective way to tie a supplied product or component back to actual revenue generated from that product or component. Many companies including ours need to make the process easier and more visible to upper management once the data is retrieved. The financial impact—favorable or unfavorable—as well as the financial risk and exposure should be captured by the supply managers and communicated up through upper management.

The lack of SCRM linkage to ERM is further evidenced in the Organization section of Table 5.8. Few supply personnel understand government legislation, geopolitical issues, or the activities being performed by the firm's risk management group. Perhaps supply chain curriculum needs to put a greater emphasis on such issues, or companies need to hire supply personnel with more varied experiences and backgrounds.

Despite the "non-trivial" amounts being spent on SCRM and most firms increasing the budget for SCRM, the overall perspective was that budgets were not sufficiently "high." Supply managers suggested that their ability to mitigate supply chain risks was often limited by a lack of money, time, or people. The current business environment and focus on lean operations suggested that securing more resources for SCRM is now even more challenging. One manager stated: "In the current state of the economy with pressure for reduced cost and leaner manufacturing, it's harder to have the resources—people and funding—to be fully prepared for these risks, which greater puts a company in the face of danger." As stated earlier, it is up to the supply manager to make a business case for SCRM. Perhaps it is the failure to make a business case that explains why the budget for SCRM is most often established in departments other than supply chain management.

Relatively few firms indicated that their company takes a proactive risk management approach. The firms that had this perspective recognized that communications and involvement with upper management was the key:

> Our top management has a reoccurring meeting where various plants get together and discuss suppliers that are putting our business at risk. Sources of risk can be financial—bankruptcy, paying sub suppliers, resources and capacity risk, or price risk. Meeting on these issues frequently allows top management to be aware of the issues and adjust business outlooks if needed.

Risk Assessment (Clause 5.4): Most firms identify a wide range of risks and then prioritize those risks in terms of potential impact and /or likelihood of occurrence. One manager cautioned that focusing on high priority risks makes good sense, but perhaps it is the interaction of multiple moderate risks that in combination result in the most significant risk. Future research might examine the use of "design of experiments" to assess risk.

The most frequently cited and persistent risk factor was supplier failure/reliability. Some firms recognized that part of the problem is their own doing. One manager commented that: "The automotive industry and their negotiating techniques have ruined and shut down suppliers. The cost pressures are immense in today's economy, forcing customers to squeeze their suppliers." Future research may explore the impact that internal company processes (e.g., lean initiatives, cost reduction or target costing programs, product variety and proliferation) have on creating supply risks.

Quite a few of the most frequently cited and increasing risk factors are beyond the control of supply managers (e.g., natural disasters, geopolitical events, increasing government regulations, currency fluctuations, etc.). Companies tended to treat such risks using dual sourcing or buffer inventories. Somewhat surprising was that fewer firms used hedging strategies or speculation techniques. Perhaps this was due to the lack of supply personnel understanding such issues as previously discussed.

Risk Treatment (Clause 5.5): Partnerships were extensively used to share risks, though few firms used joint technology development to share risk. This is somewhat surprising because it is generally agreed that risk management is most efficient and effective when done early in a product lifecycle. Given an increasing focus on "open innovation" in the last decade, perhaps more firms will partner not only for innovation but for risk reduction as well during new product development. One manager commented that this would be a challenge because SCRM analysis takes time and anything that might hold up new product development time is unlikely to be implemented.

Companies rely extensively on qualification of approved suppliers to reduce risks. One manager commented that such lists are important, but the assessments are generally based on past performance and may not be indicative of future performance. Forward-looking risk assessment measures tended to be limited and very subjective. One respondent indicated that forward-looking measures such as supplier scalability (e.g., supplier ability to develop global reach) and supplier supply chain management skills (i.e., supplier's ability to manage its own supply chain) needed to be included in supplier qualification systems to prevent future risks.

Monitoring and Review (Clause 5.6): Without ongoing monitoring and control, supplier performance may degrade after qualification and then risks will surface over time. Companies monitor and control SCRM and supply chain performance using traditional performance measures such as cost, quality, delivery, and so on. Though SCRM impacts such performance outcomes, most firms would like to develop risk specific measures to help them make the business case for more investments in SCRM. One manager commented: "I think we could have more clear-cut metrics that are directly related to supply chain risk, rather than some of the indirect ones that we have now. But to create new metrics always requires funding, which at this time is not being used for more metric development." In the meantime, firms will continue to monitor performance by conducting traditional supplier visits and using supplier scorecards. Without knowing in advance how to measure SCRM strategy performance, one option is to adopt a learning organization perspective as suggested by one manager: "I'm not sure we have an official way of reviewing if a risk strategy was as effective as others. If we avoided a risk, we consider that a success. If we still got exposed to a risk despite our strategy, we'll review lessons learned and then adjust the strategy to incorporate that."

Supply managers are rarely compensated specifically for SCRM efforts, in part due to the difficulty of proving that without risk treatment the result would have been worse. Compensation for "risk management" is generally based on traditional supply chain performance measures and one manager stated: "Risk performance evaluation is tracked through the review process, and performance ratings are given based on performance to key objectives. Employees also receive a bonus based on actual business performance—we reduce risk, business performance is strong." In most cases, however, there was no specific bonus or compensation for risk management:

> Typically, the people working on risk management are the same people working with the suppliers on a daily basis, so no further compensation is given. At a global supply chain management level, risk management is a larger part of their day-to-day responsibilities but more from a coordination of efforts level than a working level, and still no additional compensation.

Respondents seemed relatively satisfied with supply chain performance along multiple dimensions, though all respondents recognized the need for continuous improvement. Some progress was made in controlling price volatility as previously discussed. Again, whether or not these performance outcomes can be directly tied to SCRM is unclear.

Implications for Managers

The findings suggest that firms are very concerned about supply chain risks and that they spend significant effort managing those risks. However, it does not seem that firms take a long-term approach to SCRM by integrating such efforts with ERM, and that making a business case for SCRM will remain a challenge. One manager stated:

> We don't have a dedicated set of resources for risk management. We take the approach that it's everyone's responsibility. Good in theory, but during very busy parts of the year, other commitments may take the focus off risk management thus leaving us open to issues. The challenge in creating a dedicated group to manage this is always money. Is it worth it? To overcome this, you'd need to look at the cost of the resources, people, and technology and balance that against the costs that are avoided by having the group in place. This calculation would likely involve a lot of soft costs and could be difficult to get agreement on, thus making it a tougher sell.

This perspective was shared by many respondents to our survey. Given that SCRM efforts map well to the ISO 31000 standard, perhaps supply managers will be able to strengthen the business case for SCRM and create a linkage of SCRM to ERM by deploying the "missing link," the ISO 31000 standard.

Implications for Researchers

A few future research topics were already presented in the Discussion section. For example, research that includes service purchases and/or service firms is warranted. The exploration of direct cause and effect relationships is also of interest. (For example, what is the best response to a parts shortage caused by a hurricane versus a parts shortage driven by limited supply capacity?) A suggestion was also made that examining the impact and treatment of the interaction of risks might advance our understanding of SCRM. Further, research regarding the impact of buying firm strategy and process (e.g., lean initiatives, cost reduction, product proliferation) on driving supply risks was suggested. The following topics expand on such issues.

Topic 1: Can our understanding of SCRM be supported and accelerated by the adoption of the ISO 31000 framework? The literature review suggests that ISO 31000 is more comprehensive than current SCRM frameworks, that SCRM is considered a subset of ERM (Sodhi et al. 2012), and that ISO 31000 may become an internationally implemented ERM standard (Gjerdrum & Salen 2010). Perhaps SCRM researchers should adopt the ISO 31000 framework so that there can be an agreement on definitions, terms, scales, and so on, will be reached to support in-depth SCRM research.

Topic 2: Does ERM/SCRM provide appropriate return on investment? Firms with well-established SCRM strategies and structures respond more effectively, at least in the short term, to major supply disruptions than do firms without such structures. However, such significant disruptions tend to be rare. It has been suggested that different structures and approaches to SCRM provide different results. For example, one effort found that SCRM implementation impacts supply performance, but reactive SCRM provided better disruption resilience and reduction of the bullwhip effect, while preventive SCRM provided better values concerning flexibility and safety stock (Thun & Hoening 2011). Ultimately, does having an established department, system, and resources dedicated to SCRM pay for itself in the long term, and if so, what is the appropriate structure?

Topic 3: Related to topic 2, what is the most effective organizational structure for effective SCRM? Initiatives such as Six Sigma have called for different levels of specialization (e.g., black and green belts), yet still maintain that quality is the responsibility of each person. Even lean initiatives call for a somewhat hierarchical structure of expertise (e.g., group leader, team leader), yet maintain that waste reduction and flow are everyone's responsibility. Should a separate SCRM department be created or should it be part of the ERM organization? Should a hierarchical structure of risk experts be developed, or should SCRM be part of each supply person's everyday responsibilities? Or, perhaps the most effective SCRM approach would be to outsource it. The increased use of 3PL/4PL, supply chain consultants, information brokers and analysts such as D&B, government or industry regulations (e.g., GAAP, SOX, etc.), and international standards (e.g., ISO 9000, ISO 14000) already provide support for SCRM outsourcing.

Topic 4: To what extent should SCRM be integrated into new product development efforts? Collaboration with suppliers for new product development has increased in the past decade. A primary objective of such efforts is to innovate, but part of all such processes is to address technology risks early. How can firms most effectively "design for supply risk" without delaying new product development efforts? Perhaps the "rapid plant assessment" process (Goodson 2002) provides a good starting point for a "rapid risk assessment" process.

Topic 5: What is the role for IT, and how can companies more efficiently integrate new IT to support SCRM? This research suggests that firms use IT for SCRM by gathering and disseminating data, communicating with suppliers, measuring performance, and managing inventory. However, few firms used IT for SCRM by creating data warehouses, integrating suppliers into new product development, analyzing network designs analysis, or optimizing inventory. Advancements in IT applications, including, for example, cloud computing, tablets, and mobile devices, enable firms to gather and distribute real-time data. Research that identifies proper strategies for the use and effective adoption of such tools is warranted.

REFERENCES

Armstrong, J.S. & Overton, T.S. 1977. Estimating Nonresponse Bias in Mail Surveys. *Journal of Marketing Research*, 14(3): 396–402.

AS/NZS. 2004. AS/NZS 4360:2004, *Risk Management Standard*. Australia: Wellington.

Ballou, B. & Heitger, D. 2005. A Building Block Approach for Implementing COSO's Enterprise Risk Management—Integrated Framework. *Management Accounting Quarterly*, 6(2): 1–10.

Beasley, M., Clune, R., & Hermanson, D. 2005. ERM: A Status Report. *The Internal Auditor*, 62(1): 67–72.

Black, S. & Porter, L. 1996. Identification of the Critical Factors of TQM. *Decision Sciences Journal*, 27(1): 1–21.

Blackhurst, J., Wu, T., & O'Grady, P. 2005. PDCM: A Decision Support Modeling Methodology for Supply Chain, Product and Process Design Decisions. *Journal of Operations Management*, 23(3–4): 325–343.

Bowling, D. & Rieger, L. 2005. Making Sense of COSO's New Framework for Enterprise Risk Management. *Bank Accounting & Finance*, February/March: 35–40.

Capon, N., Kaye, M., & Wood, M. 1994. Measuring the Success of a TQM Programme. *International Journal of Quality and Reliability Management*, 12(8): 8–22.

Chapman, C. 2003. Bringing ERM into Focus. *The Internal Auditor*, 60(3): 30–35.

Chiang, C.Y., Kocabasoglu-Hillmer, C., & Suresh, N. 2012. An Empirical Investigation of the Impact of Strategic Sourcing and Flexibility on Firms' Supply Chain Agility. *International Journal of Operations and Production Management*, 32(1): 49–78.

Curkovic, S., Melnyk, S., Calantone, R., & Handfield, R. 2000. Validating the Malcolm Baldrige National Quality Framework through Structural Equation Modeling. *International Journal of Production Research*, 38(4): 765–791.

Dean, J. & Bowen, D. 1994. Management Theory and Total Quality: Improving Research and Practice through Theory Development. *Academy of Management Journal,* 19(3): 392–418.

Eisenhardt, K. 1989. Building Theories from Case Study Research. *The Academy of Management Review,* 14(4): 532–550.

Flynn, B., Schroeder, R., & Sakakibara, S. 1994. A Framework for Quality Management Research and an Associated Instrument. *Journal of Operations Management,* 11(4): 339–366.

Giannakis, M. & Louis, M. 2001. A Multi-Agent Based Framework for Supply Chain Risk Management. *Journal of Purchasing and Supply Management,* 17(1): 23–31.

Gjerdrum, D. & Salen, W. 2010. The New ERM Gold Standard: ISO 31000:2009. *Professional Safety,* 55(8): 43–44.

Glaser, B. & Strauss, A. 1967. *The Discovery of Grounded Theory: Strategies for Qualititative Reasearch.* Chicago: Aldine.

Goodson, R.E. 2002. Read a Plant—Fast. *Harvard Business Review,* 80(5): 105–113.

Hallikas, J., Karvonen, I., Pulkkinen, U., Virolainen, V.M., & Tuominem, M. 2004. Risk Management Processes in Supplier Networks. *International Journal of Production Economics,* 90(1): 47–58.

Hauser, L. 2003. Risk Adjusted Supply Chain Management. *Supply Chain Management Review,* 7(6): 64–71.

Holschbach, E. & Hofmann, E. 2011. Exploring Quality Management for Business Services from a Buyer's Perspective Using Multiple Case Study Evidence. *International Journal of Operations & Production Management,* 31(6): 648–685.

Hoyt, R. & Liebenberg, A. 2011. The Value of Enterprise Risk Management. *Journal of Risk and Insurance,* 78(4): 795–822.

Inderfurth, K. & Kelle, P. 2011. Capacity Reservation under Spot Market Price Uncertainty. *International Journal of Production Economics,* 133(1): 272–279.

ISO. 2009a. ISO 31000:2009, Risk Management—Principles and Guidelines. International Standards Organization, Geneva.

ISO. 2009b. ISO Guide 73:2009, Risk Management—Vocabulary. International Standards Organization, Geneva.

Kern, D., Moser, R., Hartman, E., & Moder, M. 2012. Supply Risk Management: Model Development and Empirical Analysis. *International Journal of Physical Distribution & Logistics Management,* 42(1): 60–82.

Khan, O. & Burnes, B. 2007. Risk and Supply Chain Management: A Research Agenda. *The International Journal of Logistics Management,* 18(2): 197–216.

Kleindorfer, P.R. & Saad, G.H. 2005. Managing Disruptions in Supply Chains. *Production and Operations Management,* 14(1): 53–68.

Kumar, S. & Verruso, J. 2008. Risk Assessment of the Security of Inbound Containers at U.S. Ports: A Failure, Mode, Effects, and Criticality Analysis Approach. *Transportation Journal,* 47(4): 26–41.

Laeequddin, M., Sardana, G.D., Sahay, B.S., Abdul Waheed, K., & Sahay, V. 2009. Supply Chain Partners Trust Building Process through Risk Evaluation: The Perspectives of UAE Packaged Food Industry. *Supply Chain Management,* 14(4): 280–290.

Liu, Z. & Cruz, J. 2012. Supply Chain Networks with Corporate Financial Risks and Trade Credits under Economic Uncertainty. *International Journal of Production Economics,* 137(1): 55–67.

Manuj, I. & Mentzer, J.T. 2008. Global Supply Chain Risk Management. *Journal of Business Logistics,* 29(1): 133–156.

Martin, C., Mena, C., Khan, O., & Yurt, O. 2011. Approaches to Managing Global Sourcing Risk. *Supply Chain Management*, 16(2): 67–81.

Matook, S., Lasch, R., & Tamaschke, R. 2009. Supplier Development with Benchmarking as Part of a Comprehensive Supplier Risk Management Framework. *International Journal of Operations and Production Management*, 29(3): 241–267.

McCutcheon, D. & Meridith, J. 1993. Conducting Case Study Research in Operations Management. *Journal of Operations Management*, 11(3): 239–256.

Miles, M. & Huberman, A. 1994. *Qualitative Data Analysis: A Sourcebook of New Methods*. Newbury Park, CA: Sage Publications.

Moody, M. 2010. ERM & ISO 31000. *Rough Notes*, 153(3): 80–81.

Nocco, B. & Stulz, R. 2006. Enterprise Risk Management: Theory and Practice. *Journal of Applied Corporate Finance*, 18(4): 8–20.

Purdy, G. 2010. ISO 31000:2009—Setting a New Standard for Risk Management. *Risk Analysis*, 30(6): 881–886.

Samad-Khan, A. 2005. Why COSO Is Flawed. *Operational Risk*, 6(1): 24–28.

Saraph, V., Benson, P., & Schroeder, R., 1989. An Instrument for Measuring the Critical Factors of Quality Management. *Decision Sciences*, 20(4): 810–829.

Smithson, C. & Simkins, B. 2005. Does Risk Management Add Value? A Survey of the Evidence. *Journal of Applied Corporate Finance*, 17(3): 8–17.

Sodhi, M.S., Son, B.G., & Tang, C.S. 2012. Researcher's Perspective on Supply Risk Management. *Productions and Operations Management*, 21(1): 1–13.

Tang, C.S. 2006. Perspectives in Supply Chain Risk Management. *International Journal of Production Economics*, 103(2): 451–488.

Tang, O. & Musa, S.N. 2011. Identifying Risk Issues and Research Advancements in Supply Chain Risk Management. *International Journal of Production Economics*, 133(1): 25–34.

Thun, J.H. & Hoening, D. 2011. An Empirical Analysis of Supply Chain Risk Management in the German Automotive Industry. *International Journal of Production Economics*, 131(1): 242–249.

Tummala, R. & Schoenherr, T. 2011. Assessing and Managing Risks Using the Supply Chain Risk Management Process (SCRMP). *Supply Chain Management*, 16(6): 474–483.

VanderBok, R., Sauter, J., Bryan, C., & Horan, J. 2007. Manage Your Supply Chain Risk. *Manufacturing Engineering*, 138(3): 153–161.

Voss, C., Tsikriktsis, N., & Frohlich, M. 2002. Case Research in Operations Management. *International Journal of Operations & Production Management*, 22(2): 2002, 195–219.

Wu, D., Olson, D., & Birge, J. 2011. Introduction to Special Issue on "Enterprise Risk Management in Operations." *International Journal of Production Economics*, 134(1): 1–2.

Zsidisin, G., Ellram, L., Carter, J., & Cavinato, J. 2004. An Analysis of Supply Risk Assessment Techniques. *International Journal of Physical Distribution & Logistics Management*, 34(5): 397–413.

Zsidisin, G. & Hartley, J. 2012. A Strategy for Managing Commodity Price Risk. *Supply Chain Management Review*, Mar/Apr (2): 46–53.

Zsidisin, G. & Wagner, S. 2010. Do Perceptions become Reality? The Moderating Role of Supply Chain Resiliency on Disruption Occurrence. *Journal of Business Logistics*, 31(2): 1–20.

6

A Longitudinal Study of Supply Chain Risk Management Relative to COSO's Enterprise Risk Management Framework

INTRODUCTION

Risk management is a critical component of strategy development and execution, and a driver of firm success. Yet, the number of firms that apply a systematic approach to risk management is somewhat limited (Beasley et al. 2005; Bowling & Rieger 2005). Corporate-wide risks may be managed through enterprise risk management (ERM), which establishes a framework and set of tools for systematically managing risks, and identifies, assesses, and manages risks throughout the value chain (COSO 2004).

Supply chain risk management (SCRM) is an integral component of ERM. This research focuses on SCRM within the context of the ERM framework proposed by the Committee of Sponsoring Organizations (COSO) of the Treadway Commission (COSO 2004). There is a shortage of SCRM empirical research, and this shortage is especially critical in addressing current practice (Sodhi et al. 2012). Paired longitudinal data from 17 respondents who worked for the same firm over a two-year period are analyzed to assess factors that affect decisions to develop a systematic approach for SCRM, the relative impact of SCRM, and changes in approach over time.

Respondents recognize the need for ERM and SCRM, but integration of strategies, processes, and systems is lacking. Despite the recognized need, corporate structures and budgets are not sufficiently designed to mitigate corporate and supply risks. There appears to be a reduction in spending on SCRM, and a slip in the supply groups' understanding of corporate risk management activities.

Respondents are increasing the use of information gathering, monitoring/auditing of a supplier's processes, approved supplier lists, credit/financial analysis, and hedging strategies to manage risk. They are relying less on joint technology development initiatives to mitigate risk. Respondents are generally satisfied with supply performance, and improvements in logistics reliability and in reduced material price volatility were reported.

The remainder of this chapter is organized as follows. The literature review explores ERM and SCRM practices. Next, the research method is presented, followed by the data analysis. The chapter concludes with a discussion of the findings, with an emphasis on identifying SCRM strategies and framing the findings within the context of the COSO ERM framework.

LITERATURE REVIEW

A systematic approach to risk management is needed to manage the global competitive environment and increasingly complex supply chains, particularly given increased pressure to comply with a wide range of regulations, laws, and industry guidelines. Enterprise risk management (ERM) has emerged as a critical approach to mitigate such risks and to proactively take advantage of risk opportunities (Hoyt & Liebenberg 2011; Nocco & Stulz 2006). ERM, which has also been identified as "integrated risk management" and "holistic risk management" (Hoyt & Liebenberg 2011), represents an approach to identify, analyze, and proactively plan responses to a wide range of risks (Bowling & Rieger 2005; Chapman 2003).

ERM can positively impact a firm's performance (Hoyt & Liebenberg 2011; Smithson & Simkins 2005). However, a small percentage of firms have developed a detailed understanding of ERM, and ERM implementation is limited (Chapman 2003; COSO 2010). Though ad hoc risk management may provide some benefits, silo approaches to risk management lead to inefficient and ineffective risk management systems (Hoyt & Liebenberg 2011).

This research adopts the Committee of Sponsoring Organizations (COSO) of the Treadway Commission (COSO 2004) ERM framework (Figure 6.1) to examine the extent of integration and comprehensiveness of SCRM practices, and to determine if the COSO framework is appropriate for SCRM planning and execution. The COSO framework was adopted because it is an effective ERM approach, its adoption rate is increasing,

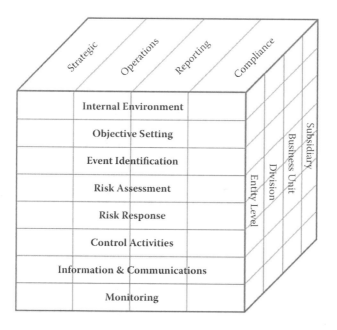

FIGURE 6.1
COSO ERM framework.

and it appears that it is becoming an ERM best practice (Moody 2011; Young & Hasler 2010).

The COSO ERM framework consists of the eight components described in Table 6.1. These components support attainment of a firm's objectives, and all eight components need to be integrated to provide effective ERM (COSO 2004; Sobel 2006). The framework indicates that risk management cuts across four objectives, described in Table 6.2 (Ballou & Heitger 2005; COSO 2004). Further, the framework emphasizes that each organizational level (i.e., subsidiary, business units, division, entity) needs to manage risks, initiated by the "entity level" then aggregated across all levels so that risks may be managed holistically (Chapman 2003; COSO 2004). COSO formally defines ERM as "…a process, effected by an entity's board of directors, management and other personnel, applied in a strategy setting and across the enterprise, designed to identify potential events that may affect the entity, and manage risks to be within its risk appetite, to provide reasonable assurance regarding the achievement of entity objectives."

TABLE 6.1

Interrelated Components of the COSO ERM Framework

Component	Description
Internal Environment	Reflects alignment of the firm's risk philosophy, its appetite for risk, the risk management and ethical culture, human resource policies and practices, assignment of responsibility, and the organizational structure to manage risks.
Objective Setting	Identifies the firm's competitive strategy or positioning (e.g., low cost, high quality, etc.) and related objectives in four areas: strategy, operations, reporting, and compliance, which in turn drives objectives throughout the value chain.
Event Identification	Identifies possible internal and external events, and the potential interrelatedness of those events, that impact a firm's ability to realize its strategy and objectives. Positive impact events are "opportunities" that are channeled back to strategic planning, while negative impact events are risks that should be managed through an integrated risk management process to help determine how such risks might be managed.
Risk Assessment	Examines the likelihood, frequency, and the impact (e.g., financial, reputation, etc.) of events across a range (e.g., best to worst case) of possible outcomes associated with the events.
Risk Response	Identifies, assesses, and selects risk response options that align with the organization's risk tolerances and risk appetite. Options include avoidance (e.g., not engaging in the activity), reduction (e.g., rebalancing the risk, reallocating resources, robust business process, etc.), sharing (e.g., insurance, partnering, contractual agreements, hedging, etc.), and acceptance.
Control Activities	Establishes that risk policies and procedures are in place and properly executed, and that the risk management initiatives are effective. Such controls may include required authorizations, supervision, segregation of duties, reconciliations, and verifications, for example.
Information and Communications	Requires that internal and external sources be used to provide appropriate and timely risk-related information that enables people to execute their responsibilities. Such communications need to be integrated throughout the value chain and impacted organizations.
Monitoring	Ensures that an ERM is present and determines how well it is working so that it can be revised and/or expanded.

TABLE 6.2

Objectives of the COSO ERM Framework

Objective	Description
Strategic	Mission driven high-level goals and objectives (governance, strategic objectives, business model, external forces, etc.)
Operations	Resource development, management, and allocation (business processes, upstream value chain, downstream value chain, etc.)
Reporting	Information gathering, analysis, and communication (information technology, financial, internal, intellectual property, etc.)
Compliance	Conformance with laws and regulations (Securities & Exchange Commission, environmental, legal, contractual, etc.)

Though ERM is touted as a strategic imperative, there is limited empirical evidence that ERM is efficient and effective (Hoyt & Liebenberg 2011). ERM implementation requires significant resource commitments and a corporate-wide cultural shift (Ballou & Heitger 2005), at times without an appropriate return on the effort (Samad-Khan 2005). Even COSO cautions that an ERM framework is not a cure-all and that ERM implementation is a significant challenge (Landsittel & Rittenberg 2010).

A survey of researchers found that 74.2% of respondents believe supply chain risk management (SCRM) is a subset or extension of ERM (Sodhi et al. 2012). While there has been an increasing amount of SCRM research, there is no consensus on the definition or scope of SCRM (Sodhi et al. 2012). For example, a three-step SCRM process has been proposed: (1) specifying sources of risks and vulnerabilities, (2) assessment, and (3) mitigation (Kleindorfer & Saad 2005). Other researchers have proposed a four-step process (Hallikas et al. 2004; Jüttner et al. 2003), while others have proposed a five-step process (Manuj & Mentzer 2008). Although common elements appear across all these frameworks, there is not yet agreement on what components and definitions constitute a "standard" SCRM process. The SCRM frameworks also overlap with some of the elements of the COSO framework, but are not as comprehensive. For example, the COSO framework begins with a requirement that the internal environment establishes the philosophy, culture, and organizational structure to support risk management. It also requires ongoing monitoring of the risk management processes, changes in risk, and performance outcomes. These two steps are either omitted or not emphasized in most of the SCRM frameworks. This comprehensiveness provides further support for selecting the COSO framework to examine SCRM.

The advancement of research in a discipline (e.g., just-in-time manufacturing, supply chain management) may be accelerated through the development and validation of frameworks and concepts generated through exploratory empirical research. For example, the total quality management (TQM) discipline leveraged standardized frameworks to advance theory building and testing (see, for example, Black & Porter 1996; Capon, Kaye, & Wood 1994; Curkovic, Melnyk, Calantone, & Handfield 2000; Dean & Bowen 1994; Flynn, Schroeder, & Sakakibara 1994; Saraph, Benson, & Schroeder 1989). By leveraging such frameworks, TQM research moved from a focus on case studies (the current state of SCRM research) to testable models and specific research hypotheses, linking the theoretical concept of TQM to empirical indicants. Operational definitions and standardized frameworks have contributed to TQM theory building by identifying the constructs associated with TQM, developing scales for measuring these constructs, and empirically validating the scales. SCRM research is still in its infancy stages and would benefit from the development of standardized frameworks and concepts.

Despite the lack of agreement on broad SCRM frameworks, a variety of supply risks and risk management strategies have been identified. Supply risks have been classified as supplier, market, and item risks (Zsidisin 2003), for example. Specific risks include order fulfillment errors, information distortion, labor disputes, natural disasters, capacity shortages, supplier bankruptcy, exchange rate risks, government regulations, single sourcing, and port delays, for example (Blackhurst et al. 2005; Manuj & Mentzer 2008; Tummala & Schoenherr 2011; Zsidisin & Hartley 2012).

Different risks require different SCRM processes (Zsidisin & Wagner 2010). Supply chain risk management strategies include environmental scanning (Zsidisin et al. 2004), use of capable suppliers (Manuj & Mentzer 2008), dual sourcing (Khan & Burnes 2007), contingency planning (Kleindorfer & Saad 2005), supplier credit analysis (Kern et al. 2012), inventory buffers (Tang 2006), integration of information systems and supply chain modeling (Giannakis & Louis 2001), and speculation, hedging, and forward buying (Zsidisin & Hartley 2012), for example.

Firms face multiple supply risks, whether in combination or isolation. Other risks include supplier reliability/failure, information errors, natural disasters, shrinkage, capacity shortages, financial instability, currency exchange rate fluctuations, port security, and increased government regulations, for example (Blackhurst, Wu, & O'Grady 2005; Kumar & Verruso 2008; Liu & Cruz 2012; Manuj & Mentzer 2008; Tummala & Schoenherr

2011; Zsidisin & Hartley 2012). Each risk might require a specific SCRM technique (Zsidisin & Wagner 2010).

SCRM treatment options include evaluation and trust building (Laeequddin, Sardana, Sahay, Abdul Waheed, & Sahay 2009), use of dual sources (Khan & Burnes 2007), environmental scanning (Zsidisin, Ellram, Carter, & Cavinato 2004), combined capacity reservation contracts and spot markets (Inderfurth & Kelle 2011), qualification and use of capable suppliers (Manuj & Mentzer 2008), supplier quality management initiatives (Holschbach & Hofmann 2011), buffer inventory (Tang 2006), contingency plans (Kleindorfer & Saad 2005), credit analysis (Kern, Moser, Hartman, & Moder 2012), strategic sourcing and flexibility (Chiang, Kocabasoglu-Hillmer, & Suresh 2012), forward buying or hedging (Zsidisin & Hartley 2012), and supplier development (Matook, Lasch, & Tamaschke 2009), for example. Despite the plethora of risks and risk management approaches, few firms have a structured SCRM approach (Martin, Mena, Khan, & Yurt 2011).

RESEARCH METHOD

The research questions were: (1) Is SCRM approached from a systematic and corporate-wide perspective? (2) What strategies and processes are used to manage supply risks and are they effective? And (3), have SCRM challenges, strategies, processes, or outcomes changed over time? From the responses to these questions, managerial implications and future research questions were developed.

This exploratory research used a purposeful sample (Eisenhardt 1989; Miles & Huberman 1994). Criterion for participation included that the company would agree to identify an informed respondent, reply in a timely manner, and be open to longitudinal research. Targeted respondents worked for companies that support supply management education and professional associations. A cross section of industries was targeted to support generalizability.

The first survey was sent to 67 firms. A 68% response rate (46 responses) was realized. Non-respondents suggested that company policy prevented them from fully participating or that they would not be able to complete the survey within the time limits. The second survey was sent to 58 firms. A 66% response rate (38 responses) was realized. Respondent and company names were compared across the two surveys. This matching process identified 17 people who responded to both surveys and who were with the same company at the time of both surveys, allowing for paired t-tests of 17 data sets. The number of paired responses was about as expected because of career transitions anticipated over the two-year period.

LIMITATIONS

The research findings are based on 17 paired responses. The seemingly small sample size might limit the generalizability of the findings. However, the research was structured as a two-year longitudinal study, which required responses from the same person at the same company. It was anticipated that supply professionals would move into new positions or move to other organizations, so the sample size is about the size expected. The majority of responses came from manufacturing firms. Inclusion of service firms in future research is warranted. Finally, perceptual measures were used as is often the case in survey research. Future efforts might include objective measures (e.g., actual risk management spending). An attempt was made to gather objective data, but few firms were willing to provide such data. The research findings should be considered with the above limitations in mind.

RESULTS

Table 6.3 indicates that the majority of responses were from manufacturing firms. The companies are all based in North America and have global sales. Table 6.4 (sales volume) and Table 6.5 (number of employees) reflect firm size. Table 6.6 suggests that respondents are in positions of knowledge about SCRM.

The results are presented relative to the eight components of the COSO framework. Components 1 and 2 (internal environment and objective setting) and components 3 and 4 (event identification and risk assessment) are presented in combined sections, respectively. The tabulated data are sorted from high to low mean values based on the second survey data. All "agree/disagree" questions are scaled from "1 = strongly disagree" to "7 = strongly agree." All "extent of use" questions are scaled from "1 = not used" to

TABLE 6.3

Respondent Industry Profile

Description	Number
Aerospace and defense	1
Automotive	5
Construction	1
Consumer products	1
Electronics manufacturers	2
Health care	2
Manufacturing, diversified	4
Retail	1

TABLE 6.4

Respondent Sales Profile

Sales ($)	Count
50M–99M	1
100M–499M	3
500M–999M	3
1B–9B	4
10B–49B	3
50B–99B	3
Over 100B	0

TABLE 6.5

Respondent Employment Profile

Employees	Count
Under 50	0
50–99	1
100–499	1
500–999	1
1,000–4,999	3
5,000–9,999	3
Over 10,000	8

TABLE 6.6

Respondent Titles

Title	Count
Procurement or Supply Chain Leader/Manager/Coordinator	6
Strategic/Senior Buyer	3
Operations/Quality Manager	6
Supply Chain Analyst	2

"7 = extensively used." Given the exploratory nature of this research, a significance level of $p = 0.10$ was used for the paired two-tailed difference tests.

Internal Environment and Objective Setting

Table 6.7 provides descriptive statistics related to the internal environment and objective setting. Consistent with the application of the framework, four subcategories were developed: need, approach, budget, and organization.

TABLE 6.7

Internal Environment and Objective Setting

	p (t-test)	Survey 1		Survey 2	
		Mean	SD	Mean	SD
Need					
Without a systematic analysis technique to assess risk, much can go wrong in a supply chain.	0.39	6.12	0.78	6.41	1.06
Managing supply chain risk is an increasingly important initiative for our operations.	0.45	5.82	1.19	6.12	0.93
It is critical for us to have an easily understood method to identify and manage supply chain risk.	0.69	5.65	1.00	5.47	1.42
We are very concerned about our supply chain resiliency and the failure implications.	0.88	5.24	1.20	5.29	1.26
My workplace plans on evaluating or implementing supply chain risk tools and technologies.	0.34	5.24	1.68	4.76	1.71
Approach					
There is no single set of tools or technologies on the market for managing supply chain risks.	0.67	5.29	1.72	5.47	1.33
We are currently using some form of supply chain risk management tools and services.	0.43	4.59	1.91	4.88	1.69
Managing supply chain risks is driven by reactions to failures rather than being proactively driven.	0.30	4.41	1.00	4.76	1.44
Supply chain risk initiatives are driven from the bottom up rather than top down.	0.50	4.06	1.68	4.35	1.66
Proactive risk mitigation efforts applied to the supply chain is common practice for us.	0.18	4.65	1.50	3.88	1.73
Budget					
We do plan to invest nontrivial amounts in managing supply chain risks.	0.25	4.94	1.82	4.47	1.37
Funding for managing supply chain risks will come from a general operations budget.	0.66	3.76	2.05	4.12	2.03
We have a dedicated budget for activities associated with managing supply chain risks.	0.26	3.82	1.88	3.24	2.11
Our spending intentions for managing supply chain risks are very high.	0.05	3.53	1.59	2.76	1.44

Continued

TABLE 6.7 *(Continued)*

Internal Environment and Objective Setting

	p (t-test)	Survey 1		Survey 2	
		Mean	SD	Mean	SD
Organization					
Supply chain employees understand government legislation and geopolitical issues.	0.76	3.65	1.27	3.53	1.46
I fully understand the activities being performed by our risk management group.	0.01	4.65	1.62	3.29	1.36
My workplace uses supply chain risk managers who work closely with corporate risk management.	0.57	1.94	1.25	2.18	1.24
We are planning to outsource all or some of our risk management functions.	0.40	2.24	1.44	1.88	1.32

Need: Firms indicated that there is a significant need to make SCRM part of their strategic planning and processes. There is recognition that risk impacts company objectives and that risks need to be managed proactively. The observations are relatively consistent across surveys 1 and 2, and there are no statistically significant differences for any items. Despite perceived SCRM importance, some of the results discussed below suggest that firms are not sufficiently allocating or developing resources for SCRM.

Approach: Risk management requires an integrated approach. Such integration presents a challenge, which is reflected by the high level of agreement that no single set of tools or technologies exist to manage risks. Although there are no statistically significant differences between survey 1 and 2 items for this data category, there appears to be a substantial drop (−0.71) in proactive SCRM approaches. Given the absence of a single set of risk management tools and technologies as well as a relatively reactive approach to SCRM, perhaps respondents are managing risks on an ad hoc basis using traditional supply chain management practices (e.g., spending, contract, and inventory management, demand planning, benchmarking, building long-term partnerships, etc.).

Budget: Only 18% of respondents somewhat agreed that spending intentions for SCRM were high, and there was a statistically significant decrease in agreement to this survey item. Though all the firms allocate funds for SCRM, only slightly more than half agreed that nontrivial amounts are being spent. Approximately half of the firms indicated that there was a dedicated budget for SCRM.

Organization: Organizational readiness for SCRM was low. Though respondents indicated that they have no intention to outsource risk management, internal SCRM competencies and integration are lacking. Approximately 71% of the respondents disagreed that they understood the activities performed by the risk management group, and there was a statistically significant decline in agreement with that item. Approximately 82% of firms had limited use of supply risk managers who worked closely with corporate risk management. Perhaps the corporate function is involved with SCRM but there is limited coordination of risk management activities across the organization.

Event Identification and Risk Assessment

Table 6.8 indicates that supplier reliability and continuous supply is a top risk factor for supply chains. Though specific risk issues (e.g., not being able to fulfill a spike in consumer demand) may be carefully evaluated,

TABLE 6.8

Event Identification and Risk Assessment

	p (t-test)	Survey 1		Survey 2	
		Mean	SD	Mean	SD
Supplier reliability and continuous supply is the top risk factor for our supply chain.	0.72	5.47	1.37	5.29	1.61
Risks of moving manufacturing facilities overseas are carefully evaluated.	0.65	5.12	1.41	4.94	1.60
Risks of not being able to fulfill a spike in consumer demand are carefully evaluated.	0.35	4.53	1.46	4.82	1.29
Key metrics are in place to measure the risk associated with key suppliers.	0.20	5.12	1.54	4.47	1.55
A key part of our supply chain management is documenting the likelihood and impact of risks.	1.00	4.06	1.30	4.06	1.30
We can actually exploit risk to an advantage by taking calculated risks in the supply chain.	0.36	4.35	1.54	4.00	1.66
Taxes such as excise and VAT impact our supply chain decisions.	0.77	4.12	1.73	4.00	1.90
We apply high levels of analytical rigor to assess our supply chain practices.	0.16	4.65	1.62	3.88	2.03

only slightly more than half the firms indicated that documenting the likelihood and impact of risks is a key part of supply chain management. There were no statistically significant differences between survey 1 and 2 data for this category of items.

Respondents reviewed a list of potential risks and rank ordered the five risks that would have the greatest impact (e.g., 1 = most severe, 2 = second most severe, etc.) on supply chain or company performance. Table 6.9 summarizes the second survey data. Only those risks that were selected three or more times are listed. "Supplier failure/reliability" and "bankruptcy/ruin/default of suppliers" were the most frequently selected and had the highest average impact, which might explain the firms' increased emphasis on consistent supplier monitoring and approved supplier lists (discussed subsequently). The next three highest-ranked factors cannot be directly

TABLE 6.9

Current Supply Chain Risk Impact Factors

Risk	1	2	3	4	5	Freq	Weighted Points	Average Weight
Supplier failure/reliability	4	4	5	1		14	53	3.79
Bankruptcy, ruin, or default of suppliers, shippers, etc.	7	1	2			10	45	4.50
Natural disasters or accidents (tsunamis, hurricanes, fires, etc.)	1	1	2	1		5	17	3.40
Energy/raw material shortages and power outages		1	1	2	1	5	12	2.40
Geopolitical events (terrorism, war, etc.)		1		3	1	5	11	2.20
Intellectual property infringement	1	1		1	1	4	12	3.00
Commodity cost volatility			1	1	1	1	4	10	2.50
Logistics failure	1				3	4	8	2.00
Contract failure		2			1	3	9	3.00
Strike—labor, buyers, and suppliers	1	1		1		3	8	2.67
Legal liabilities and litigation			2		1	3	7	2.33
Attracting and retaining skilled labor			1	1	1	3	6	2.00
Return policy and product recall requirements				2	1	3	5	1.67
Information delays, scarcity, sharing, and infrastructure breakdown				1	2	3	4	1.33

Note: 1 = highest risk (then reverse scaled).

controlled or influenced by supply, emphasizing the need for SCRM and ERM integration.

Respondents were presented with the same list of risks and were asked to identify if the risk would increase, remain the same, or decrease in the next two years. Table 6.10 summarizes the second survey, sorted from the highest to lowest increase. Many macroeconomic factors (e.g., currency exchange, inflation, geopolitical events, laws and regulations) top the list of greatest increase. This suggests that the skill sets of supply risk managers may need to continue to expand well beyond traditional supplier evaluation and monitoring to include broad economic and financial skills, and/or the need for greater integration of SCRM with ERM.

TABLE 6.10

Projected Change in Supply Chain Risks

Risk	Decrease	No Change	Increase
Currency exchange, interest, and /or inflation rate fluctuations	1	2	14
Commodity cost volatility	2	2	13
Banking regulations and tighter financing conditions	2	3	12
Government regulations (SOX, SEC, Clean Air Act, OSHA, EU)	0	7	10
Energy/raw material shortages and power outages	1	7	9
Geopolitical events (terrorism, war, etc.)	0	9	8
Customs acts/trade restrictions and protectionism	1	8	8
Bankruptcy, ruin, or default of suppliers, shippers, etc.	4	5	8
Customer-related (demand change, system failure, payment delay)	1	8	8
Logistics failure	3	7	7
Port/cargo security (information, freight, vandalism, sabotage, etc.)	0	10	7
Language and educational barriers	5	5	7
Strikes—labor, buyers, and suppliers	1	9	7
Insurance coverage	0	10	7
Supplier failure/reliability	6	5	6
Intellectual property infringement	1	10	6
Natural disasters or accidents (tsunamis, hurricanes, fires, etc.)	1	11	5

Continued

TABLE 6.10 *(Continued)*

Projected Change in Supply Chain Risks

Risk	Decrease	No Change	Increase
Ethical issues (working practices, health, safety, etc.)	2	10	5
Legal liabilities and issues	1	11	5
Return policy and product recall requirements	1	11	5
Diminishing capacities (financial, production, structural, etc.)	4	8	5
Contamination exposure—food, germs, infections	1	11	5
Tax issues (VAT, transfer pricing, excise, etc.)	0	13	4
Contract failure	4	10	3
Unfamiliar business and property laws	2	12	3
Lack of trust with partners	5	9	3
Measuring tools—metrics translate differently	2	12	3
Attracting and retaining skilled labor	4	10	3
Degree of control over operations	4	10	3
Fraud or scandal	1	13	3
Weaknesses in the local infrastructures	2	13	2
Internal and external theft	2	13	2
Property development—local codes and requirements	1	14	2
Obtaining proper bonds and licenses	0	17	0
Information delays, scarcity, sharing, and infrastructure breakdown	7	10	0

Risk Response

Table 6.11 classifies risk responses by the categories of acceptance, reduction, and shared risks as suggested by COSO. (A fourth category, avoidance, was not explicitly studied in this effort.) The table suggests that regardless of the strategies and practices used, companies will need to accept that some risk impacts will be felt due to supply disruptions. Inventory management (e.g., buffers, safety stock) remains a widely used risk acceptance tactic.

Reduction activities emphasized the use of qualified suppliers. There was a statistically significant increase in the already extensive use of approved supplier lists. Very few firms (30%) identified postponement as a risk reduction approach, which is somewhat surprising given the increased discussion of "postponed differentiation" over the last decade.

TABLE 6.11

Risk Response

Response Category	p (t-test)	Survey 1		Survey 2	
		Mean	SD	Mean	SD
Acceptance					
Inventory management (buffers, safety stock levels, optimal order, and production quantity)	0.77	5.18	1.59	5.29	1.10
Our suppliers are required to have secure sourcing, business continuity, and contingency plans	0.78	4.44	1.71	4.29	1.69
Contingency planning (jointly with suppliers)	0.54	4.00	1.32	4.29	1.36
We have placed an increased focus on inventory management to deal with supply risks	0.31	4.59	1.23	4.06	1.75
We are prepared to minimize the effects of disruptions (terrorism, weather, theft, etc.)	0.87	3.41	1.23	3.35	1.69
Reduction					
Using an approved list of suppliers	0.08	5.59	1.54	6.35	0.86
Multiple sourcing (rather than sole sourcing)	0.55	4.12	1.41	3.94	1.85
Postponement (delaying the actual commitment of resources to maintain flexibility)	0.29	4.00	1.32	3.47	1.37
Sharing					
Partnership formation and long-term agreements	0.43	5.12	0.93	4.88	1.32
Supplier development initiatives	0.33	4.53	1.50	4.82	1.63
Speculation (forward placement of inventory, forward buying of raw materials, etc.)	1.00	4.24	1.79	4.24	1.35
Hedging strategies (to protect against commodity price swings)	0.10	3.18	1.42	3.94	1.48
We are hedging our raw material exposure to reduce input cost volatility	0.82	3.47	1.50	3.59	1.58
Joint technology development initiatives	0.00	3.88	1.22	2.59	1.42

Risk sharing emphasizes development of strong supplier relationships, which is consistent with the increased use of approved suppliers identified earlier. Though not used extensively, there was a statistically significant increase in the use of hedging strategies. This is one likely driver of the improvement in reduction of material price volatility (discussed later).

TABLE 6.12

Control Activities

Activity	p (t-test)	Survey 1		Survey 2	
		Mean	SD	Mean	SD
Credit and financial data analysis	0.03	4.35	1.80	5.41	1.23
Spend management and analysis	0.91	5.24	1.64	5.18	1.38
Contract management (e.g., leverage tools to monitor performance against commitments)	0.16	4.18	1.85	4.88	1.36
Business process management	0.13	4.35	1.46	4.82	1.19
Inventory optimization tools	0.46	4.65	2.00	4.35	1.80
We use network design and optimization tools to cope with uncertainty in the supply chain	1.00	3.41	2.06	3.41	1.50
Training programs	0.71	3.35	1.46	3.24	1.25

Few firms are extensively pursuing joint technology development initiatives to share risk, and there was a statistically significant reduction in the use of this practice. Given a recent emphasis on "open innovation" and that risk is most effectively and efficiently addressed at early lifecycle stages, this result is also somewhat surprising.

Control Activities

There was a statistically significant increase in the use of credit and financial data analysis (Table 6.12), perhaps driven by the recent trend of supplier bankruptcies and the increased use of approved supplier lists. Other control activities such as spend analysis and business process management are also used, though the degree of integration of such tools is unclear. Training and network optimization tools to ensure that risk management practices are properly executed were used to a lesser extent.

INFORMATION AND COMMUNICATIONS

Table 6.13 indicates that information gathering and good communications with suppliers are widely used risk management practices. There is a statistically significant increase in the already extensive use of information

TABLE 6.13

Information and Communication

Item	p (t-test)	Survey 1		Survey 2	
		Mean	SD	Mean	SD
Information gathering	0.09	5.65	1.22	6.12	1.11
Establishing good communications with suppliers	0.43	5.41	1.06	5.71	1.26
Forecasting techniques (e.g., to pre-build and carry additional inventory of critical items)	0.87	4.76	1.44	4.71	1.40
Our company uses real-time inventory information and analytics in managing the supply chain	0.60	4.12	1.65	4.35	1.84
Visibility (detailed knowledge of what goes on in other parts of the supply chain, e.g., finished goods inventory, material inventory, WIP, pipeline inventory, actual demands and forecasts, production plans, capacity, yields, and order status)	0.62	4.12	1.17	4.35	1.50
Data warehousing	0.66	4.24	1.75	4.06	1.43
Supply chain risk information is accurate and readily available to key decision makers	0.90	3.65	1.37	3.71	1.76
Demand signal repositories	0.89	3.71	2.05	3.65	1.73
Network design analysis programs	0.55	3.06	1.98	2.88	1.45

gathering, emphasizing the importance of information for risk management decision making. Despite higher levels of information gathering and communications, there is a relatively low level of confidence that information is accurate and readily available.

MONITORING

Table 6.14 reflects a statistically significant increase in the use of consistent monitoring of a supplier's process. The consistent analysis of processes, coupled with the already extensive use of supplier measurement and supplier visits, supports risk mitigation efforts. Directly determining SCRM effectiveness is difficult, so standard supply measures (e.g., on-time

TABLE 6.14

Monitoring

Item	p (t-test)	Survey 1		Survey 2	
		Mean	SD	Mean	SD
Supplier performance measurement systems	0.69	5.12	1.93	5.29	2.05
Visiting supplier operations	0.88	5.12	1.22	5.18	1.33
Consistent monitoring and auditing of a supplier's processes	0.02	4.00	1.73	5.12	1.87
Benchmarking (internal, external, industry-wide, etc.)	0.90	4.53	1.77	4.47	1.37
We have placed an emphasis on incident reporting to decrease the effects of disruptions	0.77	4.18	1.67	4.00	1.58
We actively benchmark our supply chain risk processes against competitors	0.76	3.24	1.60	3.12	1.58

delivery) are generally used. Few firms benchmark their risk management processes relative to best in class.

Performance Outcomes

Table 6.15 suggests that most firms are relatively satisfied with SCM performance outcomes. The firms in this study realized a statistically significant

TABLE 6.15

Satisfaction with Performance

Item	p (t-test)	Survey 1		Survey 2	
		Mean	SD	Mean	SD
Logistics and delivery reliability	0.05	4.82	0.88	5.47	1.07
Meeting customer service levels	0.46	5.12	0.86	5.29	0.69
Damage-free and defect-free delivery	0.36	5.47	0.72	5.24	0.83
Supplier reliability and continuous supply	0.29	4.82	0.95	5.18	0.95
Order completeness and correctness	0.48	4.88	0.86	5.06	1.20
Reduced disruptions in the supply chain	0.82	4.76	0.97	4.82	0.95
After sales service performance	0.37	4.35	1.32	4.71	0.92
Inventory management	0.12	4.00	1.32	4.71	1.53
Reduced material price volatility	0.06	3.59	1.46	4.41	1.06
Lower commodity prices	0.12	3.71	1.05	4.24	1.20

increase in logistics/delivery performance and in reduced material price volatility. These improvements may be driven by past practices, as well as the increased use of the practices identified in this research (e.g., consistent supplier performance monitoring, information gathering, hedging strategies).

DISCUSSION

Respondents indicated that there is a need for ERM and SCRM, and that there was some management support for such initiatives. This recognition of need might suggest that the firms have implemented proactive and integrated SCRM. However, a limited set of firms have the approach, budget, and/or organization to holistically manage risk. There was a statistically significant decrease in spending intentions for risk management and in the understanding of corporate risk management activities. While most participants suggested this funding drop was driven by resource limitations, one manager suggested that recent increased economic activity and stability in the supply chain has driven a funding drop: "...since the [economic] crisis has eased, it [risk management] has not been a high priority as in past years. The data is still collected and reviewed but not at a high management level. There has been a drop off of importance of the supply risk management program since we are seeing stability in the supply chains."

Few firms used supply risk chain managers who worked closely with corporate risk management, and there appears to be limited understanding of the activities being performed by corporate risk management groups. One manager stated that it is a "lack of experience and lack of planning to reduce risk, and a lack of experience of procurement professionals" that is limiting SCRM preparedness and implementation. This limited approach was not universal though. One manager indicated:

> Supply risk management is very important to our Materials Department as well as the company. Our Supply Base Management department is responsible for developing, maintaining, and executing contingency plans for the supply base. Supply risk management is included in the job description for the Supply Base Management department. Each Supply Base Analyst is responsible for his/her suppliers. If a contingency plan is executed, other resources are appointed to assist with the plan until the supply risk

is mitigated. Maintaining our production schedules and keeping the lines running is priority number one and to date we have not impacted the line, even with the natural disasters in Japan and Thailand.

Firms will always contend with risk and are unlikely to be able to effectively and efficiently mitigate all risks, which suggests that firms may need to focus on the highest impact and/or most likely to occur risks. The survey data indicated that supplier failure is the most common and highest risk factor, and this was reflected by one analyst: "Day to day the largest failure is nonconforming product and failure to deliver on-time or the required amount." A statistically significant increase in the consistent monitoring and auditing of supplier processes was reported, which is most likely in response to this significant risk.

Bankruptcy and default of suppliers was another high-risk impact factor. A statistically significant increase was found in the use of credit and financial data analysis to control risks. Many firms rely on external reports such as the Dun & Bradstreet Supplier Evaluation Risk rating. One supply manager indicated they use internal analysis coupled with financial analysis from an outside consulting firm to assess financial risk: "Primarily we're looking at supplier financial risk. We work with an external firm to provide financial reports on our suppliers and monitor spending and risk with them. We also use supplier scorecards that look at cost/quality/delivery which drives good and frequent communication with the supply base which helps pick up on any underlying risk issues."

Currency exchange, interest rate changes, inflation and commodity cost volatility were all of growing concern. To mitigate such risks, a variety of techniques were used. One supply manager stated: "… we monitor our core commodity markets on a regular basis. We also have implemented policy of only doing business in USD and hedging currency risks from a corporate level. We also establish long-term global contracts with multiple air/ocean and trucking carriers." Overall, there was a statistically significant increase in the use of hedging strategies by the firms.

Also of growing concern were the uncertainty and impact of regulations and laws (e.g., SOX, Clean Air Act, etc.). A supply executive commented: "Major concerns are labor practices, environmental implications, and the upcoming world custom codes" (WCO SAFE Framework, EU Community Customs Code). These increasing regulatory pressures further highlight the importance of corporate and legal department involvement in mitigating "supply" risk.

Risk responses included avoidance, acceptance, reduction, and sharing. Though avoidance was not explicitly examined in this research, one manager commented that avoiding global sourcing risks is an option: "Natural disasters could be more evident and have more of an impact, and global financial markets could cause companies to look to keep stuff close to home."

A common risk reduction approach was to qualify and use approved suppliers. This approach to risk management might unintentionally lead to other risks. For example, one risk of using approved suppliers is the potential to adopt single sourcing when perhaps dual/multiple sourcing would be most appropriate, as one respondent warned: "We single source most items so we are held hostage to suppliers in regards to price and lead times." Another manager commented that developing relationships with suppliers has become more difficult: "there is less loyalty to supply base/ partnership with the 'Internet generation' of suppliers."

As expected, companies make extensive use of information and communication to identify, assess, and manage risks. Respondents indicated that there was a statistically significant increase in information gathering, for example. Such processes are fundamental to SCRM, as one manager noted:

> The major failure mode today in the supply chain would be communication, internal and external. I bring this point up, because this seems like a very small issue, but it can cause significant problems. Communications internally to plants, customers, or suppliers are crucial to any supply chain. It is always better to over-communicate or to re-confirm what was agreed upon to all parties to make sure understanding of the goal is agreed upon.

Despite the importance of information and communication, there was not a high level of confidence that risk information was accurate and readily available to support decision making. Companies have ideas regarding what information is needed, just not a common method of gathering and using such information, as exemplified by this manager's comment: "Our company currently uses way too many systems to run the supply chain which increases the risk of disconnect and error." An integrated information system resolved the issue for one company:

> SAP is our infrastructure that facilitates all of our major activities. If a process is not done through SAP then there is no way to track and control the

process. SAP is a major part of how we identify and analyze risk, because it provides that data and signals for our company to make decisions. We have multiple reports that are run off the data from SAP that drive our decision making and give us early warning on potential issues before they occur.

CONCLUSION AND FUTURE RESEARCH

Implementation of SCRM is a challenge. The most significant challenge may be establishing the commitment and culture needed to manage risks holistically, perhaps because risk management outcomes cannot be directly measured. Standard supply measures such as on-time delivery, and not line disruptions, reflect supply risk management performance but cannot directly measure it. One manager commented: "The most significant challenge is the inability for firms to seriously consider, continue to be proactive, and create contingency plans that are updated and kept current given the uncertainty to measure and quantify the actual ROI of such risk reduction efforts." Extending contingency planning throughout the value chain provides a higher level of risk mitigation but is challenging to implement, as one manager noted: "The biggest challenge is making suppliers understand the importance of having a solid contingency plan for their own business. A lot of suppliers consider this work as a paperwork only exercise and don't put the necessary effort or diligence into the plan. It takes a lot of training and consulting to make them true believers."

Supply managers will need to be persistent in communicating to upper management the importance of SCRM to secure the support, budget, and resources necessary to treat risks and meet corporate objectives. One sourcing manager emphasized this point:

As managers, you are the voice for your associates and those who may not get the face time with the people who can affect change. The metrics speak for themselves, so managers need to be able to relate the needed resources to areas in the supply chain that need improvement. In-stocks, fill-rate, turns, inventory, and vendor compliance are all areas with risk that need adequate resources to meet goals.

The COSO framework provides a good structure for supply managers to not only identify and treat risks, but to communicate the importance of

SCRM to corporate executives. These concepts, coupled with the shortage of SCRM empirical research (Sodhi et al. 2012), and the following topics may be particularly appropriate for future research.

Area 1: In the Long Term, Does Dedicating Resources Specifically for SCRM and/or ERM Provide an Appropriate Return on Investment?

Major supply disruptions garner a lot of attention and have significant business impacts. Companies with dedicated proactive risk response organizations and teams generally respond faster in the short term to such disruptions than do firms without such programs, so it is increasingly suggested that firms should adopt proactive ERM/SCRM approaches. Perhaps institutional theory (DiMaggio & Powell 1983; Oliver 1991) is driving companies to adopt formal ERM/SCRM structures. In the long term, what is the appropriate level of resources, budget, and time that a firm should spend on structured risk management programs as opposed to maintaining a "just in case" budget to support contingency responses?

Area 2: Coalescing around a Standard Risk Framework

We reviewed SCRM frameworks and noted that the COSO framework provides a more comprehensive framework that is already adopted in various industries. Existing SCRM frameworks have advanced our understanding of SCRM, but has it reached the point that researchers should agree to a common framework and will the COSO ERM framework become the de facto standard? SCRM is generally believed to be a subset of ERM (Sodhi et al. 2012) and COSO is expected to be widely adopted (Moody 2011; Rubenstein et al. 1976), so it may be a reasonable choice. If this standard is widely accepted, will it lead to a relatively standardized set of tools and templates so that risk management research may become more standardized?

Area 3: Impact and Utilization of ERP and Other Information Technology Tools

Firms in this study used a variety of information-based technology and applications for supply management efforts that support risk management (e.g., information gathering, partnership formation, supplier measurement, communications, inventory management, spend management, etc.). However, there was limited indication that IS/IT is being used in "new" ways (e.g., joint technology development, data warehousing, network design analysis programs, demand signal repositories, inventory optimization tools, etc.) to proactively understand, model, and cope with increasing levels of supply risks.

IT/IS tools are becoming increasingly sophisticated and pervasive with the growth of technologies such as Internet-based systems, cloud computing, in-memory computing, and mobile device interfaces. These tools should provide the technology necessary to evaluate and monitor supply chain risk drivers. The question will be how quickly can such tools be adopted and how effective will they become? What is preventing adoption of current tools throughout the supply chain, and what might slow the adoption of newer tools?

Area 4: Growth of the Risk Management Function within Organizations

Just as there has been a change in organizations to grow from isolated functions of production management, purchasing, and transportation to the more holistic supply chain management function, will there be a similar growth in the risk management function? Will this continue to be something that is more of an afterthought by people with direct line responsibilities, or will acceptance of the COSO framework lead to more firms adopting a corporate risk management officer and risk management organization? Will SCRM become a common organizational structure in firms? Should each function develop their own risk management structure and budget (e.g., financial risk management, project risk management, design risk management) or should all risk management be centralized?

Further, should SCRM or components of SCRM be outsourced? Firms already rely on external agents to assess and predict supplier financial performance. Further, suppliers often must or voluntarily comply with external standards (e.g., ISO 9000, GAAP, SOX, etc.). To what extent are such issues supportive of or detrimental to risk management outcomes?

Area 5: Link between Open Innovation and Risk?

Firms such as P&G, Phillips, and Ford increasingly collaborate with suppliers during early stage product development to achieve innovation.

Though risk management is part of that process, few firms in this study integrated supplier into product development specifically to reduce risks. Since risk is best addressed in early development, is this a potentially important process for firms to adopt? One complaint is that assessing supplier risk delays the development process. Will supply personnel increasingly need to adopt rapid process assessment techniques to contribute to early stage risk mitigation efforts?

REFERENCES

Ballou, B. & Heitger, D. 2005. A Building Block Approach for Implementing COSO's Enterprise Risk Management-Integrated Framework. *Management Accounting Quarterly*, 6: 1–10.

Beasley, M., Clune, R., & Hermanson, D. 2005. ERM: A Status Report. *The Internal Auditor*, 62: 67–72.

Black, S. & Porter, L. 1996. Identification of the Critical Factors of TQM. *Decision Sciences Journal*, 27(1): 1–21.

Blackhurst, J., Wu, T., & O'Grady, P. 2005. PDCM: A Decision Support Modeling Methodology for Supply Chain, Product and Process Design Decisions. *Journal of Operations Management*, 23: 325–343.

Bowling, D. & Rieger, L. 2005. Making Sense of COSO's New Framework for Enterprise Risk Management. *Bank Accounting & Finance*, February/March: 35–40.

Capon, N., Kaye, M., & Wood, M. 1994. Measuring the Success of a TQM Programme. *International Journal of Quality and Reliability Management*, 12(8): 8–22.

Chapman, C. 2003. Bringing ERM into Focus. *The Internal Auditor*, 60: 30–35.

Chiang, C.Y., Kocabasoglu-Hillmer, C., & Suresh, N. 2012. An Empirical Investigation of the Impact of Strategic Sourcing and Flexibility on Firms' Supply Chain Agility. *International Journal of Operations and Production Management*, 32(1): 49–78.

COSO. 2004. Enterprise Risk Management—Integrated Framework. Committee of Sponsoring Organizations of the Treadway Commission.

COSO. 2010. Current State of Enterprise Risk Oversight and Market Perceptions of COSO's ERM Framework. Committee of Sponsoring Organizations of the Treadway Commission.

Curkovic, S., Melnyk, S., Calantone, R., & Handfield, R. 2000. Validating the Malcolm Baldrige National Quality Framework through Structural Equation Modeling. *International Journal of Production Research*, 38(4): 765–791.

Dean, J. & Bowen, D. 1994. Management Theory and Total Quality: Improving Research and Practice through Theory Development. *Academy of Management Journal*, 19(3): 392–418.

DiMaggio, P. & Powell, W. 1983. The Iron Cage Revisited: Institutional Isomorphism and Collective Rationality in Organizational Fields. *American Sociological Review*, 48: 147–160.

Eisenhardt, K. 1989. Building Theories from Case Study Research. *The Academy of Management Review*, 14: 532–550.

Flynn, B., Schroeder, R., & Sakakibara, S. 1994. A Framework for Quality Management Research and an Associated Instrument. *Journal of Operations Management,* 11(4): 339–366.

Giannakis, M. & Louis, M. 2001. A Multi-Agent Based Framework for Supply Chain Risk Management. *Journal of Purchasing and Supply Management,* 17: 23–31.

Hallikas, J., Karvonen, I., Pulkkinen, U., Virolainen, V. M., & Tuominem, M. 2004. Risk Management Processes in Supplier Networks. *International Journal of Production Economics,* 90: 47–58.

Holschbach, E. & Hofmann, E. 2011. Exploring Quality Management for Business Services from a Buyer's Perspective Using Multiple Case Study Evidence. *International Journal of Operations & Production Management,* 31(6): 648–685.

Hoyt, R. & Liebenberg, A. 2011. The Value of Enterprise Risk Management. *Journal of Risk and Insurance,* 78: 795–822.

Inderfurth, K. & Kelle, P. 2011. Capacity Reservation Under Spot Market Price Uncertainty. *International Journal of Production Economics,* 1331: 272–279.

Jüttner, U., Peck, H., & Christopher, M. 2003. Supply Chain Risk Management: Outlining an Agenda for Future Research. *International Journal of Logistics,* 6: 197–210.

Kern, D., Moser, R., Hartman, E., & Moder, M. 2012. Supply Risk Management: Model Development and Empirical Analysis. *International Journal of Physical Distribution & Logistics Management,* 42: 60–82.

Khan, O. & Burnes, B. 2007. Risk and Supply Chain Management: A Research Agenda. *The International Journal of Logistics Management,* 18: 197–216.

Kleindorfer, P.R. & Saad, G.H. 2005. Managing Disruptions in Supply Chains. *Production and Operations Management,* 14: 53–68.

Kumar, S. & Verruso, J. 2008. Risk Assessment of the Security of Inbound Containers at U.S. Ports: A Failure, Mode, Effects, and Criticality Analysis Approach. *Transportation Journal,* 47(4): 26–41.

Laeequddin, M., Sardana, G.D., Sahay, B.S., Abdul Waheed, K., & Sahay, V. 2009. Supply Chain Partners Trust Building Process through Risk Evaluation: The Perspectives of UAE Packaged Food Industry. *Supply Chain Management,* 14(4): 280–290.

Landsittel, D. & Rittenberg, L. 2010. COSO: Working with the Academic Community. *Accounting Horizons,* 24, 455–469.

Liu, Z. & Cruz, J. 2012. Supply Chain Networks with Corporate Financial Risks and Trade Credits under Economic Uncertainty. *International Journal of Production Economics,* 137(1): 55–67.

Manuj, I. & Mentzer, J.T. 2008. Global Supply Chain Risk Management. *Journal of Business Logistics,* 29: 133–156.

Martin, C., Mena, C., Khan, O., & Yurt, O. 2011. Approaches to Managing Global Sourcing Risk. *Supply Chain Management,* 16(2): 67–81.

Matook, S., Lasch, R., & Tamaschke, R. 2009. Supplier Development with Benchmarking as Part of a Comprehensive Supplier Risk Management Framework. *International Journal of Operations and Production Management,* 29(3): 241–267.

Miles, M. & Huberman, A. 1994. *Qualitative Data Analysis: A Sourcebook of New Methods.* Newbury Park, CA: Sage Publications.

Moody, M. 2011. COSO Framework Proves Efficacious. *Rough Notes,* 154: 130–132.

Nocco, B. & Stulz, R. 2006. Enterprise Risk Management: Theory and Practice. *Journal of Applied Corporate Finance,* 18: 8–20.

Oliver, C. 1991. Strategic Responses to Institutional Processes. *Academy of Management Review,* 16: 145–179.

Rubenstein, A.H., Chakrabarti, A.K., O'Keefe, R.D., Souder, W.E., & Young, H.C. 1976. Factors Influencing Success at the Project Level. *Research Management,* 16: 15–20.

Samad-Khan, A. 2005. Why COSO Is Flawed. *Operational Risk,* 6: 24–28.

Saraph, V., Benson, P., & Schroeder, R. 1989. An Instrument for Measuring the Critical Factors of Quality Management. *Decision Sciences,* 20(4): 810–829.

Smithson, C. & Simkins, B. 2005. Does Risk Management Add Value? A Survey of the Evidence. *Journal of Applied Corporate Finance,* 17: 8–17.

Sobel, P. 2006. Building on Section 404: Investments in Sarbanes-Oxley Compliance Can Provide a Solid Foundation for Enterprise Risk Management Projects. *The Internal Auditor,* 63: 38–44.

Sodhi, M.S., Son, B.G., & Tang, C.S. 2012. Researcher's Perspective on Supply Risk Management. *Productions and Operations Management,* 21: 1–15.

Tang, C. S. 2006. Perspectives in Supply Chain Risk Management. *International Journal of Production Economics,* 103: 451–488.

Tummala, R. & Schoenherr, T. 2011. Assessing and Managing Risks Using the Supply Chain Risk Management Process (SCRMP). *Supply Chain Management,* 16: 474–483.

Young, G. & Hasler, D. 2010. Managing Reputational Risks: Using Risk Management for Business Ethics and Reputational Capital. *Strategic Finance,* 92: 37–46.

Zsidisin, G. 2003. Managerial Perceptions of Supply Risk. *Journal of Supply Chain Management,* 39: 14–25.

Zsidisin, G. & Hartley, J. 2012. A Strategy for Managing Commodity Price Risk. *Supply Chain Management Review,* March/April: 46–53.

Zsidisin, G. & Wagner, S. 2010. Do Perceptions Become Reality? The Moderating Role of Supply Chain Resiliency on Disruption Occurrence. *Journal of Business Logistics,* 31: 1–20.

Zsidisin, G., Ellram, L., Carter, J., & Cavinato, J. 2004. An Analysis of Supply Risk Assessment Techniques. *International Journal of Physical Distribution & Logistics Management,* 34: 397–41.

7

Global Procurement and Supply Risk Management Processes at Steelcase Inc.

STEELCASE BACKGROUND

Steelcase Inc. (SCS) is a global, publicly traded company with fiscal 2012 revenue of approximately $2.75 billion and nearly 10,000 employees around the world. They compete in the global office furniture industry with a portfolio of solutions that address three core elements of an office environment: interior architecture, furniture, and technology. SCS encompasses three core brands: Steelcase, Turnstone, and Coalesse and several sub-brands, including Nurture, the health care division (Steelcase 2012). Suppliers provide design, production, and service support and are a key to SCS's competitive success. Suppliers are evaluated and selected using a range of criteria including sustainable business practices, financial stability, legal and ethical compliance, quality, cost, delivery, and technical competence, for example.

RISKS IN THE STEELCASE SUPPLY CHAIN

SCS has grown over the years, and many of their suppliers have grown with them resulting in long-standing relationships with a relatively stable and proven supply base. To this extent, SCS has been operating in a relatively low-risk environment with regard to its supply chain. SCS still has to manage the many supply risks that all global firms face on a daily basis, but having a high degree of familiarity and strong relations with qualified suppliers helps proactively mitigate the risks.

Supply chain risks are not driven solely by supplier performance issues (e.g., late deliveries) or uncontrollable external events (e.g., hurricanes) or actions taken by internal SCS buyers (e.g., submitting a late request to qualify a new supplier). Sound business strategies and practices have increased supply risk as well. For example:

- During the economic downturn, few suppliers were being added to the approved supplier list while some approved suppliers went out of business for reasons beyond their control. The default of a current supplier and the transition to a new supplier increased risks.
- SCS adopted lean principles and practices that have had a positive impact on business results. However, such practices highlight the sensitivity of the plant to supply chain performance. Without a reliable lean supply chain, SCS faced potential material shortages.
- Within the last decade, SCS entered new markets (e.g., health care, higher education), which drove a surge in R&D and the introduction of many new products requiring new suppliers and new supplier capabilities. During these tough economic times, SCS decided to accept higher supply risk in return for shorter product development cycles for the products introduced into these markets.
- SCS plant consolidations and closings that were key to SCS's long-term health stressed their suppliers. A local supplier that supplied to a plant in California, for example, might now need to serve a plant in Texas. Not only did logistics challenges drive risk, but so did the need to redevelop the buyer–supplier relationships based on new localized behavior.
- When SCS went from a private to a public firm, more restrictions were placed on the flow of detailed day-to-day and long-term information due to regulations regarding insider information concerns. SCS employees who were used to ready access to financial and strategic planning information now received a tidal wave of information once a quarter just as the general public does. Though information is still made available as needed, decreased information fluidity can drive increased risk.

GLOBAL PROCUREMENT PROCESS

Historically, people outside of the supply group had not considered how corporate strategic moves and economic transitions impacted supply chain risks. Further, it was not widely recognized what supply was doing to reduce risk from an initial qualification process and to mitigate risk on a day-to-day basis. Procurement was not viewed as a risk management discipline or even as a group that could help drive different points of view during new product development or help the company grow by finding suppliers of new materials, innovations, and capabilities.

To improve business processes and outcomes, and to some extent highlight the importance of supplier lifecycle and supply risk management, the vice president of global operations made it a key objective to reinvent the supplier qualification and development process. A key principle to developing the new Global Procurement Process (GPP), shown in Figure 7.1, was to "begin with the end in mind." That is, if the expectations of the relationship are defined up front, that definition of need enables selection of the best possible candidate. If the principle is followed through lifecycle management, the relationship can be better managed and performance continuously improved.

A primary objective of the new GPP is to enable internal customers to make fact-based decisions tied to business needs in an information rich environment across the entire lifecycle of the project and relationship, rather than just issuing requests for proposals (RFPs) and making decisions based strictly on quotes. The process for supply chain risk management (SCRM) is embedded in this GPP.

The six primary processes in the GPP are interdependent and interactive. The Supplier Quality Group (SQG) is primarily responsible for "strategic needs identification" and "supplier qualification." These two processes, discussed in detail subsequently, have a significant influence on the rest of the GPP and overall risk implications. The supply chain leaders (SCLs) (a.k.a. buyers) are primarily responsible for the other four processes. "Supplier selection" is the actual award of business. "Supplier launch and readiness" is the ramp up to production. "Supplier fulfillment" is day-to-day lifecycle management. "Supplier performance reporting and

FIGURE 7.1
Steelcase Global Procurement Process (GPP).

corrective action" deals with continuous improvement and performance assessment relative to objectives and then taking appropriate countermeasures when required.

Though the SQG and SCL support each other throughout the GPP, they have a primary responsibility for different processes for a reason. The SCLs are under constant pressure to manage and reduce costs, and to ensure reliable and speedy delivery. Pursuit of such objectives might drive decisions that unintentionally increase risks. The SCL group could not be as effective as they are if they had to constantly analyze risks on their own. Therefore, the SQG group focuses on how different risk factors might impact SCL objectives.

The GPP is fundamentally a risk management process, though it is presented as supplier qualification, selection, and management process because SCS did not want people to feel that they were going through purely an engineering exercise in risk management. The concept of risk seems to be distant to some people, so without being overly explicit about it, this process gets people to buy-in to the fact that risk exists, to be sensitive to risk, and to realize that potential degradation of supplier performance can be predicted to some extent. The GPP drives a long-term perspective in relationship and risk management.

SCS is in the process of implementing the GPP globally. Collaboration software such as SharePoint will enable the global procurement team to standardize the process, pool information, and track projects globally. All of the assessments will be captured in a project management database so that reviews can be done of past projects, lessons learned can be incorporated into future processes, and new projects can rely on past assessments of suppliers that might fit the new project needs.

STRATEGIC NEEDS IDENTIFICATION AND SUPPLIER QUALIFICATION

The first two stages of the GPP focus on meeting the needs of the SCL while mitigating risk, as suggested in Figure 7.2. The "strategic needs identification" process starts when the SQG and Product Category Lead (PCL) semiannually interview innovation leaders. These business needs are communicated to the SCL. The SCL identifies a new material or part

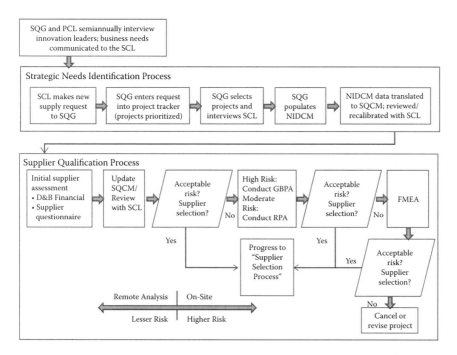

FIGURE 7.2
Needs identification and qualification processes.

need and contacts the SQG. The SQG asks three questions: Who are you? What are you looking for? and What project are you working on? This gets the project on a project tracker sheet where projects are prioritized and then selected for action. Once a project is initiated, information is solicited from all key stakeholders then funneled down to develop the two output tools that will be used to engage the rest of the GPP: the "Needs ID Ticket" and the "Qualification Criteria Matrix," as shown in Figure 7.3.

The SQG interviews the SCL using the needs ID ticket, which is also known as the Needs ID Criteria Matrix (NIDCM), shown in Table 7.1. SQG will enter information received from SCL into the form. For example, one question is "Do you have a preference on supplier location?" The SCL may respond "Southeast Asia, or perhaps China or India." Then, the SCL will be asked to identify on a scale of 0 to 5 how important that is to SCL. Zero indicates not at all a consideration, whereas 5 would be an absolute requirement. This importance ranking is entered into the first (leftmost) column. The interviews only last about half an hour, but they are critical to the whole process because they identify the needs from a business perspective that will be used throughout the GPP to guide decisions.

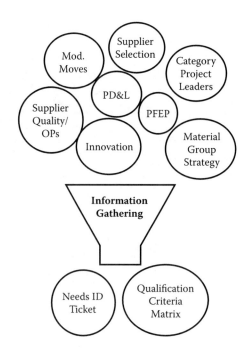

FIGURE 7.3
Strategic needs identification process.

The interview strikes a balance between a too generic process that does not capture sufficient detail (e.g., just asking "what do you need") and a full-scale detailed assessment of all potential risk factors which would become overly burdensome and time consuming for the SCL. The interviews are personal communications and interchanges between the SQG and SCL so that it is clear that there will be mutual support of the objectives throughout the project lifecycle.

The questions on the NIDCM were designed to ensure that for each purchase decision a broad set of differentially weighted issues are addressed up front, even if it would seem at first take that the purchase decision is relatively risk free. Through the interviews the SQG develops a strong sense of how sensitive the internal customer is to a specific issue or type of risk. The NIDCM will be reviewed with SCL and recalibrated if needed.

The SQG then maps the data from the NIDCM to the Supplier Qualification Criteria Matrix (SQCM) shown in Table 7.2. A coding scheme is used to map the importance rating and qualitative information from a single question on the NIDCM to one or more items on the SQCM. Not all items on the SQCM will be ranked (weighted) at this point. Items without any correlating information are either broader or narrower

TABLE 7.1

Steelcase Needs ID Criteria Matrix

Needs ID Criteria Matrix	*Date:*
Material Group:	*MG Leader:*
Process Stakeholders: i.e., QE, ME, PE, PCL	
Qualification Start Date:	*Target Date for Completion:*

	What are you buying?
	Are there engineering, material, or test specifications that must be met?
	Describe the process or equipment requirements (i.e., 200t press, 5 axis router, machine bed size, secondary operations, welding, adhesives, finishing).
	Do you require the supplier to provide product/material lot traceability, material tracking to mfg. dates?
	Do the products require any certifications (EICC, UL, CE, TUV, RoHS, BIFMA Level 1–4, PVC Free, FSC)?
	Is there an existing supplier? Who is it?
	Have you identified any candidates? Who are they?
	What is the annual spending and material/piece volume? (Actual data or projection?)
	Do you have a preference on supplier location?
	Will the product be made to order (specials, ATP, low quantity) or made to stock (supplier-held inventory, minimum runs, high volume/high production runs, large lots minimal changeovers)?
	Will the supplier manage inventories for us?
	Does it matter what markets the supplier serves (automotive, furniture, consumer goods, etc.)?
	Will this product/material have specific lead-time requirements (4/2/4 capable; Specials Eng.; ATP)?
	What engineering and R&D capabilities does the supplier require (rapid prototyping; product design; material testing; mfg. eng.; lifecycle management; help desk; customer support)?
	Do you require any quality systems or process certifications, environmental certifications (ISO certified, TS, AS, internal)?
	Will you require the supplier to provide financial reports (P&L and balance sheets)?

in scope and provide some sort of supporting information. The individual items on the SQCM are grouped into 12 primary risk categories shown plus three special processes (welding, finishing, and adhesives). Each category has multiple measures/questions, though only the measures for "company culture" are shown (to save space in this chapter). This SQCM

TABLE 7.2

Steelcase Supplier Qualification Matrix

Weight	*Note*: **Numbers shown are fictitious: For demonstration only**	Target	Score	
	Company Culture	12	10	81%
	Does the organization have a clearly defined corporate strategy with no major strategic changes expected?			
	Does the organization's culture promote growth and change?			
3	Is the company agreeable and forthcoming with all requested financial information?		2	
5	Does the organization appear to have an acceptable level of financial health?		3	
	Does the organization conduct business in an atomic supply and demand market?			
	Does the organization have an outstanding brand image that aligns with overall Steelcase business behavior?			
4	Is the organization located in an area where it is well insulated from geopolitical risk?		2	
	Does the company have significant experience conducting business in multiple languages?			
	Does the organization have the capability to exchange information via EDI/SUS/XML?			
	Customer satisfaction			
	Environmental and corporate social responsibility			
	Facilities safety and cleanliness			
	Visual management deployment			
	Research and development			
	Scheduling systems			
	Quality system deployment			
	Supply chain integration			

Continued

TABLE 7.2 *(Continued)*

Steelcase Supplier Qualification Matrix

Weight	*Note*: **Numbers shown are fictitious: For demonstration only**	Target	Score
	Inventory management, product flow and use of space		
	People, teamwork, skill level and motivation		
	Equipment and tooling condition and maintenance		
	Special processes—welding		
	Special processes—finishing		
	Special processes—adhesives		
	Total Profiling Score		
	Supplier rating		
	Qualification criteria met		
	Needs improvement		
	Needs significant improvement		
	Stop/override by VP		

will be used during "supplier qualification" to rate and compare suppliers on the key business requirements.

The SCL is not involved in the initial population of the SQCM, but the matrix is reviewed with the SCL to see if another recalibration is required prior to the "supplier qualification" process. The SQCM is the tool that standardizes the information to be used throughout the process, but it is not a static document. Project needs will be recalibrated as progression is made through the rest of the qualification process.

The supplier qualification (SQ) process is a risk and gap analysis that drives the decision to qualify, develop, or not qualify a supplier. The amount of information gathered, the level of detail analyzed, and the allocation of resources for the SQ process depends on the situation. The first two steps in each SQ process are completion and analysis of: (1) a financial report (e.g., D&B Supplier Evaluation Risk Rating and Supplier Stability Indicator); and (2) a "Candidate Supplier Questionnaire" that suppliers access and complete via the Steelcase.com supplier site. The questionnaire prompts the supplier to respond to a series of questions grouped into five categories: (1) company profile; (2) Customs-Trade Partnership Against Terrorism (C-TPAT); (3) manufacturing capabilities; (4) supply chain management; and (5) research and development. A coding key is used to map measurements from both the financial report and the supplier questionnaire to the previously initiated SQCM. Still, not all items on the SQCM will have a needs/risk weight or performance score.

Referring to Table 7.2, the "weight" number (ranging from 0 to 5) is the need ranking that may be recalibrated. The "target" cell is the sum of the need (risk) weights. The individual scores near an item (ranging from 0 to 3) are the performance dimensions derived from the financial report and supplier questionnaire. The total score is an average of the weight and performance products. For example, total score = $[(3 * 2) + (5 * 3) + (4 * 2)]/3 = 9.67 \sim 10$.

The SQCM provides a quantitative and relatively objective way to choose between competing suppliers. The SCL and SQG can compare suppliers by risk category, line item by line item, and total risk. It is at this point that the firm starts getting a strong sense of the risk level, and it might also be the point at which needs are recalibrated. The initial calibration of risk occurred during the interviews, but it is a very high level, subjective perspective. Risk perception was recalibrated somewhat after the NIDCM and SQCM were completed, but it is not until the tools are used with the internal customer that the needs analysis is more fixed and a detailed perception of risk is developed.

If the SCL is leaning toward a supplier that does not have the highest score or does not perform as well on some of the highest-rated need factors, it may be that the project needs to be changed or because the SCL has some subjective criteria that they are now considering. Either way, by referring to the NIDCM and/or SQCM, everyone can be made aware of the potential risk of not selecting the most qualified or aligned supplier. Then, perhaps the needs weighting will be revised because the project needs have changed, or the SCL will revisit their supplier selection. Generally, if an item is rated with an importance of 5 by the SCL is not achievable, it is likely a deal-breaker for that supplier.

Until this point, only "remote analysis" has taken place (no plant visits). In the past, SCS may have conducted an on-site assessment for all potential suppliers because "that's the way we always do it." However, SCS realized that for many purchases they might have spent more on the risk assessment than they would have on the combined cost of the purchased part and responding to risk situations driven by the purchased part. So SCS now first determines if the remote analysis is sufficient before conducting on-site assessments.

If the remote assessment is not sufficient, depending on the situation and perception of risk, the firm will conduct either a Rapid Plant Assessment (RPA) process or an internally developed full-scale supplier Global Business Process Assessment (GBPA). Both are on-site assessments and use the same 12 categories and special categories of need/risk as the SQCM. Again, the term "risk" is not generally used outside of the SQG. Approximately 70–80% of assessments are remote only, 15–20% RPA, and 5–10% GBPA. Despite the fact that SCS has not spent huge resources on the assessments, they have not had any critical problems in supply chain.

RAPID PLANT ASSESSMENT

To further assess risk, SCS may use a modified version of the RPA that was developed by Dr. Gene Goodson (2002). The categories on the RPA are the same risk categories used in the SQCM. The RPA is completed in two hours or less by a team of four to five people. Each SCS representative has primary responsibility for a few of the risk categories. The SCS team studies the supplier's annual reports, analyst reports, prior assessment data, industry characteristics, project needs, and so on, prior to the visit. SCS does not want the supplier to prepare anything prior to the visit, so the supplier is not informed in advance. SCS does not bring a copy of the assessment to the plant visit, and no notes are taken since doing so could impede communication and detract from picking up visual cues. The team meets immediately after the RPA to summarize the findings and develop the RPA rating sheet.

GLOBAL BUSINESS PROCESS ASSESSMENT

In higher-risk situations, SCS will conduct the more in-depth Global Business Process Assessment (GBPA). Those items previously ranked as critical needs on the SQCM and NIDCM will be explored in great detail during the plant visit. SCS will inform the supplier in advance, and provide them with initial rankings, comments, concerns, and key areas of assessment. The supplier will also be provided with a checklist that they will have to fill out prior to the meeting, which can then be verified on-site. SCS wants to ensure the supplier is prepared and has the necessary resources to conduct the in-depth GBPA when it is scheduled. SCS will also request in advance supplier documents, policies, and procedures. The GBPA form is similar to the SQCM shown previously. However, the GBPA will have more details regarding specific ranking criteria and almost every item will be assessed. The scores on the GBPA are mapped to a summary report (Table 7.3) and provided to the supplier immediately prior to the end of the GBPA process.

TABLE 7.3
STEELCASE SUPPLIER GBPA REPORT

Supplier Business Process Assessment

Supplier:	Sales (volume):
Rated By:	Employees:
Tour Date:	Industry:
Location:	Technologies:
Overall Score:	Other Comments:

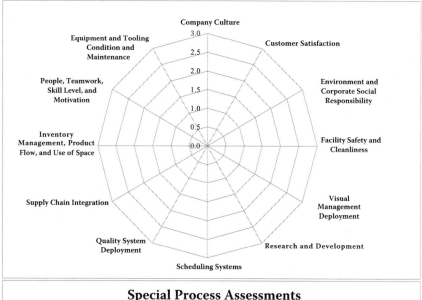

Assessment Disposition	
Number of Critical Issues	

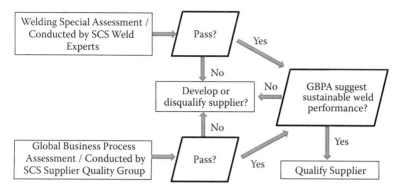

FIGURE 7.4
GBPA and special assessment alignment.

A key part of the qualification process is linking engineering or product performance special assessments to the business process assessments to determine the sustainability of the engineering or product performance as suggested in Figure 7.4. Highly qualified technical personnel will conduct the special assessments, while SQG conducts the GBPA and integrates the two assessments to determine whether or not the qualities observed at the detailed product level are also being observed at a higher business process or cultural level. For example, a special assessment of a complex weld station process might initially indicate that the supplier was highly qualified to perform that operation. However, nine months later the supplier's weld performance might degrade significantly. If the business assessment indicated that the corporate culture was low, or that there was not much emphasis on continuous improvement, or employee retention was a problem, for example, the degradation of the weld performance might have been predicted. This alignment of assessments tests whether or not specific competencies are isolated to a department and if they are sustainable.

A "Qualification Review" form (Table 7.4) is completed using the RPA or GBPA information for each candidate supplier. This form enables the SCL and SQG to make a fact-based supplier selection decision. It also makes transparent the level of risk associated with each potential supplier.

PROCESS FAILURE MODE AND EFFECTS ANALYSIS

In rare cases of extremely high risk, SCS may conduct a full-scale PFMEA. Only one supply chain PFMEA has been conducted in the last seven years. It involved a new supplier, material, and process technology that could

TABLE 7.4

SCS Supplier Qualification Review

Qualification Review
Material Group:
MG Leader:
Date:

Candidate

	Section	# of Questions on the GBPA	RPA	GBPA
A	Company Culture	9		
B	Customer Satisfaction	8		
C	Environment and Corporate Social Responsibility	13		
D	Facility Safety and Cleanliness	5		
E	Visual Management Deployment	8		
F	Research and Development	8		
G	Scheduling Systems	5		
H	Quality System Deployment	12		
I	Supply Chain Integration	11		
J	Inventory Management, Product Flow, and Use of Space	11		
K	People, Teamwork, Skill Level, and Motivation	8		
L	Equipment, Tooling Condition, and Maintenance	4		
M	Special Process — Welding	1		
N	Special Process — Finishing	1		
O	Special Process — Adhesives	1		

Point Totals:

RPA	GBPA

Total Rating Points Available

Risk Level	Supplier Rating
Minimum Risk	Qualification Criteria Met
Low Risk	Needs Improvement
Moderate Risk	Needs Significant Improvement
High Risk	Stop / Override by VP

Number of Critical Issues from the GBPA

have resulted in a very high-risk relationship. The existing assessment tools were not sufficient to assess risk, so a member of the SQG who had been involved with the design of FMEA utilized a cross-functional team to apply PFMEA to this case. It proved to be an effective tool, as the supply chain relationship was not pursued in large part due to this assessment.

The initial PFMEA template and guidelines were developed using information gathered from published articles and texts. Rather than gathering information by directly using the PFMEA templates, the interview guide shown in Table 7.5 was used to simplify the interview process. This interview guide

TABLE 7.5

PFMEA Worksheet

Cause/ Problem Statement	Result of Problem	Severity	Occurrence	Detection	Action Item	Assigned to	Target Date

put PFMEA topics into non-PFMEA language and ensured that data gathered would be in terms familiar to and driven by the buyers. For example, the buyers would be asked, "What do you see as potential problems or causes of problems? How severe are the problems? How often do you think this might occur? How could we detect the problem or know about it?"

SQG then populated the PFMEA form shown in Table 7.6. It is an Excel-based form that guides the user through the process. The "Item and Function" column in the PFMEA would be populated using the terms recorded during the interviews so that the processes and issues would be familiar to all stakeholders. Each project would have a new set of topics that were derived from the interviews.

Each major heading in the PFMEA has a comment box that provides instructions. Scales were developed for the severity, likelihood of occurrence, and likelihood of detection columns as shown in Tables 7.7, 7.8, and 7.9, respectively. People generally agreed to and understood the meaning of the scales, but there was often disagreement regarding the actual assignment of a number to a risk issue. The probability ranking was the most challenging because the ranges were inherently a bit more difficult to interpret and agree upon.

Agreement on a number was only part of the process. The greatest benefit of the process was the discussions that enabled the team to identify and analyze the critical issues from a cross-functional point of view. It was expected that people from different functions would perceive risk differently, so the discussions gave the team an opportunity to explore what the issues really were from a variety of perspectives. This process facilitates a fact-based, decision-making agreement by following a process which engages all the stakeholders in a structured, formal risk review.

Though the PFMEA proved to be effective, PFMEA has not jumped out to SCS as something that needs to become part of the standard tool set and process, so for the short to intermediate term at least there will likely be a limited use of supply chain PFMEA. However, there is some consideration that the PFMEA will be updated as supply becomes more involved

TABLE 7.6

Steelcase Supply Process PFMEA

Supply Process Failure Mode Effects Analysis

Review team:		Process stakeholders:		Date		Tollgate 1 completed:
Supplier:		**Key project dates:**				Tollgate 2 completed:
Product:						Tollgate 3 completed:

													Anticipated Results to Proposed Action(s)			
Item and Function	Potential Failure Mode	Effects of Failure	Projected Severity at 1st ship Rank 1–10	Cause(s) or Mechanism(s) of Failure	Projected Probability of Occurrence at 1st ship Rank 1–10	Key Process or Product Characteristic Yes/No	Current Design Controls	Projected Probability of Detection at 1st ship Rank 1–10	Ranking or Priority Number (Calculated 4×6×9)	Proposed Action(s)	Responsibility and Planned Completion Date	Severity Rank 1–10	Probability of Occurrence Rank 1–10	Probability of Detection Rank 1–10	Ranking or Priority Number (Calculated 13×14×15)
1	2	3	4	5	6	7	8	9	10	11	12	13	14	15	16
Part and/or Product															
Liability									0						0
New Technology									0						0
Process Complexity (Delivery, Performance)									0						0
Process Complexity (Cost)									0						0
Specifications (Incoming quality)									0						0

Continued

TABLE 7.6 (Continued)

Steelcase Supply Process PFMEA

Item and Function	Potential Failure Mode	Effects of Failure	Projected Severity at 1st ship Rank 1–10	Cause(s) or Mechanism(s) of Failure	Projected Probability of Occurrence at 1st ship Rank 1–10	Key Process or Product Characteristic Yes/No	Current Design Controls	Projected Probability of Detection at 1st ship Rank 1–10	Ranking or Priority Number (Calculated 4×6×9)	Proposed Action(s)	Responsibility and Planned Completion Date	Anticipated Results to Proposed Action(s)			
												Severity Rank 1–10	Probability of Occurrence Rank 1–10	Probability of Detection Rank 1–10	Ranking or Priority Number (Calculated 13×14×15)
1	2	3	4	5	6	7	8	9	10	11	12	13	14	15	16
Business															
Core Competency									0						0
Ownership									0						0
Capacity									0						0
Quality System									0						0
Financial									0						0
Environmental									0						0
Facilities									0						0
EDI/TradeWeb									0						0
Relationship															
Segmentation									0						0
Finished Goods									0						0
Sole/Single/Multi Source									0						0
Lead Time									0						0
Logistics									0						0

TABLE 7.7

Steelcase PFMEA Degree of Risk Severity Ranking

Degree of Severity Ranking

Degree	Description	Median Ranking
Very high	When a potential failure mode affects safe operation of the product and/or involves non-conformance with government regulations. May endanger people or product. Assign "9" if there will be a warning before failure, assign "10" if there will *not* be a warning before failure.	10 9
High	When a high degree of customer dissatisfaction is caused by the failure. Does not involve safety of people or product or compliance with government regulations. May cause disruption to subsequent processes/operations and/or require rework.	8 7
Moderate	When a moderate degree of customer dissatisfaction is caused by the failure. Customer is made uncomfortable or is annoyed by the failure. May cause rework or result in damage to equipment.	6 5 4
Low	When a failure will cause only slight annoyance to the customer.	3 2
Minor	When a failure is not likely to cause any real effect on subsequent processes/operations or require rework. Most customers are not likely to notice any failure. Any rework that might be required is minor.	1

TABLE 7.8

Steelcase PFMEA Degree of Risk Occurrence Ranking

Degree of Occurrence Ranking

Chance	Description	Probability	Median Ranking
Very high	Failure is almost inevitable.	1 in 2 1 in 3	10 9
High	Process is "similar" to previous processes with a high rate of failure.	1 in 8 1 in 20	8 7
Moderate	Process is "similar" to previous processes, which have occasional failures.	1 in 80 1 in 400 1 in 2,000	6 5 4
Low	Process is "similar" to previous processes with isolated failures.	1 in 15,000	3
Very low	Process is "similar" to previous processes with very isolated failures.	1 in 150,000	2
Remote	Process is "similar" to previous processes with no known failures.	1 in 1,500,000	1

TABLE 7.9

Steelcase PFMEA Degree of Risk Detection Ranking

Degree of Detection Ranking

Degree	Degree in %	Description	Median Ranking
Detection is not possible	0	Control method(s) cannot or will not detect the existence of a problem.	10
Very low	0 to 50	Control method(s) probably will not detect the existence of a problem.	9
Low	50 to 60	Control method(s) has a poor chance of	8
	60 to 70	detecting the existence of a problem.	7
Moderate	70 to 80	Control method(s) may detect the existence	6
	80 to 85	of a problem.	5
High	85 to 90	Control method(s) has a good chance of	4
	90 to 95	detecting the existence of a problem.	3
Very high	95 to 100	Control method(s) will almost certainly	2
		detect the existence of a problem.	1

in new product development processes and to support the company's strategic objectives (discussed previously). PFMEA might be more efficiently adopted because as the SCS supply manager indicated, "I believe the process will become more acceptable since we are seeing an influx of people with engineering and quality backgrounds in our sourcing organization."

FINISHED GOODS PFMEA

One of SCS's highest-risk supply issues is the purchase of finished goods (FG). FG items are delivered directly to an SCS customer from the supplier, so SCS does not see the FG prior to customer installation. FG items are generally low volume and/or specialized products that may require specific capital equipment. Items might include a special lighting fixture or a unique chair, for example. Steelcase still owns the FG design as the supplier builds to specs.

There are two keys to mitigating FG risks. First, the initial supplier qualification process conducted by SQG (discussed previously) provides confidence in the supplier process. Second, the FG services group, with support from SQG, conducts a "Probability/Likelihood of Discontinuance in Service" with an associated severity/impact analysis on a periodic basis or when market conditions change (reference Table 7.10). This process is

TABLE 7.10

Steelcase FG "Scorecard"

Supplier List			Probability/Likelihood (Discontinuance in Service) *Weight per probability* Viable financial stability 40% Change in ownership 20% Tier two reliance 20% Strategy change 20%				
Supplier	Product	SCL	Viable—Financial Stability	Change in Ownership	Tier Two Reliance	Strategy Change	Overall probability
			40% Weight	20% Weight	20% Weight	20% Weight	
			1 Low	1 Low	1 Low	1 Low	
			2 Medium	2 Medium	2 Medium	2 Medium	
			3 High	3 High	3 High	3 High	

Continued

Global Procurement and Supply Risk Management at Steelcase • 171

TABLE 7.10 (Continued)

Steelcase FG "Scorecard"

Supplier List			Severity/Impact					
Supplier	Product	SCL	Product Spend	Tooling Cost	Product Criticality	Recovery Time	Contingency Sources	Overall impact
			15% weight	10% weight	30% Weight	30% Weight	15% Weight	
			1 Very low 0–100k	1 Very low No tooling	1 Very low	1 Very Low 1 to 4 wks recovery	1 Very low—off the shelf	
			2 Low 100k–250k	2 Low Transferable/ Under 10k	2 Low	2 Low 4 to 8 wks	2 Low—multiple sources	
			3 Medium 250k–500k	3 Medium 10k–25k	3 Medium	3 Medium 9 to 12 wks	3 Medium—2–5 available suppliers	
			4 High 500k–1 MM	4 High 25k–50k	4 High	4 High 3 to 6 months	4 High—1–2 suppliers	
			5 Very high 1 MM and above	5 Very high 50k and above	5 Very high	5 Very high 6 months or more	5 Very high— proprietary products/process	
								0

similar to, but is not a textbook PFMEA. This "scorecard" provides a closed loop analysis in the qualification and lifecycle management process.

SUMMARY

Steelcase developed a new Global Procurement Process to ensure business needs are met by beginning with the end in mind. The six steps in the process are highly interdependent to ensure that supply relationships, processes, and risks are managed throughout the supply lifecycle. Needs and priorities, which are established at the initial "strategic needs identification" process, may be recalibrated as new information is made available and as situations change, but all subsequent procurement decisions are related back to the priorities. Supply chain risks are weighted and assessed relative to the priorities during the "supplier qualification" process. Depending on the level of risk, different qualification and risk management tools are used. These first two critical steps enable fact-based supplier selection and management decision making. A key to success in each step is to frame all questions and responses using language that is familiar to the end user (e.g., buyers).

REFERENCES

Goodson, R.E. 2002. Read a Plant—Fast. *Harvard Business Review*, 80(5): 105–113.
Steelcase. 2012. Steelcase, Inc. www.steelcase.com.

8

Feedback from Managers

Managers were asked questions about the effectiveness of risk management and its implementation. Select responses follow.

QUESTION 1

Managers were asked to discuss the three most significant challenges, barriers, or limiting factors that are having the most negative impact on supply risk management.

Response 1:

More focus on risk management are now not around which leads into my barrier below. Time—I still feel like a lot of our work is spent on reacting to risks rather than proactively identifying them and having contingencies. Some functions do this better than others, but it's definitely a best practice that could be shared throughout the organization.

QUESTION 1A:

What is the challenge, who/what is creating it, and what exactly is that challenge preventing you from doing?

Response 1a.1:
   (1) Private suppliers don't have to disclose financial statements so true risk isn't always understood.
   (2) Different country laws where [in] certain regions there are no requirements around providing financial info.
   (3) Suppliers owned by private equity firms, where main motivation is profit. Lack of financial info for a particular manufacturing unit in question doesn't allow the team to understand how much longer will that company be in business, be sold, or cease operation all together.

Response 1a.2:

The biggest challenge is making suppliers understand the importance of having a solid contingency plan for their own business. A lot of suppliers consider this work as a paperwork only exercise and don't put the necessary effort or diligence into the plan. It takes a lot of training and consulting to make them true believers.

Response 1a.3:

Another challenge is to depart from a single source purchasing strategy and move to dual sourcing for critical components. There are advantages and disadvantages of each. The advantages of moving to a dual sourcing strategy includes reduced supplier security risk and increased competition which can be used to lower cost and improve quality. Disadvantages include two sets of tooling ($$$), added complexity for buyers and operations, and reduced volume for each supplier, which could increase cost.

Response 1a.4:

Transportation, vendor compliance, and capacity constraints are the biggest challenges I face. These challenges prevent me from having the product available for our customers and also keeping a consistent inventory flow.

Response 1a.5:

Team is proactively doing research to understand how long has the private equity owned a business, and based on industry average, [they] can narrow down where the risk is before the business is sold or closed.

Response 1a.6:

People not understanding the value. Usually it is someone at a corporate level evaluating overall costs (working through consultants who are Ivy League "Punks" that don't know "Squat" and when approached have such an ego that when you question them they back off). Upper management needs to do a better job of understanding their own business and not hire consultants that have no experience!

Response 1a.7:

Margin stack-up from product design from Supplier part performance changes (part may meet specification limits, but actual performance has changed/drifted): Challenge is from Product Design utilizing thousands of components that each have their own specifications. Supplier may change an internal process or material that changes the actual performance of the part, which disrupts the overall performance of the Product. The challenge is this type of impact is unannounced and may severely impact (shutdown) our ability to produce products, which requires the emergency allocation of Engineering and Supply Chain resources, which are then not available to work on continuous improvement work.

Response 1a.8:

Supplier part lifecycle changes: Impact caused by suppliers discontinuing the manufacture/supply of items. Replacement items need to be evaluated or alternate supply sources need to be identified, which consumes Engineering and Supply Chain resources, which are then not available to work on continuous improvement work.

Response 1a.9:

Supplier financial viability: impact from a supplier experiencing cash flow/financial constraints. Can result in longer-term degradation of a supplier's performance, resources, and ability to support our requirements, or it may have an immediate impact of the supplier ceasing operation. When this occurs it requires/consumes Engineering and Supply Chain resources, which are then not available for continuous improvement work.

Response 1a.10:

Another challenge is to depart from a single source purchasing strategy and move to dual sourcing for critical components. There are advantages and disadvantages of each. The advantages of moving to a dual sourcing strategy includes reduced supplier security risk and increased competition, which can be used to lower cost and improve quality. Disadvantages include two sets of tooling ($$$), added complexity for buyers and operations, and reduced volume for each supplier, which could increase cost.

QUESTION 1C:

What would it take to overcome that barrier, would it be worth the effort and if so, how would you make the business case that it would be worth it?

Response 1c.1:

I believe there is no clear solution for every situation. Having thorough contingency plans for each part is a must and based from that assessment a decision needs to be made by management. Decisions could range from continuing to monitor the contingency plans to purchasing an extra set of tooling from a different supplier or a different location. Having a budget for supply security is a must even though you may never use it.

Response 1c.2:

A lot of manual headcount spent verifying, reconciling, and cleaning data to truly understand risk.

Response 1c.3:

It would take several meeting and process improvements as well as additional capital to address these challenges. Often, we just look for a Band-Aid or quick fix and don't get to the root of the issues so they are never fully addressed. I absolutely feel it would be worth the effort as the better our supply chain the more profitable we are as an organization.

Response 1c.4:

The two biggest challenges I see are cost and data. On cost, it takes a significant investment to create redundancy through the supply chain. This includes duplicating tools and test equipment to implement a dual-source strategy. It also includes qualification resources from our company to qualify a second source. Our company has estimated that to meet our goal of being able to recover 80% of revenue in less than 13 weeks assuming a factory is completely wiped out (as in Japan or Thailand), it would cost us $30M of up-front investment. On data, the other issue is if we know where we have risk through our embedded supply chain. Our company has done significant work to gather data to understand the country of origin for our 1st tier supply chain. Understanding our sub-tier supply chain is data we do not presently have access to except for some specific commodities.

Response 1c.5:

We are moving in the right direction. We have recently formed Strategic Sourcing teams with visibility and influence across various divisions and multiple groups within our company. We are being granted additional headcount requests as we continue to show value in professional supply chain functions through making large profitability impacts by executing strategic projects and contracts with our Suppliers. As we centralize in key areas of the business, this will be a continued focus for us and I would expect to see great progress in this area in the near future.

Response 1c.6:

Metrics. Although we do have scorecards that address delivery, cost reductions, and quality, risk is not a part of this scorecard so it's not as "in your face" as other metrics are. To overcome this, a globally recognized and agreed upon metric would need to be created and incorporated into the scorecard. Sounds simple enough, but oftentimes it's the agreement of so many different global business units that are the biggest hurdle. It should be easy enough to make the business case for this, but we do a pretty good job dealing with risk now, so upper management might take the "if it ain't broke, don't fix it" approach.

Response 1c.7:

Changing Economics. One way to overcome this change is information. Good information can give companies an advantage in dealing with potential supply risks such as strikes, capacity issues, exchange rate changes, and delivery issues.

Response 1c.8:

Challenge 1: The other issue is that many suppliers provide parts to other OEMs who are also ramping up production. Our assessment relies on the supplier's integrity to provide information on other OEMs production schedules and sometimes we have situations of shared production lines, etc. It is a systemic problem that would take a large culture shift for our company, driven from the top down and including organization changes. It would take extensive effort to provide a business case, but I imagine it would be worth it. I would assess the metrics of our production lines downtime due to short parts supply, as well as man hours and travel costs spent managing crisis suppliers. I would also measure duplicated efforts made by our various plants (conducting individual ramp up studies, collecting and analyzing supplier responses, etc.) and the amount of time and resources spent on this. I would also measure supplier hours spent responding to multiple ramp-up request studies, instead of one study issued at the corporate level.

Response 1c.9:

Challenge 2: Company Culture of Affiliate Suppliers. Oftentimes our biggest issues with parts suppliers is our affiliated suppliers. The culture has eroded over the years and management capability is lacking. There is a dependence on us to fix the major problems, and a general thought that we will not let the supplier fail, which encourages a reliance on our company. Not sure how I would make a business case for this one, but similar to issue 1, I would measure hours and resources spent at affiliates ensuring parts supply.

Response 1c.10:

What I always tell people is follow the money trail—numbers don't lie and working for a company that is highly run by a bunch of "bean counters"— they listen when you tell them what the impact of non-compliance is.

Response 1c.11:

Allocation of additional funding/resources would be required to overcome the barrier. It would be worth the effort to improve quality, customer satisfaction, and ultimately reduce Engineering and Supply Chain resources that are consumed with Supplier Risk events. Business case would need to be stated in the financial trade-off of improved quality, customer satisfaction, and reduced Engineering and Supply Chain resources over the longer term. Challenge with getting support would be the longer-term/ multiyear return on investment.

QUESTION 2:

What specific measures do you use to determine that the appropriate supply risk management strategy was selected and that it was successful?

(1) Are you single sourced for this item? Yes or No
(2) If so, where are the sources and why are you limited?
    (a) If you have no other source-increase inventory and hold more stock.
    (b) If you do have other options—evaluate them through audits, financial review, and so on.

Response 2.1:

This is definitely a work in process for our company. We have various tools we use to determine quality, compliance, and business risk of our suppliers. It is definitely an area we should invest more in and standardize across sites/divisions. The only way we currently measure this is through the business performance results.

Response 2.2:

We use a large variety of Supply Chain measures, which Procurement Directors and Operations VPs review monthly. Basic measures evaluate suppliers maintaining commitments on purchase orders, i.e., On-time, Defects PPM, Purchase Price Variance inflation/deflation, Cost saving $'s, Contract Mgmt % of contracts current, Supplier Qualification projects, Supplier Development projects.

Response 2.3:

Our company monitors each of its potential suppliers using the below-weighted metrics which sum to an overall ABSC (advanced balanced score card) ranking. The ABSC will be used post launch for existing suppliers.

Business	Profit Trend
Financial—Z Score	Technology
Geographic Location	Cost
Market Cap	

Response 2.4:

Goal: 0 lost production units from troubled suppliers while managing the cost most effectively and within the set annual target.

Response 2.5:

Our only measure is whether or not our assembly lines were impacted or not. If not, our contingency plans were successful. I believe that measuring the success of the plan isn't as important as the thought and ideas generated by having a plan.

Response 2.6:

In-stocks, fill-rate, turns, backorders, inventory carrying cost, residual inventory, and cost of goods sold (COGS).

QUESTION 3:

How does top management recognize the importance of supply risk management (e.g., is supply risk management linked with corporate risk management)?

Response 3.1:

Organizational structure is one way. We have a Global Procurement Officer who is accountable for all Supply Chain Management for all operating locations around the globe. Another way is a commitment to educate internal team members on the profession of managing supply chains and the use of risk management in their processes. This education is just as important within the Supply Chain team as those stakeholders from other departments that Supply Chain services. We have a yearlong course that builds this internal Supply Chain Management knowledge base. Finally, the application of appropriate rollout strategies and processes that affect the Supply Chain initiatives across global regions. Yes, risk management is critical to effective supply chain management.

Response 3.2:

We are a small company but at the same time we are composed of automotive industry veterans and thus for a company of 50 people think and operate more like a large global automotive OEM when we think about risk. The key to risk is to identify where your exposure is and to put in place the systems and processes to mitigate risk with the plan to reduce the organization's overall percentage chance of having an event offer. Our supply risk management processes and metrics are directly linked with corporate risk management.

Response 3.3:

For our company, supply risk management has always been a concern. However, it has escalated more recently with the recent natural disasters. Before the natural disasters, a team developed an "Early Warning System" (EWS), which was patented and is used to identify supply risks in our chain, and triggers action when a supplier is considered at risk. I don't know extensive details, but it takes into consideration financial situation as well as supply shortage risk. We have recently been working to update the formulas to include some risk factor for geographic location susceptible to natural disasters. I am not sure about the link with corporate risk management. Please let me know if you would like me to follow up on that link.

Response 3.4:

The current top management recognizes the supply risk especially as events in the news from Pharma Companies in the industry are getting 483's and shutdown due to severe compliance issues. Overall, our company takes pride in its supply link and is constantly monitoring sites and personnel to make sure we are doing everything possible to maintain high standards. They are increasing the control and evaluating sources on a corporate level and expecting sites to follow standard practices (using best practices from the past and also expanding on them).

Response 3.5:

In our industry, top management has recognized supply risk management in the past two years as critical because our growth has been limited by lack of subcomponents on best-selling, most profitable vehicles. This is different from previous years where we did have growth but it was a slow growth which did not constrain the supply base; in the past two years our growth has spiked on certain products and we have run into supplier specific constraints.

Response 3.6:

Global staff in all four operating units (North America, South America, Asia, and Europe) comprised of finance and global purchasing professionals. Supply risk management group provides a regular update to the ROC (risk oversight committee), which is a board of directors driven initiative.

Response 3.7:

Supply risk management (known as Supply Security internal to our company) is very important to our Materials Department as well as the company. Our Supply Base Management department is responsible for developing, maintaining, and executing contingency plans for the supply base.

Response 3.8:

Top management at my company recognizes supply risk by investing capital into our systems, training, and people. Our stock price is a direct correlation to our supply chain success thus it has a very high level of visibility.

Response 3.9:

At our company, until last year this was something that was talked about, but not a whole lot of action was actually given. After the supply issues created because of the earthquake in Japan and flooding in Thailand, our management has made this a top priority. Dedicated teams have been formed to analyze our risk within our own manufacturing plants and our supply chain. Particularly, because our company supplies to government customers where public safety is of critical importance, our company cannot afford to be shut down because of a lack of a continuity plan.

QUESTION 4:

What resources and support does top management allocate to supply risk management? Are such allocations sufficient—if not what is most lacking?

Response 4.1:

A combination of support team members to meet the needs of the corporation's strategies. Ensuring that new products receive well-crafted supply chains to meet those needs. Specialists with supplier mgmt experience help create these supply chains. Material group leaders that drive creation and implementation of material group strategies globally. The third approach requires a team that services day to day operational needs at our plants where opportunities for continuous improvement occur which are beyond the materials management team to satisfy. We also need to support the organizational need to innovate finding appropriate supply chains for new materials and services. Finally, we also need to support our supply chain needs for providing Supply Chain management principles to our Indirect spending to pursue improvements in these important spending areas.

Response 4.2:

As it stands today our biggest resource allocation by top management to supply risk management is people. As a startup resource allocation to supply risk management is always a concern and as a direct comparison to more established businesses our current level of resource dedication is low. However, we understand this and realize that we need to invest further in both additional staffing and IT tools to further mitigate our supply risk. Our company and specifically our supply chain organization has a ramp up plan in place and we have a budget and plan to further invest in the appropriate level of additional staff and IT tools. Specifically, we plan to increase our Supply Chain staffing by 18 additional team members. Further, we plan to purchase subscriptions to commodity indexes and supplier intelligence services. In addition, we plan to procure and install an ERP system.

Response 4.3:

Our company is changing its philosophy and has dedicated much more effort in this area in the past two to three years. They have developed a tool that divisions can access to review their particular suppliers and associated risk (based on D&B ser score). This information is available by supplier or by country of origin; it is not being grouped by commodity at this point. They are working at doing some other things to enhance, but in my mind we have come a long way.

Response 4.4:

I don't know specific numbers of resources, again I could follow up if you're interested in the hard details. Our main opportunity is our lack of North American coordination. When we significantly change our production plan at our various plants (11 in North America), the risk to our supply is assessed individually. Each plant is concerned with ensuring their specific supply needs. The problem is that many of our suppliers supply multiple plants, and no one is allocated to look at North American supply capacity and potential risks as we ramp up our production (I know, this is hard to believe). North American capacity is looked at by a corporate function, but only in regard to our production, not necessarily supply base.

Response 4.5:

Our company has a team dedicated to monitoring suppliers. We have a regular audit process that is standard for all auditors to follow. I have been on audits and seen how other industries perform controls and can emphasize that our controls are much more stringent (example, food industry—much more relaxed—scary!). As far as resources—in today's environment all companies are tasked to do more with less but in the case of Supplier Risk—this is an area where we have put resources versus taking them away.

Response 4.6:

Global staff that also includes operations support group that oversees tool moves from financially troubled or bankrupt suppliers to prevent parts shortages and vehicle production disruption. The team also utilizes outside (third-party) legal counsel and financial/operational/restructuring experts.

Response 4.7:

Supply risk management is included in the job description for the Supply Base Management department. Each Supply Base Analyst is responsible for his/her suppliers. If a contingency plan is executed, other resources are appointed to assist with the plan until the supply risk is mitigated. Maintaining our production schedules and keeping the lines running is priority number one and to date we have not impacted the line due to the natural disasters in Japan and Thailand.

Response 4.8:

Systems, training, additional head count, consulting, etc. Although they have allocated support and improved our current systems, we are still lacking and need to implement more cutting-edge tools.

Response 4.9:

This has been set up as a dedicated track with a project lead, team members, and an executive sponsor to form a plan to reduce risk.

QUESTION 5:

If top management does not recognize the importance and/or does not allocate sufficient resources, what does or should supply managers do to change the situation?

Response 5.1:

This is the responsibility of every Supply Chain team member to exhibit professional behavior and to drive understanding to upper management levels that provide ongoing leadership examples how Supply Chain Mgmt provides a sustained competitive advantage to the organization.

Response 5.2:

In a case where it's believed that top management is not supporting proper resources to address risk, each manager usually devises a way to use existing resources to address the risk while also putting together a proposal on what risk is being faced, attaching a dollar figure to the impact and justifying the resources requested. Basically, it's a "here's the potential negative impact at some point, but if we spend much less than that *now*, we can avoid a bigger hit later."

Response 5.3:

The key is communication. It is the Supply Manager's role within the company to clearly and concisely communicate the organization's risks associated to supply and the business. At our company, I feel we do an excellent job of articulating our current state of play and our plan forward. Our top management is composed of automotive industry veterans "who get it" so they fully appreciate our challenges ahead and have given us the appropriate budgets for the future that will allow us to manage the business and mitigate our overall supply risk.

Response 5.4:

It is definitely recognized as important and resources are always allocated when needed, but I think we need more preventative measures from a North American corporate perspective. We miss supply and capacity concerns due to lack of detection, and inevitably our company ends up sending multitudes of people to go "fix the situation" once it becomes a crisis (crisis is defined by a supplier who has or is about to shut our company's production line down from no supply of parts) and make sure parts are getting out the door.

Response 5.5:

My opinion—Look at the cost of nonconformance—it can bring a company to its knees in a very short period. Example: A company with the peanut issue a few years ago—they realized that buying an audit from a third party without oversight could be a disaster and cost the company millions of dollars of lost revenue and also put a major scar on their reputation.

Response 5.6:

Importance is recognized but top leadership still discussing function ownership—this cannot be changed by managers and only by top executives/shareholders of the company.

Response 5.7:

N/A for our company. If a company does not recognize the importance, they should understand the impact to the company if they were shut down because of a supply security issue and begin to develop thorough contingency plans.

Response 5.8:

As managers, you are the voice for your associates and those that may not get the face time with the people who can affect change. The metrics speak for themselves, so managers need to be able to relate the needed resources to areas in the supply chain that need improvement. In-stocks, fill-rate, turns, inventory, and vendor compliance are all areas with risk that need adequate resources to meet goals.

Response 5.9:

N/A—Top management does recognize the importance and provide resources.

QUESTION 6:

How are the individuals who are responsible for supply risk management assessed and compensated for their risk management efforts?

Response 6.1:

Each employee has a Measureable Annual Performance Plan that itemizes metrics and their six month and annual review is based on the agreed upon objectives, metrics, and results.

Response 6.2:

Currently, our employees are part owners in the company thus they have a vested interest in ensuring the success of the company. Employees all have stock options in the company. Overall, Supply Chain professionals each have specific goals and their compensation is tied to meeting their goals.

Response 6.3:

I am not sure, I would need to follow up on this question. There is no specific compensation awarded for risk management efforts. For the individuals responsible for risk management, their efforts are supposed to be recognized through their normal performance reviews and corresponding annual raise/bonus.

Response 6.4:

Personnel in a role such as this have a major responsibility and therefore are compensated generously within our organization.

Response 6.5:

They are measured on cost savings for supply chain projects + reducing/removing stockouts at manufacturing locations—best performers receive bonuses/promotions similar to all other functions.

Response 6.6:

Primarily we're looking at supplier financial risk. We work with an outside company to provide financial reports on our suppliers and monitor spending and risk with them.

Response 6.7:

Main information is gathered through questionnaires, news, and industry knowledge. We are also working with our suppliers to make them more "flexible" to contend with our short lead times to our customers.

Response 6.8:

Above targets have a direct link to each team member's annual performance metric reviewed by management.

Response 6.9:

It's part of their job description.

Response 6.10:

They are assessed semiannually and awarded bonuses if the company plan is achieved.

Response 6.11 (also refers to Question 1 and Question 2):

For all three of these, our company is in the process of putting a strategy in place, so we are not yet at the point of measuring the effectiveness of what has been put in place. We are thinking through all of this real-time now. The high-level strategy that our company is driving toward is to have redundancy in place that would allow 80% of our revenue to be recovered within a quarter of a catastrophic incident.

QUESTION 7:

How is the effectiveness of supply risk management processes monitored and evaluated on an ongoing basis?

Response 7.1:

We review risk on a monthly basis with our entire supply chain group at a plant level and at a global level. During these meetings risks are identified and action plans are reviewed. Management makes sure the appropriate people are engaged and driving results. Obviously, each risk has a different course of action.

Response 7.2:

Our company will move to monitoring each of its suppliers using the below additional weighted metrics, which sum to an overall EBSC (External Balanced Scorecard) ranking. The company EBSC will be used for existing suppliers post launch.

Environment	Delivery
Responsiveness	Quality

Current and future supply opportunities will be determined based on suppliers' ability to continuously maintain high scores in the above ABSC and EBSC areas.

Response 7.3:

I believe most companies only do this when an issue occurs—wrong approach. Monitoring suppliers on a regular basis is critical—both from an audit standpoint and also checking their financials on a periodic basis (when companies are losing money—they generally take shortcuts, which in my opinion causes issues).

Response 7.4:

They are asked to accumulate their projects, surveys, and costs savings.

Response 7.5:

See above [Response 2.4], as well as monitoring FRR (financial risk rating) of each supplier, which is also tied to purchasing business award decisions in order not to increase supply risk by awarding a financially troubled supplier work they won't be able to perform.

Response 7.6:

Each contingency plan has to be reviewed and updated on an annual basis.

Response 7.7:

My organization measures risk on a consistent basis and makes adjustment to processes and metrics throughout the year. We have a team of analysts and managers that review our metrics and risk at the department level and work with the buyers to address areas needing improvement/adjustment.

QUESTION 8:

Managers were asked to discuss how you monitor and evaluate the performance of supply risk management strategy and processes, and then to consider several interrelated issues.

Response 8:

Our company is unique in that as a company we are really in the advanced development stages of bringing our vehicle, product, to market. Thus, as a company we do not have a history of supply risk management data from our supply base. As a result, we are taking a number of steps in order to mitigate our risk as a new company.

QUESTION 9:

What do you see as the major failure modes in the supply chain today?

Responses 9.1–9.8:

Firm1   Capacity, cost control, quality. Capacities were reduced over the last year with economic downturn and many suppliers are having a hard time bringing back labor or getting financing to increase capacity that is in line with the recovery. As a result, costs are out of control and quality is sacrificed.

Firm2   A major failure mode is the globalization of the supply chain. There is increased lead time for deliveries and possibly higher costs associated with the amount of work necessary ensuring everybody is accurate to cross into our ports and hubs. If an overseas supplier ships the wrong quantity because they read a production report wrong, it will have a negative financial impact on your inventories.

Firm10   Different parts of the supply chain reacting to changes at different rates and may cause shortages or present limits.

Firm15   Cost of quality isn't considered when globally sourcing components (i.e., a couple of air charter, scrapped or reworked material can easily wipe out a business case to source offshore).

Firm23   Communication, standardization, and technology advancement, when related to supply chain, have always seemingly penetrated the aerospace market slower than others. Due to low volumes and strict guidelines there seem to be a lack of priority to take consideration of techniques implemented more readily in commercial, industrial, and automotive markets.

Firm25   In running a lean operation, production can be impacted by a one to two date late delivery. We have encountered delays in transportation delivery due to hub consolidation and lost load issues at hubs during the consolidation process.

Firm32   Faster business cycles (financial constraint—lean staff—lack of flexibility) will cause shorter reaction times in case of risk. Increased global sourcing will increase the number of potential influencing factors. Second tier management and monitoring influence on complex SM-infrastructure in supply chains.

Firm19   The banking industry still concerns me as well as volatility of many countries for war and natural disasters. Also, in developing countries the labor force is now demanding higher wages and China is revaluing their currency, which will impact the cost of doing business in China and predicate cost increases for goods and raw materials produced there.

Question 10:

What do you see as the major failure modes in the supply chain today?

Responses 10.1–10.8:

Firm6   Lack of experience and lack of planning to reduce risk.

Firm7   Understanding of supply chain costs (material/economics), cost reduction initiatives which impact quality.

Firm25   Not evaluating total cost of the supply chain, too many companies look in a shell at their individual work centers rather than evaluating the total supply chain.

Firm31   No way to manage supplier overall risk.

Firm32   Import business to the United States is at risk, countries in Asia now adjust their currency rates, making Asian suppliers much less competitive. Tax laws are changing, which are making it more difficult to import products. Total cost analysis is not conducted when moving overseas, as we only see dollar signs in the piece of the good we buy. Companies do not investigate the total price, including freight likelihood of a quality issue that will support and supply interruption cost, and so on.

Firm12   Dependence on suppliers in emerging regions.

Firm13   Lack of qualified workforce.

Firm32   Bankruptcies will increase in next 12 months. Some supplier groups of specific commodities are consolidating due to the economic conditions. In some industries, the number of suppliers has gone down by over 50%, so in areas where you used to have 2,000 suppliers nationwide supplying the same type of commodity, there are now 100 or less.

Appendix A: Research Questionnaire Results

TABLE A.1

Final Results

General Information (Optional)

Job Title:	Duties:
Firm1 Strategic Buyer	
Firm2 N/A	
Firm3 Supply Chain Leader, Principal	Supplier approval and contract management processes
Firm4 Sr. Inventory Analyst	
Firm5 Strategic Buyer	
Firm6 Strategic Procurement Manager	
Firm7 Senior Buyer	Sourcing, cost reduction
Firm8 Supervisor, Inventory Management	Supervise a team of 5 buyers for U.S. inventory and projects for a distributor
Firm9 Supply Chain Analyst	Forecast orders from customers, manage new product implementation throughout supply chain, determine root cause of late shipments and provide corrective action operations
Firm10 Director of Supply Chain	
Firm11 Director of Supply Chain	Supply chain
Firm12 Commodity Manager	Contract negotiation and supply base transformation
Firm13 Supply Chain Coordinator	Purchasing/Inventory Management
Firm14 Supply Base Manager	Management of supplier relationships and supply base design
Firm15	
Firm16	

Continued

TABLE A.1 *(Continued)*

Final Results

Firm17	Plant Manager	Production, manufacturing process engineering, test engineering and coordination with support functions
Firm18		
Firm19	Senior Scheduler	Assurance of production schedule/material integrity that impact cost, process, and customer delivery
Firm20	Supply Base Manager	Manage all procured direct material supply
Firm21		
Firm22	Supply Chain Manager	Responsible for procurement and inventory control
Firm23	Assistant Buyer	Outside processing coordinator and assist the buyers with entering and processing purchase orders and invoice
Firm24	Project Localization Manager	Setting up our manufacturing in EC(s)
Firm25		
Firm26		SM process and systems
Firm27		
Firm28	Materials Planner	Supply chain planning, raw ingredients
Firm29	Senior Buyer—Iron Components	Sales activity
Firm30	Sales Director	Sales activity
Firm31	Supply Chain Management Program	Strategic procurement, logistics, materials, supplier quality
Firm32	Purchasing Manager	Manager of supply chain
Firm33		
Firm34	Global Sourcing Business Unit Manager	Responsible for all P&L for $8 million import/export operation for various sealing application for engineered polymer systems division
Firm 35		
Firm36	Buyer	Securing products and materials necessary for manufacturing for products
Firm37	Purchasing Manager	
Firm38	Supply Chain Manager	Management of purchasing, sourcing, logistics
Firm39	Import Analyst	Purchase, forecast, and manage import products

Continued

TABLE A.1 *(Continued)*

Final Results

Firm40	Senior Supply Chain Planner	Manage production, inventory, on-time delivery and deployment of ~$20 million in inventory; managing other projects like network planning, inventory strategy, cost savings projects, and new product launches
Firm41		
Firm42	Vice President of Purchasing	All purchasing activities
Firm43		
Firm44	Account Representative	Manage international (JP) procurement component of supply, to sub-assembly plant (MX), quality control and delivery to final assembly in (United States). Includes price negotiations, routing, cost analysis, and so on
Firm45		
Firm46	Director, Global Procurement and Supply Chain Management	Sourcing, contract administration, supplier quality

COMPANY BACKGROUND INFORMATION

The questions in this part should be answered at the level of your entire organization.

Which of the following best describes the *main activity* of your company?*

- ☐ Aerospace/defense
- ☐ Agriculture
- ☐ Automotive
- ☐ Banks/financial services
- ☐ Chemicals
- ☐ Computer hardware
- ☐ Computer software
- ☐ Consumer products
- ☐ Electronics
- ☐ Food
- ☐ Fuel, utilities and power

- ☐ Health care
- ☐ House building and construction
- ☐ Leisure industries
- ☐ Manufacturing
- ☐ Office equipment
- ☐ Public sector
- ☐ Publishing/broadcasting
- ☐ Telecommunications
- ☐ Transportation
- ☐ Other
- ☐ Please specify: _____

What is the *annual sales revenue* of your company?

- ☐ Under $10M
- ☐ $10M–$49M
- ☐ $50M–$99M
- ☐ $100M–$499M
- ☐ $500M–$999M

- ☐ $1B–$9B
- ☐ $10B–$49B
- ☐ $50B–$99B
- ☐ Over $100B

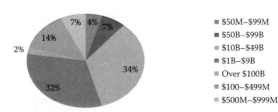

Annual sales revenue.

---

* **Manufacturing:** 39/46 includes **11** automotive first-tier suppliers, **4** automotive OEMs, **3** electronics manufacturers, and **21** other (e.g., office furniture, home appliance, pumps, seals, gauges, valves, hydraulics, aerospace, medical equipment, plumbing fixtures, seats, recreational vehicles, safety equipment, industrial doors, automation equipment, pharmaceuticals, cosmetics, home building material, child care goods, food); 28/46 can be classified as capital-intensive high-volume producers using assembly lines in operations; 11/46 can be classified as low volume producers of highly customized and engineered products. **Non-manufacturing:** 7/46 includes **3** distributors, **1** transportation management, **1** telecommunications, **1** clinical testing, and **1** retailer.

What is the *number of employees* in your company?

☐ Under 50
☐ 50–99
☐ 100–499
☐ 500–999

☐ 1,000–4,999
☐ 5,000–9,999
☐ Over 10,000

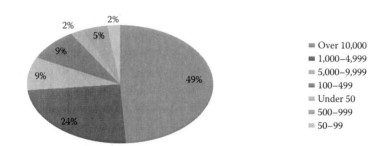

Number of employees.

What is the *ownership structure* of your company?

☐ Privately owned ☐ Publicly owned ☐ Public/privately owned

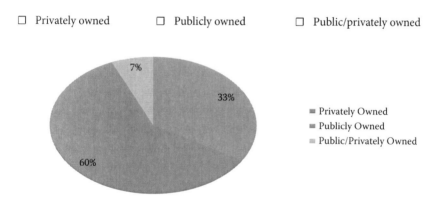

Ownership structure.

Which *geographical regions* account for your sales revenue? (Check all that apply.)

☐ Africa **(16/46 firms)**
☐ North America **(46/46 firms)**
☐ Asia **(34/46 firms)**

☐ Europe **(31/46 firms)**
☐ South America **(30/46 firms)**

MANAGING SUPPLY CHAIN RISK

Managing supply chain risk applies the techniques of risk management to the supply chain. It develops an enterprise view into the risks deep within a supply chain, and gives companies a tool that they can use to identify and manage risks to reduce their potential impact. Effective risk management includes a process that systematically identifies potential failures in the supply chain.

Which best describes your usage of supply chain risk evaluation tools, techniques, and methodologies?[*]

☐ Plan to implement an application within 1–2 years

☐ Plan to evaluate an application within 1–2 years

☐ Currently using an application

☐ No plans to use anything

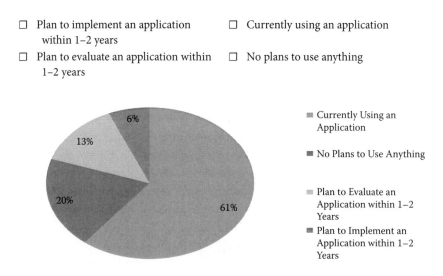

Description of usage.

---

[*] All firms agreed there is no obvious and specific single application for managing supply chain risks on the market today. 61% are actually using existing SCM applications for managing risk. In the absence of risk management applications, these firms (61%) are building risk considerations into existing traditional SCM applications (e.g., spend, contract, and inventory management, demand planning, benchmarking, etc). An additional 6% said they would like to implement an SCM risk application in 1–2 years, and another 13% said they are considering it. This indicates that while actual specific supply chain risk applications are non-existent, interest levels are very high (80%). The 80/20 rule resurfaces. Eighty percent of the firms have placed a high priority on managing supply chain risks and 20% do not.

If you are not using any tools, techniques, or methodologies for managing supply chain risks, then what is the major reason?

☐ Satisfied with current process   ☐ Cannot justify the benefits
☐ Cannot justify the costs   ☐ Lack of skill sets

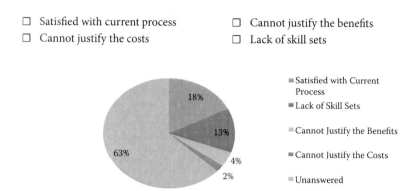

Reasons for non-usage.

Approximately how much do you plan to spend next year for managing risks in the supply chain (e.g., IT, support services, process changes, etc.)? Feel free to skip this question if you are uncomfortable with the dollar signs associated with it.

☐ Less than $500,000   ☐ $500,000–$1,000,000
☐ $1,000,000–$5,000,000   ☐ More than $5,000,000

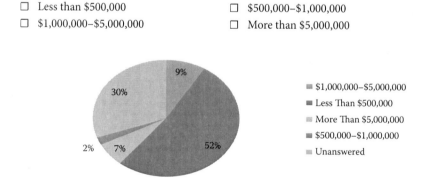

Spending plan.

Will your budget for managing supply chain risks increase, decrease, or stay the same next year?

☐ Increase ☐ Decrease ☐ No change

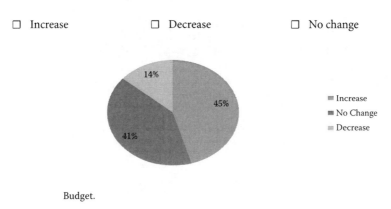

Budget.

Which area within your company usually takes ownership of investments made for managing supply chain risks?

☐ Risk Management ☐ Supply Chain/Purchasing
☐ Legal ☐ Logistics
☐ Accounting/Finance ☐ Manufacturing/Operations
☐ IT ☐ Quality
☐ Other (Please Specify)

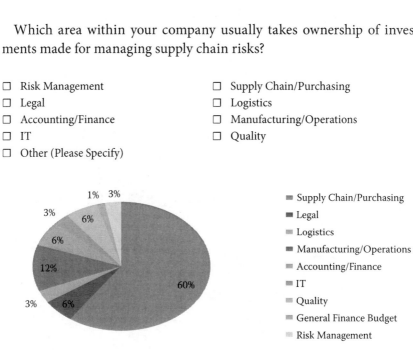

Area of investment ownership.

Where does the funding for managing supply chain risks come from in your company?

☐ General operations budget ☐ Specific departmental budget
☐ General finance budget ☐ General IT budget
☐ Specific budget to address supply chain
　　issues

- Specific Departmental Budget
- Specific Budget to Address Supply Chain Issues
- General Finance Budget
- General Operations Budget
- General IT Budget

Funding.

With a 1 to 7 scale and a sample size of 46 firms, the variance (Var.) for each question can generally be interpreted as follows. A Var. of > 2.00 implies there was a sizeable amount of variation in the responses and <2.00 implies less variation. You will notice that in general, the questions with a high mean (>5.00) had low variances (<2.00). The majority of the companies answered toward the high end (Mean >5.00) with less variation. However, there was a larger amount of variation for questions with a mean of <4.00.

Please circle a number using the 7-point scales with: 1 = Not used to 7 = Extensively used.

To what extent are the following used in managing your supply chain and risks within it?

Information gathering   1 2 3 4 5 6 7
Mean = 5.67, SD = 1.21, Var. = 1.47 (low),
Kurt = −0.41, Skew = 0.66

Training programs   1 2 3 4 5 6 7
Mean = 3.54, SD = 1.59, Var. = 2.52 (high),
Kurt = −0.85, Skew = 0.07

Continued

Joint technology development initiatives   1 2 3 4 5 6 7
Mean = 3.59, SD = 1.47, Var. = 2.16 (high),
 Kurt = –0.57, Skew = 0.37

Partnership formation and long-term agreement   1 2 3 4 5 6 7
Mean = 5.11, SD = 1.08, Var. = 1.17 (low),
 Kurt = 0.69, Skew = –0.67

Supplier development initiatives   1 2 3 4 5 6 7
Mean = 4.83, SD = 1.37, Var. = 1.88 (low),
 Kurt = –1.04, Skew = –0.10

Supplier performance measurement system   1 2 3 4 5 6 7
Mean = 5.35, SD = 1.61, Var. = 2.59 (high),
 Kurt = 0.32, Skew = –1.04

Consistent monitoring and auditing of a supplier's   1 2 3 4 5 6 7
 processes
Mean = 4.59, SD = 1.72, Var. = 2.96 (high),
 Kurt = –1.17, Skew = –0.25

Using an approved list of suppliers   1 2 3 4 5 6 7
Mean = 5.78, SD = 1.18, Var. = 1.40 (low),
 Kurt = 1.25, Skew = –1.09

Multiple sourcing (rather than sole sourcing)   1 2 3 4 5 6 7
Mean = 4.04, SD = 1.36, Var. = 1.86 (low),
 Kurt = –0.30, Skew = –3.36

Visiting supplier operations   1 2 3 4 5 6 7
Mean = 5.04, SD = 1.32, Var. = 1.73 (low),
 Kurt = –0.18, Skew = –0.27

Establishing good communications with supplier   1 2 3 4 5 6 7
Mean = 5.65, SD = 1.04, Var. = 1.08 (low),
 Kurt = –0.21, Skew = –0.074

Increasing product differentiation   1 2 3 4 5 6 7
Mean = 3.91, SD = 1.50, Var. = 2.26 (high),
 Kurt = –0.37, Skew = –0.38

Postponement (delaying the actual commitment of   1 2 3 4 5 6 7
 resources to maintain flexibility)
Mean = 3.70, SD = 1.35, Var. = 1.82 (low),
 Kurt = –0.08, Skew = –0.04

Speculation (forward placement of inventory, forward   1 2 3 4 5 6 7
 buying of raw materials, etc.)
Mean = 4.07, SD = 1.69, Var. = 2.86 (high),
 Kurt = –0.91, Skew = –0.08

Continued

Inventory management (buffers, safety stock levels, optimal orders, and production quantity) 1 2 3 4 5 6 7
Mean = 4.96, SD = 1.69, Var. = 2.84 (high), Kurt = −0.91, Skew = −0.95

Data warehousing 1 2 3 4 5 6 7
Mean = 4.09, SD = 1.76, Var. = 3.10 (very high), Kurt = −0.80, Skew = −0.01

Network design analysis programs 1 2 3 4 5 6 7
Mean = 3.25, SD = 1.94, Var. = 3.77 (very high), Kurt = −1.10, Skew = 0.43

Demand signal repositories 1 2 3 4 5 6 7
Mean = 3.42, SD = 1.85, Var. = 3.43 (very high), Kurt = −1.16, Skew = 0.06

Spending management and analysis 1 2 3 4 5 6 7
Mean = 4.85, SD = 1.53, Var. = 2.35 (high), Kurt = −0.71, Skew = −0.16

Inventory optimization tools 1 2 3 4 5 6 7
Mean = 4.78, SD = 1.66, Var. = 2.77 (high), Kurt = −0.10, Skew = −0.62

Credit and financial data analysis 1 2 3 4 5 6 7
Mean = 4.54, SD = 1.60, Var. = 2.56 (high), Kurt = −0.68, Skew = −0.32

Business process management 1 2 3 4 5 6 7
Mean = 4.65, SD = 1.37, Var. = 1.88 (low), Kurt = −0.98, Skew = −0.20

Hedging strategies (to protect against commodity price swings) 1 2 3 4 5 6 7
Mean = 3.61, SD = 1.63, Var. = 2.64 (high), Kurt = −0.65, Skew = 0.19

Contract mgmt (e.g., leveraging tools to monitor performance against commitments) 1 2 3 4 5 6 7
Mean = 4.48, SD = 1.64, Var. = 2.70 (high), Kurt = −0.67, Skew = −0.29

Benchmarking (internal, external, industry-wide, etc.) 1 2 3 4 5 6 7
Mean = 4.59, SD = 1.54, Var. = 2.38 (high), Kurt = −0.62, Skew = −0.51

Continued

Forecasting techniques (e.g., to pre-build and carry   1   2   3   4   5   6   7
additional inventory of critical items)
Mean = 4.61, SD = 1.57, Var. = 2.47 (high),
  Kurt = −0.72, Skew = −0.21

Contingency planning (jointly with suppliers)   1   2   3   4   5   6   7
Mean = 4.22, SD = 1.25, Var. = 1.55 (low),
  Kurt = −0.82, Skew = 0.07

Please circle a number using the 7-point scales with: 1 = Not satisfied to 7 = Very satisfied.

How satisfied are you with your supply chain group's performance on the following issues?

After sales service performance   1   2   3   4   5   6   7
Mean = 4.57, SD = 1.29, Var. = 1.67 (low),
  Kurt = −1.18, Skew = −0.47

Supplier reliability and continuous supply   1   2   3   4   5   6   7
Mean = 4.85, SD = 0.99, Var. = 0.98 (very low),
  Kurt = 0.46, Skew = −0.84

Inventory management   1   2   3   4   5   6   7
Mean = 4.52, SD = 1.22, Var. = 1.50 (low),
  Kurt = 0.35, Skew = −0.74

Logistics and delivery reliability   1   2   3   4   5   6   7
Mean = 4.96, SD = 1.01, Var. = 1.02 (very low),
  Kurt = −0.70, Skew = −0.32

Lower commodity prices   1   2   3   4   5   6   7
Mean = 3.98, SD = 1.27, Var. = 1.62 (low),
  Kurt = −0.08, Skew = −0.03

Reduced material price volatility   1   2   3   4   5   6   7
Mean = 3.80, SD = 1.51, Var. = 2.29 (high),
  Kurt = −0.68, Skew = −0.01

Reduced disruptions in the supply chain   1   2   3   4   5   6   7
Mean = 4.59, SD = 1.15, Var. = 1.31 (low),
  Kurt = −1.19, Skew = −0.59

Order completeness and correctness   1   2   3   4   5   6   7
Mean = 4.96, SD = 1.11, Var. = 1.24 (low),
  Kurt = 0.01, Skew = −0.31

Continued

Damage-free and defect-free delivery 1 2 3 4 5 6 7
Mean = 5.41, SD = 0.83, Var. = 0.69 (very low),
  Kurt = -0.57, Skew = -0.20

Meeting customer service levels 1 2 3 4 5 6 7
Mean = 5.07, SD = 1.20, Var. = 1.44 (low),
  Kurt = -0.23, Skew = -0.61

Visibility (detailed knowledge of what goes on in other 1 2 3 4 5 6 7
  parts of the supply chain, e.g., finished goods inventory,
  materials inventory, WIP, pipeline inventory, actual
  demands and forecasts, production plans, capacity, yields,
  and order status)
Mean = 4.26, SD = 1.29, Var. = 1.66 (low),
  Kurt = -0.07, Skew = -0.45

Please circle a number using the 7-point scales with: 1 = Strongly disagree to 7 = Strongly agree.

Managing supply chain risk is an increasingly important 1 2 3 4 5 6 7
  initiative for our operations.
Mean = 5.65, SD = 1.30, Var. = 1.70 (low),
  Kurt = 0.31, Skew = -0.88

My workplace plans on evaluating or implementing supply 1 2 3 4 5 6 7
  chain risk tools and technologies.
Mean = 4.98, SD = 1.58, Var. = 2.51 (high),
  Kurt = -0.71, Skew = -0.49

Supplier reliability and continuous supply is the top risk 1 2 3 4 5 6 7
  factor for our supply chain.
Mean = 5.35, SD = 1.34, Var. = 1.79 (low),
  Kurt = 0.20, Skew = -0.80

We have a dedicated budget for activities associated with 1 2 3 4 5 6 7
  managing supply chain risks.
Mean = 3.65, SD = 1.96, Var. = 3.83 (very high),
  Kurt = -1.45, Skew = 0.07

We apply high levels of analytical rigor to assess our supply 1 2 3 4 5 6 7
  chain practices.
Mean = 4.37, SD = 1.53, Var. = 2.33 (high),
  Kurt = -0.75, Skew = -0.19

Supply chain risk initiatives are driven from the bottom up 1 2 3 4 5 6 7
  rather than top down.
Mean = 3.67, SD = 1.56, Var. = 2.45 (high),
  Kurt = -1.24, Skew = 0.28

Continued

We are currently using some form of supply chain risk management tools and services.
    1   2   3   4   5   6   7
Mean = 4.46, SD = 1.93, Var. = 3.72 (very high), Kurt = –1.45, Skew = –0.09

Managing supply chain risks is driven by reactions to failures rather than being proactively driven.
    1   2   3   4   5   6   7
Mean = 4.39, SD = 1.36, Var. = 1.84 (low), Kurt = 0.17, Skew = –0.26

We have placed an increased focus on inventory management to deal with supply risks.
    1   2   3   4   5   6   7
Mean = 4.80, SD = 1.34, Var. = 1.81 (low), Kurt = 1.37, Skew = –1.24

We use network design and optimization tools to cope with uncertainty in the supply chain.
    1   2   3   4   5   6   7
Mean = 3.66, SD = 1.85, Var. = 3.44 (very high), Kurt = –1.18, Skew = 0

Taxes such as excise and VAT impact our supply chain decisions.
    1   2   3   4   5   6   7
Mean = 3.86, SD = 1.69, Var. = 2.86 (high), Kurt = –0.98, Skew = –0.20

A key part of our supply chain management is documenting the likelihood and impact of risks.
    1   2   3   4   5   6   7
Mean = 4.20, SD = 1.67, Var. = 2.78 (high), Kurt = –1.22, Skew = –0.02

Supply chain risk information is accurate and readily available to key decision makers.
    1   2   3   4   5   6   7
Mean = 3.87, SD = 1.57, Var. = 2.47 (high), Kurt = –0.84, Skew = 0.15

Our spending intentions for managing supply chain risks are very high.
    1   2   3   4   5   6   7
Mean = 3.37, SD = 1.57, Var. = 2.47 (high), Kurt = –0.84, Skew = 0.15

Funding for managing supply chain risks will come from a general operations budget.
    1   2   3   4   5   6   7
Mean = 3.91, SD = 1.58, Var. = 2.50 (high), Kurt = –0.70, Skew = 0.16

Continued

We do plan on investing nontrivial amounts in managing supply chain risks.   1 2 3 4 5 6 7
Mean = 4.30, SD = 1.94, Var. = 3.77 (very high),
  Kurt = –1.15, Skew = –0.14

We can actually exploit risk to an advantage by taking calculated risks in the supply chain.   1 2 3 4 5 6 7
Mean = 4.02, SD = 1.86, Var. = 3.46 (very high),
  Kurt = –0.93, Skew = –0.34

I fully understand the activities being performed by our risk management group.   1 2 3 4 5 6 7
Mean = 4.00, SD = 1.63, Var. = 2.66 (high),
  Kurt = –0.92, Skew = 0.34

We are planning to outsource all or some of our risk management functions.   1 2 3 4 5 6 7
Mean = 2.25, SD = 1.28, Var. = 1.63 (low),
  Kurt = 0.31, Skew = 0.91

Risks associated with transit delays or import operations are proactively managed.   1 2 3 4 5 6 7
Mean = 4.52, SD = 1.44, Var. = 2.08 (high),
  Kurt = 0.17, Skew = –0.58

Risks associated with efforts toward shorter production times are proactively managed.   1 2 3 4 5 6 7
Mean = 4.63, SD = 1.31, Var. = 1.70 (low),
  Kurt = 1.01, Skew = –0.71

My workplace uses supply chain risk managers who work closely with corporate risk management.   1 2 3 4 5 6 7
Mean = 2.53, SD = 1.74, Var. = 3.03 (very high),
  Kurt = 0.15, Skew = 1.12

Supply chain employees understand government legislation and geopolitical issues.   1 2 3 4 5 6 7
Mean = 3.70, SD = 1.26, Var. = 1.59 (low),
  Kurt = –0.45, Skew = –0.22

We are prepared to minimize the effects of disruptions (terrorism, weather, theft, etc.).   1 2 3 4 5 6 7
Mean = 3.70, SD = 1.31, Var. = 1.73 (low),
  Kurt = –0.41, Skew = 0.23

Continued

There is no single set of tools or technologies on the market for managing supply chain risks.
1 2 3 4 5 6 7
**Mean = 5.24, SD = 1.49, Var. = 2.23 (high),
Kurt = –0.18, Skew = –0.68**

Without a systematic analysis technique to assess risk, much can go wrong in a supply chain.
1 2 3 4 5 6 7
**Mean = 5.54, SD = 1.03, Var. = 1.05 (low),
Kurt = –0.50, Skew = –0.25**

We have placed an emphasis on incident reporting to decrease the effects of disruptions.
1 2 3 4 5 6 7
**Mean = 4.50, SD = 1.43, Var. = 2.03 (high),
Kurt = 0.25, Skew = –0.67**

Please circle a number using the 7-point scales with: 1 = Strongly disagree to 7 = Strongly agree.

Our suppliers are required to have secure sourcing, business continuity, and contingency plans.
1 2 3 4 5 6 7
**Mean = 4.62, SD = 1.71, Var. = 2.92 (high),
Kurt = –1.11, Skew = –0.30**

It is critical for us to have an easily understood method to identify and manage supply chain risk.
1 2 3 4 5 6 7
**Mean = 5.30, SD = 1.23, Var. = 1.51 (low),
Kurt = 0.064, Skew = –0.84**

Proactive risk mitigation efforts applied to the supply chain is common practice for us.
1 2 3 4 5 6 7
**Mean = 4.33, SD = 1.49, Var. = 2.22 (high),
Kurt = –0.53, Skew = –0.47**

We are hedging our raw material exposure to reduce input cost volatility.
1 2 3 4 5 6 7
**Mean = 3.78, SD = 1.49, Var. = 2.22 (high),
Kurt = –0.65, Skew = –0.42**

Key metrics are in place to measure the risk associated with key suppliers.
1 2 3 4 5 6 7
**Mean = 4.65, SD = 1.68, Var. = 2.81 (high),
Kurt = 0.37, Skew = –0.96**

Our company uses real-time inventory information and analytics in managing the supply chain.
1 2 3 4 5 6 7
**Mean = 4.76, SD = 1.52, Var. = 2.32 (high),
Kurt = –0.91, Skew = –0.44**

Continued

Risks of moving manufacturing facilities overseas are   1   2   3   4   5   6   7
carefully evaluated.
Mean = 5.65, SD = 1.15, Var. = 1.33 (low),
  Kurt = 0.09, Skew = –0.83

Risks of not being able to fulfill a spike in consumer   1   2   3   4   5   6   7
demand are carefully evaluated.
Mean = 5.22, SD = 1.25, Var. = 1.55 (low),
  Kurt = –0.31, Skew = –0.43

We actively benchmark our supply chain risk processes   1   2   3   4   5   6   7
against competitors.
Mean = 3.57, SD = 1.68, Var. = 2.83 (high),
  Kurt = –1.19, Skew = –0.21

We have had supply disruptions that have caused financial   1   2   3   4   5   6   7
hardships in the past 24 months.
Mean = 4.72, SD = 2.01, Var. = 4.03 (very high),
  Kurt = –0.70, Skew = –0.64

We are very concerned about our supply chain resiliency   1   2   3   4   5   6   7
and the failure implications.
Mean = 4.78, SD = 1.59, Var. = 2.53 (high),
  Kurt = –0.62, Skew = –0.53

Please rank order five of the following risks, which would have the greatest severity or impact on your supply chain if it occurred (e.g., 1 = most severe, 2 = second most severe, etc.). The impact might be in terms of financial losses, delivery delays, quality to the customer, loss of reputation, property damage, and so on.

- ☐ Supplier failure/reliability
- ☐ Natural disasters or accidents (tsunamis, hurricanes, fires, etc.)
- ☐ Geopolitical events (terrorism, war, etc.)
- ☐ Government regulations (SOX, SEC, Clean Air Act, OSHA, EU)
- ☐ Logistics failure
- ☐ Contract failure
- ☐ Intellectual property infringement
- ☐ Weaknesses in the local infrastructures
- ☐ Obtaining proper bonds and licenses
- ☐ Customs acts/trade restrictions and protectionism
- ☐ Ethical issues (working practices, health, safety, etc.)
- ☐ Port/cargo security (information, freight, vandalism, sabotage, etc.)

Continued

- [ ] Internal and external theft
- [ ] Property development—local codes and requirements
- [ ] Unfamiliar business and property laws
- [ ] Legal liabilities and litigation
- [ ] Return policy and product recall requirements
- [ ] Lack of trust with partners
- [ ] Language and educational barriers
- [ ] Measuring tools—metrics translate differently
- [ ] Information delays, scarcity, sharing, and infrastructure breakdown
- [ ] Attracting and retaining skilled labor
- [ ] Bankruptcy, ruin, or default of suppliers, shippers, etc.
- [ ] Degree of control over operations
- [ ] Fraud or scandal
- [ ] Strikes—labor, buyers, and suppliers
- [ ] Commodity cost volatility
- [ ] Currency exchange, interest, and/or inflation rate fluctuations
- [ ] Banking regulations and tighter financing conditions
- [ ] Insurance coverage
- [ ] Diminishing capacities (financial, production, structural, etc.)
- [ ] Customer-related (demand change, system failure, payment delay)
- [ ] Contamination exposure—food, germs, infections
- [ ] Energy/raw material shortages and power outages
- [ ] Tax issues (VAT, transfer pricing, excise, etc.)

TABLE A.2

Frequency of Responses

Risk		Frequency
Supplier failure/reliability	⬆	41
Bankruptcy, ruin, or default of suppliers, shippers, etc.	➡	22
Logistic failure	➡	20
Commodity cost volatility	➡	18
Natural disasters or accidents	➡	15
Strikes — labor, buyers, and shippers	➡	15
Diminishing capacity	⬇	10
Government regulations	⬇	9
Attracting and retaining skilled labor	⬇	8
Customer-related (demand change, system failure)	⬇	8
Lack of trust with partners	⬇	7
Currency exchange, interest, and/or inflation rate fluctuations	⬇	7
Intellectual property infringement	⬇	7
Energy/raw material shortages and power outages	⬇	6
Geopolitical event	⬇	6
Ethical issues	⬇	5
Legal liabilities and litigation	⬇	5
Information delays, scarcity, sharing, and infrastructure breakdown	⬇	5
Customs acts/trade restrictions and protectionism	⬇	4
Contract failure	⬇	4
Degree of control over operations	⬇	3
Contamination exposure — food, germs, infections	⬇	3
Measuring tools — metrics translate differently	⬇	2
Weakness in the local infrastructure	⬇	2
Internal and external theft	⬇	2
Return policy and product recall requirements	⬇	2
Banking regulations and tighter financing conditions	⬇	2
Port/cargo security	⬇	1
Tax issues	⬇	1

The numbers in Table A.2 indicate the frequency of the responses. Please list any other risks not listed above that impact your supply chain:

Do you believe the supply chain risk will increase, stay the same, or decrease in the next 1–2 years? Please check a box.	**Risk Will *Decrease* in the Next 1–2 Years**	**Risk Will Not Change in the Next 1–2 Years**	**Risk Will *Increase* in the Next 1–2 Years**
Supplier failure/reliability	☐	☐	☐
Natural disasters or accidents (tsunamis, hurricanes, fires, etc.)	☐	☐	☐
Geopolitical events (terrorism, war, etc.)	☐	☐	☐
Government regulations (SOX, SEC, Clean Air Act, OSHA, EU)	☐	☐	☐
Logistics failure	☐	☐	☐
Contract failure	☐	☐	☐

Continued

Do you believe the supply chain risk will increase, stay the same, or decrease in the next 1–2 years? Please check a box.	Risk Will *Decrease* in the Next 1–2 Years	Risk Will Not Change in the Next 1–2 Years	Risk Will *Increase* in the Next 1–2 Years
Intellectual property infringement	☐	☐	☐
Weaknesses in the local infrastructures	☐	☐	☐
Obtaining proper bonds and licenses	☐	☐	☐
Customs acts/trade restrictions and protectionism	☐	☐	☐
Ethical issues (working practices, health, safety, etc.)	☐	☐	☐
Port/cargo security (information, freight, vandalism, sabotage, etc.)	☐	☐	☐
Internal and external theft	☐	☐	☐
Property development —local codes and requirements	☐	☐	☐
Unfamiliar business and property laws	☐	☐	☐
Legal liabilities and issues	☐	☐	☐
Return policy and product recall requirements	☐	☐	☐
Lack of trust with partners	☐	☐	☐
Language and educational barriers	☐	☐	☐
Measuring tools—metrics translate differently	☐	☐	☐
Information delays, scarcity, sharing, and infrastructure breakdown	☐	☐	☐
Attracting and retaining skilled labor	☐	☐	☐
Bankruptcy, ruin, or default of suppliers, shippers, etc.	☐	☐	☐
Degree of control over operations	☐	☐	☐
Fraud or scandal	☐	☐	☐
Strikes—labor, buyers, and suppliers	☐	☐	☐
Commodity cost volatility	☐	☐	☐
Currency exchange, interest, and/or inflation rate fluctuations	☐	☐	☐
Banking regulations and tighter financing conditions	☐	☐	☐
Insurance coverage	☐	☐	☐
Diminishing capacities (financial, production, structural, etc.)	☐	☐	☐
Customer-related (demand change, system failure, payment delay)	☐	☐	☐
Contamination exposure—food, germs, infections	☐	☐	☐
Energy/raw material shortages and power outages	☐	☐	☐
Tax issues (VAT, transfer pricing, excise, etc.)	☐	☐	☐

TABLE A.3

Increase, Decrease, or No Change in Supply Chain Risk

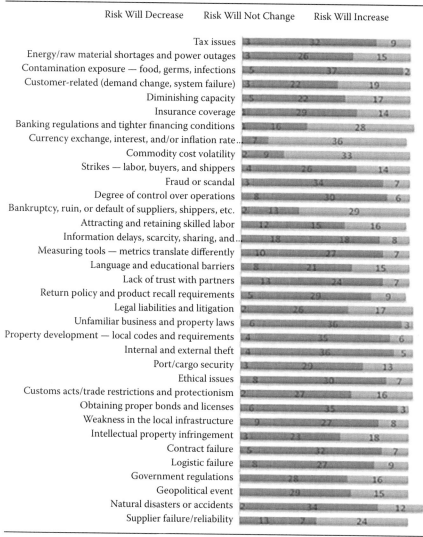

What processes and techniques does your company use to identify and analyze risk in its supply chain?

Firm1   Initial supplier evaluations, QS audits, and industry benchmarking.

Firm2   Financial risk assessment, market share risk assessment (various industry reports), and supply chain commodity strategy (short- and long-term analysis).

Continued

Firm3	Financial reports, supplier questionnaires, candidate comparison metrics (supplier profiling form, supply chain PFMEA). For lifecycle management, we have supplier report cards and our buyers conduct periodic supply chain reviews.
Firm4	We have a large number of tools and groups that are solely focused on analyzing and reducing risks.
Firm5	Supplier performance data and industry benchmarking.
Firm6	TQI
Firm7	Benchmarking, communication with suppliers, financial reviews, and supplier quality audits.
Firm8	We use reporting techniques for supplier evaluation as well as internal evaluation and have processes set in place for all the different situations that occur in business everyday. We have several methods of training employees at all levels. We also have procedures set in place to comply with ISO standards and are audited on a regular basis.
Firm9	Information and data on suppliers, logistics, and operations. Supplier metrics, supplier on-time delivery, financial analysis of suppliers. Capacity planning for operations and suppliers. Lead time analysis for project management.
Firm10	Management review.
Firm11	Primary technique is supplier scorecard and secondary technique is supplier audits.
Firm12	Raw material aggregation programs, lessons learned databases on source of supply transitions, long-term contracts, supplier development, and supplier measurement systems (OTD, PPM, financial health).
Firm13	Do not have any specific processes to analyze the risk in our supply chain.
Firm14	Supplier financial performance review, supplier operation performance review, business continuity plans from suppliers, stakeholder survey, viability process annually, and supply assurance register.
Firm15	Supplier qualification process, ERP/Kanban model for long-term capacity planning, and online supplier portal system.
Firm16	Majority of our risk is centered around oil prices/value of dollar, and ID theft/fraud.
Firm17	Supplier performance management process to evaluate and identify supplier performance trends, Dun & Bradstreet supplier risk analysis based on accounts payable performance of supplier, and supplier management process with quarterly business reviews for "strategic" suppliers.
Firm18	Historical data, research industry competitions, case studies, and consultant.
Firm19	Back-up carriers, effort to have a local supply base, corporate purchasing as a resource to apply leverage, standardized with different plants on contingency plans, material, milk-runs, and so on.

Continued

Firm20	Overall supply chain visibility and sharing of information. We have contingency plans for all commodities. We evaluate and identify high-impact suppliers on several different criteria. We use many different techniques to evaluate risk.
Firm21	Supplier selection and management processes and tools.
Firm22	We use Excel spreadsheets to monitor and analyze supply issues, we are working on duel sourcing our main items to reduce the reliance we have on our suppliers, we are also working with our suppliers to make them more "flexible" to contend with our short lead times to our customers.
Firm23	
Firm24	
Firm25	Biggest risk is evaluating sources overseas—cost is king, evaluation of supplier's capabilities should be number 1 with cost emphasized as second.
Firm26	Risk management groups in organization to monitor supplier "health," global business hot spots, logistics issues, commodity risk, and so on. Using a variety of internal and external tools. We subscribe to a variety of services that provide updated economic and business information.
Firm27	Risk analysis and monitoring technique.
Firm28	Project inventory and service levels, cross-functional team works together to attempt to mitigate, and as updates on events that could affect our S.C, arise, and cross-functional teams put in place to minimize risk.
Firm29	Sourcing recommendation sheets: A summary of quotations for new business that takes into account all cost aspect; PPM and rejects, delivery rating, financial scores, total spending with supplies, % of supplier total business.
Firm30	Internal RLA documents which include engineering and sales/marketing.
Firm31	Mostly bottom up issues, and internal training classes.
Firm32	We perform what is called a *purchase risk assessment*, which basically reviews the financial viability of a company, their ability to provide continuous supply, their technical capability and their capacity over time.
Firm33	Supply chain analysis, in-depth financial assessment on an annual basis, and on-site capability review awards of substantial projects.
Firm34	Process done extensively at top level in organization regarding key commodity markets and supplier's organization does poor job of effectively communicating from top down.
Firm35	Supplier risk analysis. Run 1× per year using metrics from previous year other factors to determine over top 10 risky suppliers.
Firm36	Open communication with key suppliers and supplier evolution.
Firm37	Supplier development, SSA = financial review yearly, visits.

Continued

Firm38 Our current risk assessment is a homegrown tool which utilizes performance data such as quality and delivery, financial risk, % of commodity ownership as well as process risk classification and component risk classification as it relates to potential for injury to patient in case of failure.

Firm39 We have multiple systems that are monitored by various teams that provide reporting and updates of potential risk. Reports include logistical, operational, and inventory risk. Each group has a unique system that is measured against our current metrics. Each analyst is responsible for his/her suppliers when issues arise.

Firm40 Integrated business process, forecasting techniques and analysis, safety stock, capacity and network planning, long-term supplier partnerships, multi-sourcing, rigorous safety and training requirements for plan operations, extensive food safety processes, mandatory ethics training for all employees, price hedging for commodities, POS data tracking with some customers to proactively identify demand trends, vendor management inventory, supplier performance measurement, and extensive product development process and stage gate process for new innovation.

Firm41

Firm42 Supplier monitoring, interview key executives, and financial review.

Firm43 Implementing and executing supplier quality management system and regular dialog with key suppliers on KPI.

Firm44

Firm45 FEMA, supplier risk assessment, and financial rankings.

Firm46 We only source to suppliers and carriers with very high level of competency.

What do you see as the major failure modes in the supply chain today?

Firm1 Design and project management skills of suppliers.

Firm2 Quality of sourcing from low-cost countries.

Firm3 Day to day the largest failure is non-conforming product and failure to deliver on time or the required amount.

Firm4 Launching new models under a strict timeline.

Firm5 Logistics, single sourcing, supplier failure (not meeting demands), and customer specifications.

Firm6 Lack of experience and lack of planning to reduce risk.

Firm7 Understanding of supply chain costs (material/economics), cost reduction initiatives, which impact quality.

Continued

Firm8	The elements not in our control—carriers causing damage who are paid by suppliers, volatility of the commodity market, and so on. We try to be proactive in dealing with these things, but for the most part they cannot be predicted.
Firm9	Suppliers' inability to deliver on time, error in forecasting customer demand, delays in supply chains due to long lead time components, honesty from suppliers.
Firm10	Lack of customer forecast and project customization versus standardization.
Firm11	MFG strategies from 1st/2nd tier supplier to BEMs given pressure to resolve lead times.
Firm12	Uncertainty in utilizing unproven suppliers in emerging regions, risk of bankruptcy in domestic suppliers who cannot either mitigate or absorb increase in raw materials and energy costs.
Firm13	Lack of sound information/communication.
Firm14	Tier 2 management, financial viability of suppliers, business management performance, and labor relations.
Firm15	Lack of emphasis at suppliers on process flow, lot size reduction, and process reliability.
Firm16	The major failure mode involves the impact of oil prices and government regulations on consumer demand models. ID theft and employee fraud have also proven a challenge in today's supply chain.
Firm17	Availability of material through the supply hierarchy, cost volatility driven by inflation, lack of consistent supplier/buyer communication.
Firm18	Infrastructure, economy, and communication.
Firm19	Disconnect between carrier and supplier at times and real-time information, EDI order feeds, timely receipts to assure accurate inventory.
Firm20	Raw material costs, supplier cash flow issues, bankruptcy, and volatility in the market.
Firm21	Inventory planning/positioning and cost containment.
Firm22	We single source most items so we are held hostage to them in regards to price and lead times.
Firm23	Companies failing to use up-to-date MRP systems, and not accepting change. By relying on old procedures, companies are missing a lot of information that can be accurate and readily available.
Firm24	For us it is suppliers doing what they say when they say it and our ability to control shipments in ever tightening deliveries for our customers.
Firm25	Not evaluating total cost of the supply chain; too many companies look in a shell at their individual work centers rather than evaluating the total supply chain.

Continued

Firm26   Lots of data available, but difficult to analyze in order to provide good information to make appropriate decisions. Difficult to keep everyone in "readiness" mode.

Firm27   Supplier reliability and logistical failure.

Firm28   Communication breakdown, supplier relationships, and late estimating variances.

Firm29   Bankruptcy, commodity pricing/volatility, and demand fluctuation and long lead times.

Firm30   Supplier maintaining the program launch timeline.

Firm31   No way to manage supplier overall risk.

Firm32   Import business to the United States is at risk, countries in Asia now adjust their currency rates, making Asian suppliers much less competitive. Tax laws are changing, which are making it more difficult to import products. Total cost analysis is not conducted when moving overseas, as we only see dollar signs in the piece of the good we buy. Companies do not investigate the total price including freight likelihood of a quality issue that will support, supply interruption cost, and so on.

Firm33   Credit crunch, decrease in industry sales volume, systematic over capacity in supply chain, raw material/energy price escalation.

Firm34   Volatility in commodity markets, plastics, PTFE, rubber, shipping costs.

Firm35   Commodity price volatility and supply chain trust.

Firm36   Over capacity, overseas material transit, over maintaining low inventory level, and customer demanding/restricting product source based on country.

Firm37   Relationship building, trust.

Firm38   Quality defects due to lack of process controls and effective quality systems at supplier, missed/late deliveries and issues with reaction time due to larger number of suppliers in low cost countries, supplier bankruptcy or other financial issues and its impact on continuity of supply.

Firm39   VMI (too many vendors with poor supply chains increase risk), unrealistic metrics, and merchandising.

Firm40   Forecast variability, commodity pricing volatility.

Firm41

Firm42   C-11, commodity pricing, and payment delay.

Firm43   Delivery reliability to promise dates and price increase request.

Firm44

Firm45   Financial and people turnover.

Firm46   Potential bankruptcies due to financial stability issues in the auto industry.

What do you see as the major failure modes in the supply chain in the future?

Firm1   Design and project management, and talent management by suppliers.

Firm2   Lead times due to energy challenges.

Firm3   Major concerns are labor practices, environmental implications, and the upcoming world custom codes (WCO SAFE Framework, EU Community Customs Code).

Firm4   The economy.

Firm5   Same as today.

Firm6   Lack of experience of procurement professionals.

Firm7   Financial instability, raw materials, and economic increases.

Firm8   The same as above, as well as the issues that come about with global expansion as well as increasing acquisitions which cause the business to get even larger.

Firm9   Raw material shortages, natural disaster delays, single sourced product, and supplier bankruptcy disruptions.

Firm10 Commodity pricing, availability, and logistics.

Firm11 Less loyalty to supply base/partnership with the "Internet generation."

Firm12 Dependence on suppliers in emerging regions.

Firm13 Lack of qualified workforce.

Firm14 Managing long supply chains, sub-tier management, financial viability, and labor relations.

Firm15 Lack of emphasis at suppliers on process flow, lot size reduction, and process reliability.

Firm16 ID theft and fraud are expected to increase, whoever is elected as the next president of the United States could drastically impact supply chain through changes in expectations as well as potential new emissions or "green" policies or regulations.

Firm17 Quality, delivery, and cost.

Firm18 Alternative energy and lack of infrastructure.

Firm19 100% system inventory integrity and ability to proactively react to customer needs from a lean delivery standpoint in response to the continued effort that inventory reductions will be on-going from customers causing more process focus and streamline need on receipts, order feeds, on-time delivery performance, and so on.

Firm20 I see the same issues plaguing the automotive supply chain as above until the market settles. At that time the bankruptcy/takeover issues will subside and customer/supplier cash flows will become healthier. Then the peaks and valleys in the market and raw material costs will be smaller and easier to ride out.

Firm21 Inventory planning/positioning, cost containment supply security.

Continued

Firm22   Material availability and price increase.

Firm23   Companies failing to use up to date MRP systems, and not accepting change. By relying on old procedures, companies are missing a lot of information that can be accurate and readily available.

Firm24   Well assuming we don't plunge into a depression here, it remains as in the previous question.

Firm25   Not evaluating the current risks around the world versus cost of the supply chain, a recent example is everyone was looking at the cost of China and now with the cost of shipping the trends has started to reverse itself. Need to focus on the risk of the commodity versus the cost of implementing the change not the short-term gain.

Firm26   Geopolitical impacts, safety of materials/products from emerging nations, meltdowns due to natural disasters.

Firm27   Legal liabilities and government regulations.

Firm28   Communication breakdown, supplier relationships, and late estimating variances.

Firm29   Transportation costs, exchange rates, commodity costs, financial stability, and market changes.

Firm30   Lack of complete understanding of supply base capabilities.

Firm31   Logistics costs, material increases, and more competition.

Firm32   Bankruptcies will increase in next 12 months. Some supplier groups of specific commodities are consolidating due to the economic conditions. In some industries, the number of suppliers has gone down by over 50%, so in areas where you used to have 2,000 suppliers nationwide supplying the same type of commodity, there are now 100 or less. The automotive industry and their negotiating techniques have ruined and shut down suppliers. The cost pressures are immense in today's economy, forcing customers to squeeze their suppliers.

Firm33   Credit crunch, decrease in industry sales volume, systematic over capacity in supply chain, raw material/energy price escalation.

Firm34   Volatility in commodity markets, plastics, PTFE, rubber, shipping costs.

Firm35   Material availability and inventory management processes/policy.

Firm36   Low inventory levels, customer demand, and long transit time.

Firm37   Sometimes you need to take calculated risk.

Firm38   Quality defects due to lack of process controls and effective quality systems at supplier, missed/late deliveries, and issues with reaction time due to larger number of suppliers in low cost countries, supplier bankruptcy or other financial issues and its impact on continuity of supply. Increased exposure to financial issues at our suppliers due to the current economic conditions.

Firm39   I think our current systems need to be updated to today's technology and a new ERP system implemented. Our company currently uses way too many systems to run the supply chain which increases the risk of disconnect and error.

Continued

Firm40 Forecast variability, commodity pricing volatility.

Firm41

Firm42 C-11, commodity pricing, and payment delay.

Firm43 Continued price pressure from prolonged economic downturn.

Firm44

Firm45 Financial due to low volumes and global capacity.

Firm46 Longer pipelines due to global sourcing.

Failure mode and effects analysis (FMEA) is a tool for identifying, analyzing, and prioritizing potential failures. FMEA is a well documented and proven technique commonly used to evaluate the risk for failures in product and process designs. Every potential failure identified is evaluated based on likelihood and severity.

If your company is *not* currently using the FMEA model, it is because…[*]

Please circle a number using the 7-point scales with: 1 = Strongly disagree to 7 = Strongly agree.

There is no noticeable "explicit" value yet.　　　　1　2　3　4　5　6　7
Mean = 4.43, SD = 1.79, Var. = 3.22 (very high),
Kurt = −0.95, Skew = −0.36

There is not enough knowledge of the FMEA procedure.　1　2　3　4　5　6　7
Mean = 5.27, SD = 1.48, Var. = 2.20 (high),
Kurt = 0.84, Skew = −0.97

FMEA is too time-consuming.　　　　　　　1　2　3　4　5　6　7
Mean = 4.10, SD = 1.52, Var. = 2.31 (high),
Kurt = −0.24, Skew = −0.38

It is too confusing or complicated.　　　　　1　2　3　4　5　6　7
Mean = 3.50, SD = 1.48, Var. = 2.19 (high),
Kurt = −1.02, Skew = 0.14

It would not be compatible with our software or processes.　1　2　3　4　5　6　7
Mean = 3.57, SD = 1.81, Var. = 3.29 (very high),
Kurt = −1.27, Skew = 0.02

It is not recognized or required by our industry.　　1　2　3　4　5　6　7
Mean = 4.21, SD = 1.64, Var. = 2.69 (high),
Kurt = −0.70, Skew = −0.42

Continued

---

[*] The majority of the companies do not use FMEA (27/46 were not users).

It is difficult for us to estimate failure modes using tools   1   2   3   4   5   6   7
such as the FMEA model.
Mean = 3.96, SD = 1.32, Var. = 1.74 (low),
  Kurt = –0.49, Skew = –0.35

Not enough failures are experienced to justify using it.   1   2   3   4   5   6   7
Mean = 3.62, SD = 1.82, Var. = 3.32 (very high),
  Kurt = –1.19, Skew = 0.12

Never heard of FMEA.   1   2   3   4   5   6   7
Mean = 2.69, SD = 2.38, Var. = 5.65 (very high),
  Kurt = –0.74, Skew = 1

If your company currently uses the FMEA model, then please answer the rest of the survey.*

    1. Are functional teams established to implement your FMEA procedure (**Yes** or **No**)?

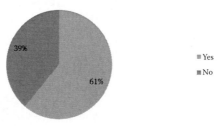

Survey item 1.

    2. Are the FMEA procedures and goals clearly communicated to all employees (**Yes** or **No**)?

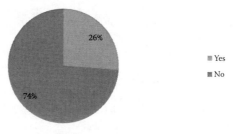

Survey item 2.

---

* Only 19/46 firms surveyed were formal users of the FMEA model.

3. Are the FMEA procedures and goals clearly communicated to supply chain employees (**Yes** or **No**)?

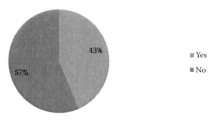

Survey item 3.

**Please circle a number using the 7-point scales with: 1 = Not an impor-
tant reason to 7 = Very important reason.**

What is the reason for using FMEA?

Needed for quality system   1   2   3   4   5   6   7
Mean = 5.62, SD = 1.91, Var. = 3.65 (very high),
Kurt = 1.57, Skew = –1.53

To improve process performance   1   2   3   4   5   6   7
Mean = 6.19, SD = 1.12, Var. = 1.26 (low),
Kurt = 2.23, Skew = –1.58

To reduce total costs   1   2   3   4   5   6   7
Mean = 5.00, SD = 1.55, Var. = 2.40 (high),
Kurt = 1.13, Skew = –1.16

Reduce total failures whether big or small   1   2   3   4   5   6   7
Mean = 6.33, SD = 0.97, Var. = 0.93(very low),
Kurt = 1.52, Skew = –1.50

Contractor/customer requirements   1   2   3   4   5   6   7
Mean = 4.86, SD = 1.85, Var. = 3.43 (very high),
Kurt = 0.03, Skew = –0.87

Required by upper management   1   2   3   4   5   6   7
Mean = 4.69, SD = 1.78, Var. = 3.16 (very high),
Kurt = –0.03, Skew = –0.90

Improve image of the company   1   2   3   4   5   6   7
Mean = 4.14, SD = 2.03, Var. = 4.13 (very high),
Kurt = –1.31, Skew = –0.29

Please circle a number using the 7-point scales with: 1 = Strongly disagree to 7 = Strongly agree.

Customer requirements were used when developing FMEA.   1 2 3 4 5 6 7
Mean = 5.05, SD = 1.80, Var. = 3.25 (very high),
Kurt = 0.58, Skew = –1.10

Management has provided the resources and provisions for enabling employees to use FMEA.   1 2 3 4 5 6 7
Mean = 4.75, SD = 1.48, Var. = 2.20 (high),
Kurt = 0.50, Skew = –0.81

The use of FMEA has led to: higher product reliability.   1 2 3 4 5 6 7
Mean = 2.69, SD = 1.64, Var. = 2.68 (high),
Kurt = 2.68, Skew = –1.80

The use of FMEA has led to: higher product quality.   1 2 3 4 5 6 7
Mean = 5.80, SD = 1.24, Var. = 1.54 (low),
Kurt = 3.81, Skew = –1.79

The use of FMEA has led to: better quality planning.   1 2 3 4 5 6 7
Mean = 5.45, SD = 1.57, Var. = 2.47 (high),
Kurt = –0.69, Skew = –0.67

The use of FMEA has led to: continuous improvement in product and process design.   1 2 3 4 5 6 7
Mean = 5.45, SD = 1.36, Var. = 1.84 (low),
Kurt = 1.42, Skew = –1.36

The use of FMEA has led to: lower manufacturing costs.   1 2 3 4 5 6 7
Mean = 4.75, SD = 1.74, Var. = 3.04 (very high),
Kurt = –0.55, Skew = –0.57

The FMEA process covers the entire global supply chain.   1 2 3 4 5 6 7
Mean = 4.21, SD = 1.87, Var. = 3.51 (very high),
Kurt = –1.18, Skew = 0.17

Global suppliers of your organization are encouraged to implement FMEA.   1 2 3 4 5 6 7
Mean = 4.74, SD = 1.73, Var. = 2.98 (high),
Kurt = –0.05, Skew = –0.70

FMEA is often too vague and causes confusion for those in the supply chain.   1 2 3 4 5 6 7
Mean = 4.11, SD = 0.88, Var. = 0.77(very low),
Kurt = 0.21, Skew = –0.78

Continued

The format of FMEA software and documentation is consistent within all participants.   1 2 3 4 5 6 7

Mean = 3.32, SD = 1.42, Var. = 2.01 (high),
Kurt = –0.74, Skew = 0.03

Design requirements are defined in quantifiable terms to all parts of the supply chain.   1 2 3 4 5 6 7

Mean = 3.58, SD = 1.26, Var. = 1.59 (low),
Kurt = –0.81, Skew = –0.57

The process ensures the inclusion of input from both suppliers and customers in SCM.   1 2 3 4 5 6 7

Mean = 3.95, SD = 1.39, Var. = 1.94 (low),
Kurt = –0.48, Skew = –0.45

FMEA is a group-oriented assignment.   1 2 3 4 5 6 7

Mean = 4.74, SD = 1.48, Var. = 2.20 (high),
Kurt = –0.84, Skew = 0.05

The current FMEA could be improved in terms of organization and efficiency.   1 2 3 4 5 6 7

Mean = 5.16, SD = 1.21, Var. = 1.47 (low),
Kurt = –0.52, Skew = –0.13

I would be more likely to use FMEA if our IT/ERP system included it.   1 2 3 4 5 6 7

Mean = 4.25, SD = 1.65, Var. = 2.72 (high),
Kurt = –0.49, Skew = –0.05

FMEA is applied in all functional areas of the company, including supply chain management.   1 2 3 4 5 6 7

Mean = 4.15, SD = 1.60, Var. = 2.56 (high),
Kurt = –1.01, Skew = –0.44

The FMEA process is the job of a few personnel and implementation is not widespread.   1 2 3 4 5 6 7

Mean = 4.37, SD = 1.50, Var. = 2.25 (high),
Kurt = –0.68, Skew = 0.17

Please circle a number using the 7–point scales with: 1 = Not an issue to 7 = Major issue.

Since using FMEA, how much of an issue and source of difficulty have the following factors been?

Obtaining accurate quality information.　　　　　　　　1　2　3　4　5　6　7
Mean = 4.05, SD = 1.23, Var. = 1.52 (low),
　Kurt = 0.84, Skew = −0.66

Finding reliable data.　　　　　　　　　　　　　　　1　2　3　4　5　6　7
Mean = 4.10, SD = 1.25, Var. = 1.57 (low),
　Kurt = 0.75, Skew = −0.74

The ability to explain a defect clearly and understandably.　1　2　3　4　5　6　7
Mean = 3.95, SD = 1.35, Var. = 1.83 (low),
　Kurt = −0.14, Skew = 0.50

Identifying preventative actions for each failure.　　　　1　2　3　4　5　6　7
Mean = 3.84, SD = 1.38, Var. = 1.92 (low),
　Kurt = −0.55, Skew = −0.25

Team commitment, members know and understand the　　1　2　3　4　5　6　7
　importance.
Mean = 4.37, SD = 1.42, Var. = 2.02 (high),
　Kurt = −0.54, Skew = 0.43

Lack of time, inability to work around members'　　　　1　2　3　4　5　6　7
　schedules to set up time.
Mean = 4.68, SD = 1.42, Var. = 2.01 (high),
　Kurt = −0.74, Skew = −0.03

Determining how much detail is necessary to complete　　1　2　3　4　5　6　7
　the analysis.
Mean = 4.53, SD = 1.35, Var. = 1.82 (low),
　Kurt = 1.54, Skew = −0.67

Lack of creativity.　　　　　　　　　　　　　　　　1　2　3　4　5　6　7
Mean = 3.37, SD = 1.30, Var. = 1.69 (low),
　Kurt = −0.78, Skew = −0.44

The team's ability to agree on potential failures and why　1　2　3　4　5　6　7
　they occur.
Mean = 3.68, SD = 1.11, Var. = 1.23 (low),
　Kurt = −0.56, Skew = 0.44

Continued

Getting the team involved, motivated, trained, and focused.

1 2 3 4 5 6 7

Mean = 4.32, SD = 1.38, Var. = 1.89 (low),
Kurt = −0.80, Skew = 0.36

Finding risk priority numbers (RPNs).

1 2 3 4 5 6 7

Mean = 3.58, SD = 1.07, Var. = 1.15 (low),
Kurt = 0.54, Skew = −0.84

Difficulty in identifying and ranking severity of the failures.

1 2 3 4 5 6 7

Mean = 3.74, SD = 1.41, Var. = 1.98 (low),
Kurt = −0.67, Skew = −0.14

Documenting all the data and requirements needed to complete the FMEA.

1 2 3 4 5 6 7

Mean = 4.00, SD = 1.56, Var. = 2.44 (high),
Kurt = −0.35, Skew = 0.10

Consistency in the assessment of each failure.

1 2 3 4 5 6 7

Mean = 4.21, SD = 1.47, Var. = 2.18 (high),
Kurt = −0.27, Skew = −0.64

Lack of management support.

1 2 3 4 5 6 7

Mean = 3.32, SD = 1.60, Var. = 2.56 (high),
Kurt = −0.92, Skew = 0.15

Confusion in FMEA terminology.

1 2 3 4 5 6 7

Mean = 3.68, SD = 1.57, Var. = 2.45 (high),
Kurt = −0.97, Skew = −0.29

The ability to overlook sets of data that are needed to assess the severity of a failure.

1 2 3 4 5 6 7

Mean = 3.79, SD = 1.47, Var. = 2.18 (high),
Kurt = −0.31, Skew = −0.52

Most personnel from various functions do not have adequate knowledge on failures.

1 2 3 4 5 6 7

Mean = 4.74, SD = 1.63, Var. = 2.65 (high),
Kurt = −0.26, Skew = −0.56

TABLE A.4

What Impact Do You Feel FMEA Currently Has in Your Business Environment?

Firm1	Lower cost of quality.
Firm2	It has helped our product entry into various markets.
Firm3	Let me first be clear that I am answering from the sourcing perspective. Our quality department uses FMEA extensively. In sourcing we have a FMEA form, but we only use it in the very highest risk situations.
Firm4	I think it's had a great impact; we've definitely made large strides and improvements. However, we still have a long way to go.
Firm5	
Firm6	Major
Firm7	
Firm8	
Firm9	
Firm10	It helps where used, but only used in engineering.
Firm11	Minimal.
Firm12	I believe the FMEA tool has an impact when it is properly utilized.
Firm13	
Firm14	It is an important part of our quality system. DFMEA + PFMEA are routinely used for product and process design. Improvements in both products and processes have been obtained.
Firm15	Has helped create more consistent support for investment in process reliability on the shop floor.
Firm16	
Firm17	
Firm18	
Firm19	
Firm20	
Firm21	
Firm22	FMEA has made a positive impact to our company. We are starting to identify and prevent problems from occurring.
Firm23	
Firm24	
Firm25	It is a tool to assist in improving out processes and get better at making the products we sell.
Firm26	Used for product development and Six Sigma projects.
Firm27	
Firm28	

Continued

TABLE A.4 *(Continued)*

What Impact Do You Feel FMEA Currently Has in Your Business Environment?

Firm29	
Firm30	Engineering process used to determine RLA.
Firm31	Mandatory to achieve quality parts/auditing.
Firm32	Currently, it has a major impact on engineering and quality, as those two functions are entrenched in reviewing and in some cases re-creating all DFMEAs related to the products we produce. We have had three recent recalls due to product failures, which has forced us to re-look at things.
Firm33	Positive, if treated as the living document it is and if it is used properly and consistently. Excellent tool for conveying lessons learned to current and new processes.
Firm34	
Firm35	
Firm36	
Firm37	It is an engineering tool for design and improvements.
Firm38	
Firm39	
Firm40	
Firm41	
Firm42	
Firm43	Drives continuous improvement throughout our functional areas. The more the effectiveness of FMEAs is demonstrated, the more the workforce embraces the importance of FMEAs and data-driven decision making.
Firm44	
Firm45	
Firm46	

TABLE A.5

How Could FMEA Be More Effectively Used to Help Reach the Organizational Goals of Your Company?

Firm1	It's the tools that lead up to it are the issue.
Firm2	FMEA is being used today and is part of our quality culture.
Firm3	I believe it would help improve process planning.
Firm4	A more widespread rollout among different functions.
Firm5	
Firm6	User friendly on all working operating systems.
Firm7	
Firm8	
Firm9	
Firm10	
Firm11	Currently used to identify new product development issues. Should include total supply chain.
Firm12	It is a tool that is utilized during green belt certification; however it appears for the most part it is put back in the "tool box" to collect dust once individuals are certified.
Firm13	
Firm14	The principles could be used as part of the supply chain risk processes.
Firm15	More overall organizational awareness and understanding.
Firm16	
Firm17	
Firm18	
Firm19	
Firm20	
Firm21	
Firm22	We need more training and practice in completing a FMEA. Once we are fully trained, this will be a very powerful tool.
Firm23	
Firm24	
Firm25	Have training courses down to the shop floor level for a general understanding.
Firm26	Adopt Six Sigma methodology and project management sourcing.
Firm27	
Firm28	
Firm29	

Continued

TABLE A.5 *(Continued)*

How Could FMEA Be More Effectively Used to Help Reach the Organizational Goals of Your Company?

Firm30	Implemented in the supplier selection process.
Firm31	More organized.
Firm32	Training and time. We need to train everyone on how to do them the *same* way, as consistency is necessary, and we need the time and resources available to dedicate to this cause, as everyone recognizes the importance. Need to prioritize these efforts in our daily workload.
Firm33	Previous program FMEAs should be heavily consulted and reviewed when creating a new one. If also kept-up-to-date, quality issues will decrease.
Firm34	
Firm35	
Firm36	
Firm37	
Firm38	
Firm39	
Firm40	
Firm41	
Firm42	
Firm43	Utilize at upper management level for business processes and objectives.
Firm44	
Firm45	
Firm46	

TABLE A.6

What Industry Trends Do You See for FMEA in the Next Several Years?

Firm1	Only best in class will use it.
Firm2	More use.
Firm3	I believe the process will become more acceptable since we are seeing an influx of people with engineering and quality backgrounds in our sourcing organization.
Firm4	I think it's going to identify the companies that are doing well and it's going to weed out the ones that aren't using it.
Firm5	
Firm6	
Firm7	
Firm8	
Firm9	
Firm10	
Firm11	With greater supply chain awareness, our company will include more cross-functional participation.
Firm12	A better understanding of the risks involved with globalization would be of great benefit. (1) Currency exchange, intellectual property infringement, increasing wage rates. (2) Correlation between logistics costs and raw material/energy costs, as well as overall impact of increase in volume/demand requirements as more companies source internationally.
Firm13	
Firm14	Unknown.
Firm15	Increased use.
Firm16	
Firm17	
Firm18	
Firm19	
Firm20	
Firm21	
Firm22	I personally feel that most companies will not incorporate FMEA to all functional areas of the company. Unfortunately, it is and will continue to be considered a tool for engineering and quality until it is taught and pushed through the supply chain issues.
Firm23	
Firm24	

Continued

TABLE A.6 *(Continued)*

What Industry Trends Do You See for FMEA in the Next Several Years?

Firm25	I see FMEA being more and more important, especially in today's environment.
Firm26	As Six Sigma methodology usage increases it is likely that OEMs and suppliers would increase.
Firm27	
Firm28	
Firm29	
Firm30	FMEA worksheets applied to supply base.
Firm31	Growing down the supply chain.
Firm32	With the new edition of the FMEA manual that AIAG just put out, it is clear that the manufacturing and auto industries feel it is an important part of everyday life.
Firm33	New AIAG FMEA 4th edition just released. Expected that the industry will take time to implement the changes and ideas in the manual. Once done, they will proceed based on how successful it was.
Firm34	
Firm35	
Firm36	
Firm37	At our company—improved products and reduced risk.
Firm38	
Firm39	
Firm40	
Firm41	
Firm42	
Firm43	More use as a business management tool instead of just a product and operations process improvement tool.
Firm44	
Firm45	
Firm46	

TABLE A.7

What Type of Advantage Has Your Company Gained over Those Who Do Not Participate in FMEA?

Firm1	When disruptions occur they are minimal in the time it takes to solve the issue.
Firm2	Ease of doing business with key customers.
Firm3	But we did avoid a supply situation that would have been disastrous a few years back. The FMEA process gave us a structured method to identify and prioritize the risks for presentation to the project team.
Firm4	Not sure.
Firm5	
Firm6	Visibility.
Firm7	
Firm8	
Firm9	
Firm10	
Firm11	Unknown.
Firm12	Individuals in the company are able to gain a better understanding of all process steps involved in a process for which they may only be involved in a small segment thereof. In addition, the ability to prioritize and address risks has mitigated some unnecessary costs, which would have impacted the business.
Firm13	
Firm14	Improved product quality and reliability.
Firm15	Better process and product reliability.
Firm16	
Firm17	
Firm18	
Firm19	
Firm20	
Firm21	
Firm22	I already identified several major risks that need to be resolved by using FMEA in my role as supply chain manager. The main advantage is customer satisfaction due to having quality products available to manufacture our double-action doors.
Firm23	
Firm24	

Continued

TABLE A.7 *(Continued)*

What Type of Advantage Has Your Company Gained over Those Who Do Not Participate in FMEA?

Firm25	Our products are more reliable. It shows a "story" and helps in the process of improvement.
Firm26	Quality improvement.
Firm27	
Firm28	
Firm29	
Firm30	None.
Firm31	Customers and validation.
Firm32	We are getting better, but I do not believe we have an advantage as of yet.
Firm33	Difficult to say. We require FMEA of all our suppliers. Thus, I am not familiar with any companies that do not use it at all.
Firm34	
Firm35	
Firm36	
Firm37	
Firm38	
Firm39	
Firm40	
Firm41	
Firm42	
Firm43	More efficient and effective use of our limited resources. Increased customer satisfaction.
Firm44	
Firm45	
Firm46	

TABLE A.8

To What Extent Could a Modified Version of FMEA Be Used to Manage Risks in Your Supply Chain?

Firm1	More wildly adopted.
Firm2	
Firm3	Disguise it as a survey or questionnaire.
Firm4	Currently I think I use it more in our logistic side versus procurement. And I think with all the increase in raw materials and commodities, it would definitely be a great impact for them to use.
Firm5	
Firm6	Tool to identify risk easily.
Firm7	
Firm8	
Firm9	
Firm10	
Firm11	Definite opportunity.
Firm12	I could see it as a great benefit in identifying potential problems which may occur in order to proactively manage the issue, as opposed to waiting until something goes wrong to put a risk mitigation plan in place.
Firm13	
Firm14	Severity, occurrence, detection, incorporated into supply chain risk management practices.
Firm15	We already have used a modified version for both supply chain management and new business opportunity evaluation.
Firm16	
Firm17	
Firm18	
Firm19	
Firm20	
Firm21	
Firm22	FMEA is more than just a software or spreadsheet. It is a thought process. In saying that, the FMEA can be modified any way necessary to be able to achieve the mind frame of what can go wrong and what will we do to prevent that failure from occurring or reduce that chance of it occurring.
Firm23	
Firm24	
Firm25	FMEA data that is electronic and integrated.
Firm26	Over 50%.

Continued

TABLE A.8 *(Continued)*

To What Extent Could a Modified Version of FMEA Be Used to Manage Risks in Your Supply Chain?

Firm27	
Firm28	
Firm29	
Firm30	Make the input format more user-friendly.
Firm31	More widely across supply chain and visibility.
Firm32	Using FMEA in the supply chain group here is a long way off. We do not have the resources to get this completed right now. Too many operational issues, and commercial issues related to commodity inflation and currency changes.
Firm33	Already being done with full FMEA, not modified.
Firm34	
Firm35	
Firm36	
Firm37	I would like to see this.
Firm38	
Firm39	
Firm40	
Firm41	
Firm42	
Firm43	There is a great opportunity for this to drive internal and external improvements in supply chain performance.
Firm44	
Firm45	
Firm46	

Index